The Epistle of James within Judaism

The Epistle of James within Judaism

The Earliest First-Century Window into Messianic Jewish Belief and Practice

A. Boyd Luter

WIPF & STOCK · Eugene, Oregon

THE EPISTLE OF JAMES WITHIN JUDAISM
The Earliest First-Century Window into Messianic Jewish Belief and Practice

Copyright © 2024 A. Boyd Luter. All rights reserved. Except for brief quotations in critical publications or reviews, no part of this book may be reproduced in any manner without prior written permission from the publisher. Write: Permissions, Wipf and Stock Publishers, 199 W. 8th Ave., Suite 3, Eugene, OR 97401.

Wipf and Stock Publishers
199 W. 8th Ave., Suite 3
Eugene, OR 97401

www.wipfandstock.com

PAPERBACK ISBN: 978-1-7252-6074-0
HARDCOVER ISBN: 978-1-7252-6075-7
EBOOK ISBN: 978-1-7252-6076-4

Cataloguing-in-Publication data:

Names: Luter, A. Boyd. [Author].

Title: The Epistle of James within Judaism : the earliest first-century window into messianic Jewish belief and practice / A. Boyd Luter.

Description: Eugene, OR: Wipf and Stock Publishers, 2024 | Includes bibliographical references and index.

Identifiers: ISBN 978-1-7252-6074-0 (paperback) | ISBN 978-1-7252-6075-7 (hardcover) | ISBN 978-1-7252-6076-4 (ebook)

Subjects: LCSH: Bible.—James—Criticism, interpretation, etc. | Jews in the New Testament. | Christianity and antisemitism. | Jewish Christians.

Classification: BS2785.2 L88 2024 (paperback) | BS2785.2 (ebook)

05/08/24

With deep affection, I dedicate this book to our grandchildren, each of whom Cici and I treasure as gifts from God:

Mia

Titus

Nate

Alex

Will

Anna

Paige

Lois Kate

Parker

Margaret

Dorothy

Caroline

Nash

Hayden

Lilly-Cate

Contents

Acknowledgments ix

1. Introduction 1
2. Background issues 7
3. "The twelve tribes in the diaspora" 38
4. "The perfect law of liberty" 60
5. "Pure and undefiled religion" 82
6. "Your *synagoge*" and "the elders of the *ekklesia*" 102
7. Echoes of the Tanakh and the teaching of Jesus in James 123
8. James on faith, works, and justification 145
9. Conclusion 172

Bibliography 177
Author Index 191
Scripture Index 193

Acknowledgments

I WISH TO EXPRESS my heartfelt thanks to the administration of The King's University for granting me a sabbatical in the Spring semester of 2022. The sabbatical freed me to undertake research related to this book in the world-class libraries at Cambridge University and Oxford University.

Further, in bringing this volume to publication, I have benefited greatly from the editing skill of Dr. Robin Parry and the design skill of Dr. Savanah N. Landerholm of Wipf & Stock Publishers. They have not only done their jobs exceptionally well, but also made the process amazingly streamlined and enjoyable.

1

Introduction

FIRST OF ALL, IT is the intention of this volume to demonstrate that the Letter of James was the earliest of the New Testament books written. Having done my best to make that case, we will have taken a huge step toward being in an optimum position to set forth the specific role of the Letter of James in the earliest period of the messianic Jewish movement.

At the beginning of this study, it is eminently fair to say that the Letter of James has sometimes been considered by scholars as *one* of the earliest books in the New Testament.[1] However, more often, James has been viewed as among the latest books in the New Testament canon to be written.[2]

A significant example of such later dating of the Letter of James is found in the New Testament introduction volume by the highly respected Roman Catholic NT scholar Raymond Brown.[3] In his "Summary of Basic

---

1. In his lengthy section on the "Author and Date" of the Letter of James, D. C. Allison Jr. (*James*, 28–29) lists the dates for James set forth by forty-four different commentators. Of these, eleven concluded James was written in 50 CE or earlier and seven more held that James was written between 50 and 62 CE, the traditional date of the death of James, the leader of the Jerusalem church.

2. The remaining twenty-six works on the Letter of James in Allison's listing (*James*, 28–29; see footnote 1 above) were dated anywhere from the 60s, *after* the death of James the Just, to as late as the middle of the second century CE, with several holding to dates well past 100 CE. That, of course, means that the traditional author of the Letter of James could not have written the letter. Thus, unless another, lesser-known figure by the name "James" (Greek *Iakobos*) wrote the letter instead, the Letter of James would be pseudepigraphal (i.e., written under the name of a well-known NT figure to attempt to get the document accepted).

3. Brown, *Introduction to the New Testament*, 726.

Information" related to the "Epistle of James," Brown states regarding the letter's date: "If pseudonymous, after the death of James *ca.* 62, in the range 70–110; most likely in the 80s or 90s."[4] Strangely, in this Summary, Brown does not offer a possible date *if* the Letter of James is *not* pseudonymous.[5] That implies he does not seriously consider the possibility that James is not pseudonymous, though, in his discussion of "The Background" of the Letter of James,[6] he speaks of the historical figure James, whom he describes as *"listed first among the 'brothers' of Jesus* in Mark 6:3; Matt 13:55 . . . ."[7] Brown's only later mention of the historical James is in passing: " . . . whether or not written by James, the NT letter that bears his name echoes in many ways traditional Jewish belief and practice."[8]

Before proceeding further, though, several windows into speculative later chronological settings here are helpful to gaze through. First, if the Letter of James is dated at any point in time following the death of the traditional author in 62 CE, the basic integrity of the letter is called into question, because that means someone else besides the *stated writer* is the actual author.[9] Second, besides the inability to establish a likely author, etc., if the Letter of James was written in the latter part of the 60s, it would only make sense to expect there would be something in it clearly reflecting the mounting Jewish Revolt against Rome (66–73 CE), such as Jewish Zealot sentiments, but none are present—certainly not any in an expected way.[10] Third, if the Letter of James was written after 70

---

4. Brown, *Introduction to the New Testament*, 726.

5. This absence is particularly strange given that, two years before the publication of Brown's NT Introduction in 1997, Brown's fellow American Catholic NT scholar Luke Timothy Johnson had registered the following opinion on the dating of the Letter of James: "James is a very early writing . . ." (Johnson, *Letter of James*, 121).

6. Brown, *Introduction to the New Testament*, 725–27.

7. Brown, *Introduction to the New Testament*, 725.

8. Brown, *Introduction to the New Testament*, 727.

9. According to Terry Wilder (citing I. Howard Marshall, from an unpublished paper), in "Pseudonymity and the New Testament," 296: "A text is pseudonymous when it is 'not by a person whose name it bears in the sense that it was written after his death by another person or during his life by another person who was not in some way commissioned to do so.'" For scholars with a high view of scripture, pseudonymity is an issue of the integrity of the document in question. It is one thing to posit authorship other than the traditional author with anonymous texts like the Gospels or Hebrews. It is a very different thing for a scholar to set forth a different author than a NT book directly states, in this case, "James" (Jas 1:1).

10. For example, there is no use of *zelotes* ("Zealot") in James and the uses of *zelos* (3:14, 16) and the verb *zeloo* (4:2) are found in contexts that are interpreted as political only with the greatest ingenuity and less than measured exegesis.

CE, it would necessarily emerge from the crushing (and somewhat historically foggy) circumstances among the Jewish (and messianic Jewish) community (or communities) following the destruction of the Second Temple and the city of Jerusalem by the Romans, none of which is seen in James.[11] Finally, if the letter was written either in the last part of the first century CE or in the first half of the second century CE—say, leading up to the Bar Kochba Rebellion in the 130s CE—the degree of speculation increases proportionately as to background issues, such as authorship, date, place of origin of the letter, original audience, etc.[12]

None of what has just been stated, however, should be taken to mean that a dating of the Letter of James later than the death of the traditional author is impossible. Rather, these thoughts have been offered to make two points: 1) the issue of when the Letter of James was written is contested among scholars; and 2) the point in time when writing of the Letter of James is understood to take place has a significant impact on the understanding of numerous other background and textual aspects of the Letter regarding first-century CE messianic Judaism. As will be explained in more detail below, both points will be dealt with in the following chapters of this book. Prior to that, though, a concise summary of the prevailing vantage point of this volume will be set forth.

The perspective of this book

This book represents a post-supersessionist perspective. The term *post-supersessionism* refers to "a family of theological perspectives that *affirms God's irrevocable covenant with the Jewish people as a central and coherent*

---

11. The only potentially significant textual argument in favor of a dating for the Letter of James after 70 CE is the *lack* of mention of Temple worship or sacrifice. However, like all "arguments from silence," there must be other ways of corroborating the point being argued beyond the lack of mention itself.

12. A marked tendency among scholars who date the Letter of James in the second century CE is to compare similar wording between James and certain extrabiblical works, e.g., the Shepherd of Hermas and the Epistle of Barnabas, from that period and assume James must also date from the second century CE, rather than the traditional explanation that the Shepherd of Hermas and Epistle of Barnabas cited the *earlier* Letter of James. While it has long been quite common for scholars to attribute identical or similar wording in a later extrabiblical work to citation of an (at least somewhat earlier) NT book, viewing such citation or allusion as going the other direction or being limited to the same narrow time period as the extrabiblical work is to go even further down the road of exegetical/historical speculation.

part of ecclesial teaching." Post-supersessionism "rejects understandings of the new covenant that entail the abrogation or obsolescence of God's covenant with the Jewish people, of the Torah as a demarcator of Jewish community identity, or of the Jewish people themselves."[13]

What this means for this volume foundationally is that it is written from a post-supersessionist perspective. Theologically—simply put, that means the author of this work does not believe that either Jesus or the church has replaced (i.e., superseded) Israel in God's plan. As such, this book rejects a view that has been the—often unchallenged—majority position throughout church history since at least the fourth century CE.[14]

It is worth asking at this point: What specifically does the post-supersessionist perspective taken by the author mean in regard to this treatment of the Letter of James? First and foremost, while the Letter of James has frequently been interpreted from a perspective in which the church has replaced Israel, it is not most naturally understood that way. The present book will make this point at numerous textual junctures throughout, showing that supersessionism muddies the textual water, so to speak, by deviating from obvious ways to interpret aspects of the Letter of James.

Second, a post-supersessionist approach to the Letter of James offers insight into how issues addressed in the letter—theological and behavioral—were understood by the early messianic Jewish community. Three of the related issues to be resolved are: 1) *Who* is addressing the issues and *where* is he located? 2) *In what timeframe* does the messianic Jewish community in view exist? and 3) *Where* is the original audience of the Letter of James located?

Third, a post-supersessionist, messianic Jewish perspective regarding the Letter of James links up much more seamlessly with the Book of Acts than does replacement theology/supersessionism. This is true without the interpreter attempting to drag early messianic Judaism across into the text of Acts at all.

---

13. The wording in this paragraph is taken from the front page of the website for the Society for Post-Supersessionist Theology (spostst.org).

14. The reference to the fourth century CE means at least from the time of St. Augustine to the present (though the impact of early supersessionist interpretation actually may have begun to become dominant a century or more earlier than Augustine). For two helpful recent surveys related to supersessionism, the first from a historical perspective and the latter a sort of contemporary "practical theology," see McDermott, "Getting the Big Picture Wrong," 33–44; and Glaser, "Dangers of Supersessionism," 101–18.

INTRODUCTION

Fourth, a careful post-supersessionist approach to the Letter of James can offer helpful perspective for Messianic Jewish believers today, as well as insight as to how gentile believers should relate to contemporary Messianic Jews.[15] In addition, such a treatment can lend insight to both groups regarding the Lord's overall plan, which includes both groups.

Survey of contents

Chapter 2 will handle *most* of the standard background issues related to the Letter of James. In the author's view, the date James was written is the most foundational issue, given its bearing on several of the other issues. The one major issue not dealt with in chapter 2 will be the identity of the original audience of the letter, because that question is the focus of chapter 3.

Chapter 3 will ask and answer the question: What is most likely meant by the wording usually translated as something like "To the twelve tribes in the Dispersion"? (Jas 1:1 NRSV). This phrase has been subject frequently over the centuries to a supersessionist interpretation. However, even when understood as speaking of dispersed Jews, there has been a somewhat surprising variety of interpretations.

Chapter 4 focuses on the meaning of "the perfect law, the law of liberty" (1:25) and similar wording elsewhere in the Letter of James. How would the wording expressed in James about the Torah be understood by messianic Jewish believers in the first century CE, as well as by Messianic Jews today?

Chapter 5 discusses James's meaning of the wording "Religion that is pure and undefiled by God" (Jas 1:27). Does it mean that the rest of the Mosaic law is to be ignored in the messianic Jewish believer's obedience, or can it be reconciled with a Torah-observant lifestyle?

Chapter 6 inquires as to the most likely meaning of what is most naturally literally translated from the Greek text as "synagogue" (Greek *synagoge*) in 2:2. Why is this word usually rendered as "assembly" or "meeting"? Though it is not always the case, supersessionist assumptions have often been in play. Chapter 5 also brings to center stage the following

---

15 I cap Messianic when referring to contemporary Messianic Jews and Messianic Judaism, as is conventional. When speaking of first-century Jewish followers of Yeshua I speak of messianic Jews and messianic Judaism. This signals an intention to avoid anachronism when considering early Jewish followers of Yeshua, while at the same time acknowledging real connections between the ancient and modern movements.

wording in 5:14: "Call for the elders of the church," with "church" being the standard translation of the Greek *ekklesia*. What does this single use of *ekklesia* in the Letter suggest, both about the wider setting from which that document emerged and those to whom it was sent?

Chapter 7 deals with citations—and potential echoes—of the Hebrew Bible in the Letter of James. Though there are a surprisingly limited number of actual quotations from the Tanak in James, those that appear are each used to strong effect. In addition, the likely allusions to the Tanak reflect that the mind of James, the author, is saturated with the Hebrew scriptures. Chapter 6 also probes the extent to which the Letter of James may also be saturated with the teaching of Messiah Jesus. That is especially true regarding what appears to be considerable echoing of the Sermon on the Mount, notably the version in Matthew 5–7.

Chapter 8 explores what has been the most controversial portion of the Letter of James over the centuries: 2:14–26. What has prompted the controversy? The relationship between faith and works regarding "justification" set forth by James *appears* to be in direct conflict with Paul's approach to justification in his letters to the Romans, Galatians, and Ephesians. But is that the case?

The book will close with a conclusion that will review the findings from each of the previous chapters regarding the text of James and their meaning for understanding first-century CE messianic Judaism. It will then seek to draw helpful inferences for Messianic Jewish belief and practice today.

2

Background issues

IT WOULD BE IDEAL if biblical books could be adequately interpreted just by studying the text, without requiring any awareness of their backgrounds. Sadly, it is not possible to proceed very far toward truly understanding most scriptural books—with the possible exception of Proverbs and some of the psalms which are anonymous in regard to authorship[1]—without making a diligent effort to determine at least: 1) who wrote the document; 2) when it was written; 3) where it was written; 4) to whom it was addressed and the location of the intended audience; 5) the type (or types) of literature the document embodies; and 6) the structure of the document (because, in the ancient biblical world, authors often emphasized various points they wanted to communicate to the audience with structural cues).

In this chapter, in the following order, the background issues of date, author, provenance (i.e., where the Letter was written), literary genre (i.e., the type of literature the author has chosen for this letter), and the structure of the Letter of James will be addressed. As stated in the introduction, the issue of the identity of the original readers of the Letter of James will be discussed in chapter 3.

The date of the Letter of James

In order to give a sense of the range of possible dating for the Letter of James, important examples from commentators whose works have appeared in the past two decades will be listed, first among those from other

---

1. Even then, close consideration of specific subtypes of Hebrew proverbial or hymnic literature is essential to accurate interpretation.

than conservative backgrounds, then by evangelicals. Following that, the most important evidence concerning the dating issue will be considered.

The dating of James among significant recent broader New Testament scholars

Dale C. Allison, Jr., whose International Critical Commentary volume on the Letter of James appeared in 2013, places the dating of the letter in the range of CE 100–120.[2] Recently, however, in one chapter, Richard Bauckham has effectively neutralized Allison's contentions regarding James on all fronts . . . except one: its *date*.[3] However, by that statement, I do not mean Bauckham joins Allison in late-dating James. Rather, Bauckham did not, in that otherwise exceptional chapter, in any way focus on when in the lifetime of the author of James the letter was likely written.

Helpfully, though, Bauckham had earlier written the "James" commentary segment for the *Eerdmans Commentary on the Bible*,[4] in which he cautiously provides at least a general date range of composition for the Letter of James: "James' letter may . . . be of a very early date."[5] Assuming the chronological ranges of fairly recent scholarly discussions of the dating of James, and that Bauckham's position on when to date James remained roughly where it was in 2003, "a very early date" would likely fall between the mid to late-40s and the mid-50s CE.[6]

Also in decided contrast with the conclusion on dating by Allison, Catholic New Testament scholar Luke Timothy Johnson, in his 2004 book of essays on James, *Brother of Jesus, Friend of God*,[7] states on the dating issue: "I propose that we . . . take as our premise that the letter is indeed early and authentic . . . ." This wording matches closely what

---

2. Allison, *James*, 29. His exact words are "a date of 100–120 would seem to fit the bill."

3. Ironically, Bauckham's chapter is included in the same edited volume as Allison's "The Fiction of James and Its *Sitz im Leben*." See Richard Bauckham, "Messianic Jewish Identity in James," in *The Catholic Epistles: Critical Readings*, 85–98.

4. Bauckham, "James," 1483–92.

5. Bauckham, "James," *Eerdmans Commentary*, 1483.

6. Slightly out of the stated time range of the past two decades, Rainer Reisner, in his "James" segment in the *Oxford Bible Commentary*, 1257, stated that the dating of the Letter of James should be in "the middle of the 40s" (or even slightly before).

7. Johnson, *Brother of Jesus, Friend of God*, 3.

Johnson had written in his 1995 Anchor Bible commentary on *The Letter of James*: "James is a very early writing . . . ."[8]

The dating of James among significant recent evangelical New Testament scholars

On the evangelical side of the aisle, a sampling of the views of significant commentators on the dating of James in the last two decades finds both early datings and a narrower range of possible dates. The first of this group of commentaries published, the 2008 volume in the Zondervan Exegetical Commentary on the New Testament, by Craig Blomberg and Mariam Kammell, states that James is "probably the first NT document written."[9] The next commentary is Dan McCartney's 2009 Baker Exegetical Commentary on the New Testament series on James, which, like Blomberg and Kammell, does not specify a date, but clearly agrees with the view he titles "The Letter Was Written Before Paul's Letters."[10] Next is Scot McKnight's 2011 *The Letter of James* in the New International Commentary on the New Testament series. McKnight concludes James was written in "the 50s."[11] Moving closer to the present day, in 2020, Aida Besancon Spencer's *A Commentary on James*, in the Kregel Exegetical Library series, set forth the earliest of all dates encountered in my research, leaning toward the earlier part of the period "AD 34–48."[12] Finally, Doug Moo's second edition of *The Letter of James* in the Pillar New Testament Commentary series appeared in 2021, in which he suggests "James was written in the mid-40s . . . ."[13]

Nothing has been said yet about the evidence each scholar considered in making his or her decision on the dating of James or why he or she

---

8. Johnson, *Letter of James*, 121.

9. Blomberg and Kammell, *James*, 35.

10. McCartney, *James*. McCartney also said, helpfully, "James's context is more characteristic of the first half of the first half than that of the second century."

11. McKnight, *Letter of James*, 38.

12. Spencer, *Commentary on James*, 33–34.

13. Moo, *Letter of James*, 32. It is also worth noting that, besides the first edition of Moo's PNTC volume (2000), he has also contributed two editions of the James commentary in the TNTC series (1985 and 2015), likely making Moo the most published recent higher-profile commentator on James.

understood that evidence the way they did. This study turns first to what is behind the weighing of the major evidential factors[14] on that topic.

A succinct appraisal of key issues relevant to the dating of the Letter of James

In my view, the answers to the following four questions[15] provide *adequate* information to draw a reasonably considered conclusion of when the Letter of James was written:

1. If James, the half-brother of Jesus,[16] did write the Letter of James,[17] what is its possible range of dating?
2. How does the apparent date-related background of the Letter of James stack up with relevant material in the Book of Acts?
3. How does the data about the organization of the community in James relate to a possible dating for the Letter of James?
4. What is the relationship between the teaching on "justification" in the Letter of James and the apostle Paul's view?

Answering question 1

Strong extrabiblical tradition records the date of death of James, the brother of Jesus, as being 62 CE.[18] Assuming that is correct, *if* James wrote

---

14. Because of space limitations, not all "reasons" adduced as evidence regarding the date of the Letter of James will be discussed, just the ones I have concluded after careful consideration are most significant.

15. Some scholars would consider the questions I have chosen—and even other questions I have not chosen—to be insufficient to provide the needed information to make an informed decision on the dating of James. I respect that perspective, but I believe the four stated questions do provide the basic information needed to make a valid determination of dating.

16. In most cases throughout this book, James will be referred to as the brother of Jesus, not half-brother, although that is the most accurate description, since his mother was Mary, but he was conceived by the Holy Spirit, while James's mother was Mary and his father was Joseph. However, since Paul calls James "the Lord's brother" in Gal 1:18, it certainly would seem appropriate to refer to James the same way.

17. The traditional view of the authorship of James, which has remained the scholarly consensus, is that it was written by the brother of Jesus. See the further discussion on the authorship of James later in this chapter.

18. According to L.T. Johnson (*Letter of James*, 99–100), the *date* of James's death

the letter bearing his name,[19] the *latest* possible dating for the writing of the Letter of James is the very early 60s.

Moving backward in time from the early 60s, there are apparently three mentions of James the brother of Jesus, also the leader of the Jerusalem church, by name[20] in the Book of Acts (12:17; 15:13; 21:18). Acts 15:13 reflects the role of James as the decisive voice in the discussion at the Jerusalem Council, which event is likely dated in 49 CE.[21] Acts 21:18 takes place at the end of Paul's Third Missionary Journey, probably in 57 CE.[22]

Though hardly impossible, it appears unlikely the Letter of James was written during the time frames of Acts 15 or 21, because James's Jewish audience in the Dispersion (Jas 1:1) also would have needed to be informed about the findings of the Jerusalem Council regarding the gentiles. Both contexts (Acts 15 and 21) do refer to the act of writing a document (Greek *episteilai* ["to write"]; 15:20; see also 21:20] and *grapsantes* [also "to write"] 15:23] or *epistolen* ["letter"; 15:30])—a very important document. The "letter" in question was written at the conclusion of the Jerusalem Council by a group of church leaders (15:23-29; see also 21:25)—not a single figure (i.e., James). And the "letter" was sent to "the believers of gentile origin in Antioch and Syria and Cilicia" (15:23). Thus, the "letter" in view in Acts 15 and 21 addresses a completely different ethnic audience than "the twelve tribes in the Dispersion" (Jas 1:1), to whom the Letter of James was sent.

The remaining mention of James in Acts is in 12:17. That is the initial passage in Acts in which James, the brother of Jesus,[23] is spoken of in a leadership role in the Jerusalem church. In that passage, Peter, having been

---

being 62 CE is solidly confirmed by Josephus. However, the *details* of his death, notably Eusebius's versions from Clement of Alexandria and Hegesippus, are not on nearly as solid ground.

19. I.e., as opposed to the Letter of James being a pseudepigraphon.

20. Although not mentioned specifically, James was almost surely also intended in the grouping described in Acts 1:14 as being in "the room upstairs" (1:13) by the wording ". . . and Mary the mother of Jesus, as well as his brothers."

21. E.g., in his entry on "Chronology," in the *Dictionary of the Later New Testament and Its Developments* (187, 193), Paul Maier dates the Jerusalem Council in 49 CE. Richard Longenecker concurs with a 49 CE dating for the Apostolic Council ("Acts," 9:443).

22. In the conclusion to a very precise discussion, Loveday Alexander ("Chronology of Paul," 122-23) specifies that the relevant events in Acts 21 took place in 57 CE.

23. Note that this passage cannot possibly be speaking of the other high-profile "James" (i.e., "the brother of John"), because he has just been killed by Herod Agrippa I, as stated in Acts 12:1-2.

miraculously released from imprisonment in Jerusalem, instructed those who been praying for his release to "Tell this to James and to the believers."[24] At that point, "[Peter] left and went to another place" (i.e., certainly outside of Jerusalem, where he would have been taken back to prison, if apprehended—and quite possibly outside of Judea or even Palestine [12:17)]. The dating of this event is perhaps a year or two before 44 CE,[25] when the death of Herod Agrippa I took place, as recorded in Acts 12:20–23.[26]

With Peter having left the Jerusalem leadership, James was the obvious successor as leader of the mother church, as the wording "James and the believers" in 12:17 strongly infers. Therefore, if a "pastoral letter" was to be written from the Jerusalem church during that time of persecution to those who had fled Jerusalem and the surrounding areas in Palestine, James was the obvious candidate to do so. Based on the inference noted above from Acts 12:17, such a letter could have been written somewhere between 42 to 44 CE, several years before the Jerusalem Council.

Answering question 2

While Acts 12:17ff. certainly reflects a plausible time in which the Letter of James could have been written, that passage is not the only relevant text in Acts regarding the dating of James. Recently, Aida Spencer has advanced a view arguing for yet an earlier dating of James. She concludes: "If it is true that James writes to diaspora Jews before the issue of the inclusion of Gentiles becomes prominent, then the letter needs to be set between Acts 8–15."[27] In Spencer's view, the issue of "the inclusion of Gentiles" begins to become "prominent" in Acts 10 (i.e., related to Cornelius, the gentile centurion) then peaks in the run-up to the Jerusalem Council in Acts 15, which Spencer dates in AD 48–49.[28] In this scenario, James must be dated *earlier* than 48 CE.

In addition, Spencer holds that "the dispersion to which James refers is probably the earliest one that affected the messianic Jews in Jerusalem

---

24. Unless otherwise stated, all scripture citations are from *The New Revised Standard Version Bible*, 1989.

25. Rainer Reisner, in *Paul's Early Period*, states: "[I]t is probable that Agrippa begins his actions against the original Jerusalem church to please the Jews immediately during his first Passover festival (cf. Acts 12:3)" in 41 CE.

26. See Braund, "Agrippa," in *ABD*, I:99.

27. Spencer, *Commentary on James*, 32.

28. Spencer, *Commentary on James*, 32–33.

(Acts 8:1)."[29] In favor of her understanding is that, cognate with the Greek *te diaspora* (lit. transl. "the Diaspora") in Jas 1:1, is the cousin[30] verb *diaspeiro*, which is used in Acts 8:1, 4; 11:19,[31] speaking of those scattered by the persecution following the death of Stephen. Thus, the immediate circumstances behind the writing of James *could be* as early as the late 30s or early 40s.

Answering question 3

There is limited data related to the spiritual community found in the Letter of James. The only two terms obviously related to either Jewish or Christian worship settings or polity are *synagogen* (2:2) and *ekklesias* (5:14).

The noun *synagoge* is used thirty-four times in the Gospels, always of Jews gathering for worship (or *where* they gathered [e.g., Luke 7:5]). In Acts, *synagoge* is used nineteen times, with eighteen speaking of a specific Jewish synagogue in Jerusalem (6:9), Damascus (9:2, 20), or a city on Paul's apostolic mission field. The nineteenth use is in 15:21, which speaks of (Jewish) synagogues "in every city" (i.e., throughout at least the eastern Roman Empire).

By contrast, Jas 2:2 is not only the lone use of *synagoge* in the Letter of James but it is its sole use in the New Testament Epistles. Since the author and readers of the Letter of James certainly appear to be believers in Jesus as Messiah (see 2:1),[32] the data just reviewed make it likely the worship setting in 2:2 is best understood as a messianic Jewish "synagogue"[33] and the inclusion of *synagoge* there should *not* be rendered as "assembly"[34] or "meeting."[35]

Of the well over a hundred uses of *ekklesia* in the NT, three are in the Gospels, twenty-three are in Acts, 68 in the Epistles and twenty in

---

29. Spencer, *Commentary on James*, 31.

30. I.e., cognate.

31. It appears to be significant for the point being made here that 8:1, 4; 11:19 are the *only uses* of *diaspeiro* in the Book of Acts.

32. A lit. translation of Jas 2:1 is "My brothers, do not hold with favoritism the faith in our glorious Lord Jesus Christ" (Greek *Adelphoi mou, me en prosopolempsias echete ten pistin tou kyriou hemon Iesou Christou tes dokses*).

33. So translated and interpreted by, e.g., Johnson, *Letter of James*, 221–22; and Spencer, *Commentary on James*, 123–24.

34. As in, e.g., NRSV; ESV; NASB 2020.

35. As in, e.g., NIV; CSB.

Revelation. James 5:14 is the only usage of *ekklesia* in the Letter. For the purposes of this treatment, besides Jas 5:14, the uses in Acts are particularly relevant, given the previous material from Acts discussed in answering questions 1 and 2.

The corporate designation of believers in Jesus as Messiah as *ekklesia* appears initially in Acts in 5:11. Significantly, *ekklesia* occurs again in 8:1, 3, at the beginning of the persecution that started with Stephen's martyrdom. There is thus no chronological difficulty with the usage of *ekklesia* in Jas 5:14 matching up with these early uses of *ekklesia* in Acts. In fact, an early side-by-side dating of Jas 5:14 and the early chapters of Acts (notably 8:1, 3)—in the mid-40s, at the latest—makes even more sense when it is considered that *synagoge* (2:2) and *ekklesia* (5:14) refer to the same people (i.e., those with faith in Jesus as Messiah, placing them spiritually in his *ekklesia* [Matt 16:18], but who, given their Jewish backgrounds, worship as/in a *synagoge*).

In addition, the wording "the elders of the church" in Jas 5:14 does not point to the organization of gentile churches, even though the only other use in the NT of the exact wording "the elders of the church" is in Acts 20:17 (Greek *tous presbyterous tes ekklesias* in both passages),[36] referring to "the elders" of the primarily gentile church in Ephesus (20:17a). After all, Israel in the Hebrew Bible had leaders called "elders" (e.g., Num 11:16). Then, in the Gospels, there were Jewish "elders" in Galilee (e.g., Luke 7:3) and Jerusalem (e.g., Matt 21:23). In the early chapters of Acts, among other things, the Jewish "elders" were involved in dragging Stephen before the Sanhedrin (6:12). Then, late in Acts, "the chief priests and the elders of the Jews" were the authorities who "brought charges" against Paul in Jerusalem (25:15).

However, in Acts 11:29–30, the text states the collection taken by the church in Syrian Antioch for the relief of the brethren living in Judea (11:29) was received by "the elders" of the church in Jerusalem (11:30). According to Reisner:

> Reference to the elders (*presbyteroi*) as recipients of the collection (Acts 11:30) suggests that this occurred during the period after the execution of James the son of Zebedee and after Peter's flight from Jerusalem, when the leadership of the church there passed to a committee of elders under the leadership of James the brother of Jesus, though this admittedly provides only an

---

36. See my discussion of the usage of *presbyteros* ("elder") in Luke and Acts in Forrest and Roden, *Biblical Leadership*, 334–48.

approximate dating to the period after A.D. 41–42.... Given the dating of the Judean famine..., however, the last conceivable year seems to be A.D. 45.[37]

If Reisner's range of dating is correct, even working with his "last conceivable year"[38] (45 CE), the Jerusalem church recognized leadership by elders by the mid-40s CE. That conclusion is consistent with the slightly later (i.e., 49 CE) mention of "elders"[39] at the Jerusalem Council (Acts 15:2, 4, 6, 22, 23), where James, the Lord's brother, appears to have been the presiding officer (15:13–21).[40]

All in all, the considerations above concerning the uses of "synagogue" and "church" as largely equivalent ideas in the Letter of James appear to support an early dating for the letter. That date is 45 CE or earlier.

Answering question 4

If James is understood as being written in the mid-40s (or earlier), it must be recognized that there would be *no direct relationship* between James's teaching on "justification" and Paul's teaching on that topic. Why do I say that? Because *the ramifications* of Paul's view on "justification by faith alone" likely would not have become widely known in Jerusalem until shortly before the time of the Jerusalem Council in Acts 15 (49 CE).

Think about it. Yes, it is clear Paul did meet with Peter, James, and John, the three "pillars" of the Jerusalem church (Gal 2:9), about Paul's gospel message (2:2), as well as the gentile mission led by Paul and the Jewish mission led by Peter (2:7–9). However, as McKnight concludes,[41] that meeting did not take place until 46 CE. Thus, the dates of Gal 2:1–10

---

37. Reisner, *Paul's Early Period*, 134. Other scholars, however, date the relief visit in Acts 11:27–30 slightly later. For example, Moo states: "The famine-relief visit cannot be dated any more precisely than 45–47" (*Galatians*, 12).Even with Moo's slightly later range of dating, though, there is still overlap dating of the year 45 CE.

38. Reisner, *Paul's Early Period*, 134.

39. The repeated phrase "the apostles and the elders" in Acts 15:2, 4, 6, 22, 23 certainly implies that "the elders" were fully accepted as leaders in the Jerusalem church alongside "the apostles."

40. Also, at the end of his Third Missionary Journey, in Acts 21:18, Paul immediately chooses to "visit James; and all the elders were present," strongly inferring James's pastoral leadership in the Jerusalem church, alongside "the elders."

41. McKnight, *Galatians*, 88, employing a chart from a handout by Professor Murray Harris, then at Trinity Evangelical Divinity School.

and the Jerusalem Council set forth above allow that what James wrote about "justification" in Jas 2 was recorded *prior to* widespread knowledge of Paul's perspective on justification on James's part by a year or more.

In sum: the answers to the four questions posed above, taken at face value, point to a date for the Letter of James *no later than the mid-40s*. That likely makes James the earliest New Testament document. Also, as will be seen a number of times throughout this book, such an early date has important implications for a fully accurate understanding of early messianic Judaism.

The authorship of the Letter of James

The issue of the authorship of James has already come into play to a degree.[42] Question 1 above asked: If James, the half-brother of Jesus, did write the Letter of James,[43] what is its possible range of dating?

I took the liberty to ask that question in the Dating section of the chapter for a very good reason: because James, the half-brother of Jesus (Matt 13:55; Mark 6:3), is the only "James" found in the New Testament well-known enough to state as an opening ascription of authorship "James, a servant of God and of the Lord Jesus Christ" (Jas 1:1) and expect for that wording to be understood and held in high authority.

The name translated "James" in English Bibles renders the Greek *Iakobus*, which is the Greek equivalent of the Hebrew "Jacob." Since Jacob is the name of one of the patriarchs of Israel, it was a reasonably common name in the first century CE. There are four men named James/Jacob in the New Testament and, strikingly, all four are included in one paragraph in the first chapter of Acts (1:12–14). Only three, however, are mentioned by name in that paragraph: James the brother of Andrew, James son of Alphaeus, and James the father of Judas (not Judas Iscariot, because he betrayed Jesus [e.g., Matt 26:14–15, 47–50] and was already

---

42. It is impossible to keep all such background issues completely separated for obvious reasons. For example, if a biblical book was written on a certain date, somebody (i.e., the author) wrote the book, and that book was written from a certain place (i.e., provenance) to a certain person or group of people (i.e., original audience) in a certain style (i.e., literary genre), which could mark the document as coming from a specific time and place. However, it is still important to consider each issue on its own as much as can be done reasonably.

43. The traditional view of the authorship of James, which has remained the scholarly consensus, is that it was written by the brother of Jesus.

dead by his own hand [Acts 1:18–19]). The fourth James is included in 1:14, among the "brothers" of Jesus.

Of the first three named in 1:13, James the brother of Andrew was a prominent apostle, one of three who made up the apostolic inner circle of Jesus, along with his brother, John, and Simon, better known as Peter.[44] It is exceedingly unlikely this James wrote the Letter of James, because he was killed by King Herod Agrippa I, as recorded in Acts 12:1–2, "probably in AD 44,"[45] and could easily have been jailed by Herod Agrippa as early as 41.[46]

Although one of the original twelve apostles, "James son of Alphaeus," other than in Acts 1:13, is mentioned only in the other lists of the apostles in the Gospels (Matt 10:3; Mark 3:18; Luke 6:15 [and possibly in Mark 15:40, as "James the younger"). Moo considers James son of Alphaeus to be "rather obscure" and "probably not well-known enough to have written an authoritative letter . . . under his own name."[47]

James the father of Judas (Acts 1:13) is mentioned strictly to differentiate his son, Judas (transliterating the common Jewish name "Judah"), from Judas Iscariot. This is seen most clearly in the list of apostles in Luke 6:16: ". . . and Judas son of James, and Judas Iscariot, who became a traitor."

James the brother of Jesus was not a believer in Jesus as Messiah during Jesus's public ministry, given that John 7:5 states clearly, "Even his brothers were not believers in him." However, in 1 Cor 15:7, as part of the apostle Paul's list of Jesus's post-resurrection appearances, Paul writes, "Then he appeared to James, then to all the apostles," before he mentions the risen Lord's appearance to him (15:8).

By the time 1 Corinthians was written (56 or 57 CE), James, the brother of Jesus, had been the recognized leader of the Jerusalem church for over a decade and, in that role, would have been well-known even to the Corinthian church. That is why all Paul says in 15:7 is "James." No further description was needed.

---

44. The closeness to Jesus of this inner circle of Peter, James, and John is demonstrated in two major events in Jesus's public ministry: 1) taking those three up on the Mount of Transfiguration with him (Matt 17:1–7); and 2) taking them apart from the other apostles to pray in the Garden of Gethsemane (26:26–37).

45. Moo, *Letter of James*, 11–12.

46. Reisner, *Paul's Early Period*, states: "[I]t is probable that Agrippa begins his actions against the original Jerusalem church to please the Jews immediately during his first Passover festival (cf. Acts 12:3)" in 41 CE.

47. Moo, *Letter of James*, 11.

This is the only passage in the New Testament that directly states what likely was the circumstance of the salvation of James: the resurrected Jesus appearing to his brother (15:7), perhaps not completely unlike Jesus's appearance to Paul on the Damascus Road (see Acts 9; 22; 26). After his conversion, James apparently witnessed to his brothers "Joseph and Simon and Judas" (i.e., transliterated as "Jude" [see Matt 13:55]), and they also believed. That appears to be how all the younger brothers of Jesus, now believers in him as Messiah, came to be in the Upper Room (Acts 1:13) in Acts 1:14, only a few days before the feast of Pentecost in Acts 2.

The above survey demonstrates that James, the brother of Jesus, was the only "James" mentioned in the New Testament well-known enough to self-identify at the beginning of his letter as "James, a servant of God and of the Lord Jesus Christ," and expect his identity to be understood by his audience. In addition, his known position as head of the Jerusalem church would have provided the authority necessary for the Letter of James to be fully accepted by his audience. Thus, there is the highest likelihood that James, the brother of Jesus, was the author of the Letter of James.[48]

The location of the author of the Letter of James

If the Letter of James was written by James, the brother of Jesus in the mid-40s of the first century CE, there is no strong reason as to why it would have been written from anywhere else besides Jerusalem. After all, as the leader of the mother church from at least the earlier 40s (Acts 12:17) until his death in 62 CE, he would have been in residence in Jerusalem.

Any view that posits another location for the writing of the Letter of James is necessarily based on speculative perspectives on the date and authorship of the Letter. That is the case because the only geographical clue in the text to the author's location is that, for Jews, the only logical place from which to send a letter to "the twelve tribes *in the dispersion*" (Greek *en te diaspora* [lit. transl. "in the diaspora"]) is Jerusalem. In Jewish eyes, Jerusalem was the center of the world, from which any religious "dispersion" would spread out.

---

48. The only other options are that: 1) some completely unknown "James" wrote the letter, an idea offered by, e.g., Kummel (*Introduction to the New Testament*, 411); or 2) someone else who wrote under the name of, and attempting to draw on the authority of, James, the brother of Jesus, an approach championed recently by Allison (*James*, 3–32). Suffice it to say that neither view is compelling.

The literary genre of the Letter of James

The next background issue concerning the Letter of James to be handled in this chapter is the type of literature it is.[49] On that topic, first and foremost, it must be recognized that James is a "letter." That identification may seem completely obvious to many, at first glance, but it has been contested in the past, primarily because, in certain ways, it does not proceed like a letter—especially a New Testament letter.

For example, the Letter of James identifies no individuals among the audience, as do most letters in the New Testament. Upon initial readings, it appears to move quickly from topic to topic, more like wisdom literature in the Hebrew Bible than other New Testament letters. Also, it does not end like most New Testament letters, not concluding with a greeting (e.g., Heb 13:24) or a benediction (13:20–21).

However, as Bauckham explains regarding the important initial wording, "James . . . to the twelve tribes of the Dispersion: Greetings":

> James has the only feature of the ancient letter form which was essential: the letter-opening. It is true that most ancient letters had both a stereotyped letter-opening and also a somewhat less stereotyped letter-closing (in Greek letters usually at least "Farewell!"). James lacks a formal letter-closing. But the letter-closing, though normal, was not essential.[50]

That being the case, James is *more* than just an ancient letter. As Karl-Wilhelm Niebuhr, referring to the same wording mentioned above in Jas 1:1 (i.e., "James . . . to the twelve tribes in the Dispersion"), states:

> Owing to its opening, the Epistle of James functions as an "apostolic diaspora letter." . . . We can refer to a tradition of Greek diaspora letters with religiously based claims to authority that show up in various works of early Jewish literature. . . . The authors of the diaspora letters have the task, the divine commission, of strengthening the identity of the people of God living in

---

49. See the full discussion of the genre issue by Johnson (*Letter of James*, 16–24), who concludes the Letter of James is "protreptic discourse in the form of a letter" (24). Johnson explains that protreptic discourses "often contain the same elements of memory, model, imitation, and maxims that are found also in paraenesis" (20). In contrast, Allison (*James*, 71–76)—writing almost two decades later than Johnson and reflecting considerable newer research—views James as "a diaspora letter" (76).

50. Bauckham, *James: Wisdom of James*, 12.

the diaspora. They fulfilled this commission by articulating the will of God for the situation and with their recipients in mind.[51]

Simply put, if James, the brother of Jesus, wrote the Letter of James: 1) it is written communication by an apostolic figure;[52] 2) it is written to an audience "in the Diaspora" (1:1); and 3) it is, ultimately, structured as a letter, as explained above.

Thus, because the Letter of James fits Niebuhr's description very closely, the Letter is best understood as an *apostolic diaspora letter*. Certainly, careful consideration of other such genres as the commonly held views of paraenesis[53] (i.e., moral or ethical instruction) or wisdom[54] is completely appropriate. However, such genre identifications can be readily subsumed under the overall genre understanding for the Letter of James as an "apostolic diaspora letter."

The structure of the Letter of James

In recent times, there has been a great deal of published research regarding the structure of the Letter of James.[55] However, there is nothing approaching a consensus on this issue. Scot McKnight made that point quite effectively in his careful and detailed discussion on the structure of the Letter of James,[56] in which he compares ten outlines of the Letter—all of which received at least a partly favorable reception from scholars in some quarters, but none of which fully persuaded McKnight—before cautiously offering his own structuring of James.[57]

---

51. Niebuhr, "Epistle of James in Light of Early Diaspora Letters," 67–84.

52. That "James, the Lord's brother" (Gal 1:19) is apparently called an apostle by Paul is adequate reason to refer to the Letter of James as an "*apostolic* diaspora letter."

53. The fountainhead of much of the thinking behind the momentum to view the Letter of James as paraenesis was Martin Dibelius, notably in his commentary on James (*Commentary on the Epistle of James*).

54. An apparent exponent of the "wisdom" view is Donald Burdick, in his "James" segment in the *Expositor's Bible Commentary*, 12:164.

55. See, for example, Mark Taylor's excellent survey of the development of thought on the structure of the Letter of James: "Recent Scholarship on the Structure of James," 86–115.

56. McKnight, *Letter of James*, 47–55.

57. McKnight, *Letter of James*, 55. It is fair to observe that several of those ten outlines utilize each other to varying degrees, though none are in completely detailed agreement.

Over the years, others have offered various partial (i.e., one passage or one section of the book) or overarching (i.e., whole book) inverted parallel (i.e., chiastic)[58] outlines of the Letter of James, but without much success in terms of the reactions of other scholars. However, it is not as if all possibilities of inverted parallel structures related to James have been summarily dismissed. For example, in 2006, Mark Taylor and George Guthrie offered a chiastic structuring of Jas 2:1—5:6 that has drawn positive attention.[59]

Because there is no widespread agreement on the outline of the Letter of James, there is also relatively little commonality regarding an overall theme (or themes) of the Letter. But that is always an "iffy" proposition unless a book's structure clearly points to the overarching topic. Significantly, that is precisely what chiastic (i.e., center-facing) outlines do.

An example of a chiastic structure of over half of the Letter of James is Taylor's and Guthrie's outline of Jas 2:1—5:6 below:[60]

Letter body: Living the "law of liberty" (2:1—5:6)

A Body opening (2:1–11)
  B So speak and so act (2:12–13)
    C Wrong acting, speaking (2:14–3:12)
      D *Righteous vs. worldly wisdom (3:13–18)*
    C' Prophetic rebuke (4:1–10)
  B' Do the law, do not judge it (4:11–12)
A' Body closing (4:13–5:6)

This type of inverted parallel/center-facing structure, which was very common in both Hebrew and Greek passages (or entire books) throughout the Bible,[61] spotlights its main point in the middle of the textual

---

58. The term "chiastic" comes from the Greek letter Chi, which, as a capital letter looks like an English 'X.' What is focused on to be applied to structure is that the X crosses in the middle. Thus, the main focus of a chiasm (or chiastic structure) is in the middle of the outline, not the beginning or end.

59. See Taylor and Guthrie, "Structure of James," 681–705.

60. Cited by McKnight, *Letter of James*, 54. Italics mine.

61. In previous publications, for example, I have laid out book-length chiastic structures of Ruth (in Luter and Davis, *Ruth and Esther*; *Song of Songs*—for the Evangelical Exegetical Commentary series); Philippians (with M. Lee, in *New Testament Studies*); Hebrews (in *Kesher* and in Luter, *God's Land Promise to Israel*); James (in Wells and Luter, *Inspired Preaching*); and Revelation (also in *Inspired Preaching* and

segment. In this case, Taylor and Guthrie believe their section entitled "Righteous vs. worldly wisdom," covering Jas 3:13–18, is the central focus of the wider section 2:1—5:6.

Although Taylor and Guthrie are to be heartily commended for their careful work regarding their structuring of Jas 2:1—5:6, I cannot agree with it. Instead, I believe the entire Letter of James is center-facing, not just 2:1—5:6, and, with the whole letter to work with, the spotlighted center of James proves to be 3:1–12.[62] That will be seen in my structural understanding of the whole letter, which is presented in the next section of this chapter.

A fresh overall chiastic structuring of James

In the outline below, four things need to be emphasized. First, in an inverted parallel outline such as this, the corresponding parts of the first and second halves of the book (i.e., A and A'; B and B'; C and C'; D and D'; E and E'; and F and F') "mirror" each other in one of three possible ways: a) they say the same thing in the same or similar words; b) they say opposite things; or c) like 2 + 2 = 4, the content of the two halves fit together to create a larger point. The interactions of these structural "pairs" will be explained more below in going through the overall structure of the Letter of James.

Second, section G (3:1–12) has no corresponding section. It is the structural center of the Letter of James, making the point the author wanted to emphasize the most to his audience. More will be said about this in moving through the following discussion of the structure.

Third, not only does the book-wide structure of the Letter of James face to the center, but so do each of the sections that make up that overall outline of the book. When smaller sectional chiasms make up an entire biblical book, it becomes considerably more likely that the overall book-length chiastic outline is valid.

God's Land Promise to Israel). The outline of James in this chapter is an adapted version of what I published in 2002 in *Inspired Preaching*.

62. This is not to say that no other outline of the Letter of James besides the chiastic structure I submit below is legitimate. I, for example, know of three different completely valid outlines that cover the entirety of the Book of Revelation: one linear, one chiastic, and one covering the seven blessing statements of the Apocalypse, the first of which is in 1:3 and the seventh in 22:14.

Fourth, in the book-length outline below, the pairs within each sectional chiasm are listed as being "even" or "odd" numbered. The significance of that observation is that chiasms with an *even* number (e.g., made of four, six, or eight parts) are *less* focused toward the center of a structure, while chiasms with an *odd* number (i.e., having an unpaired point in the center) of parts *always* focus strongly on the midpoint. The main point of this observation is that the two outside layers of the overall book structure (i.e., the A and B layers) seen below both are made up of sectional chiasms with an even number of subsections, making them less focused thematically. However, all the other paired layers of the Letter (i.e., C, D, E, and F), plus the central section (G), contain an odd number of subsections, meaning they are more focused thematically. This means the structure of the Letter of James is communicating that there is more of an overall thematic focus on its middle layers, notably on its central section (3:1–12).

Introduction (1:1). Author, audience, and greeting

A (1:2–4) Dispersed ones, view trials as opportunities to grow to maturity
(*even* numbered internal chiasm)
  B (1:5–8) Wisdom through the prayer of faith
  (*even* numbered internal chiasm)
    C (1:9–21) The temporary nature of wealth, the nature of temptation, the giving Father, and the need to be patient and resist anger.
    (*odd* numbered internal chiasm)
      D (1:22–27) Be a doer of the Word who bridles the tongue and keeps yourself unstained by the world.
      (*odd* numbered internal chiasm)
        E (2:1–13) It is sinful and lawless to show partiality and be merciless toward your neighbor
        (*odd* numbered internal chiasm)
          F (2:14–26) Faith is displayed by faithful works
          (*odd* numbered internal chiasm)
            G (3:1–12) The grave danger of the abuse of the tongue, especially by teachers
            (*odd* numbered internal chiasm)
          F' (3:13–18) Wisdom is displayed by wise behavior
          (*odd* numbered internal chiasm)
        E' (4:1–10) It is sinful to be worldly, not humble, and double-minded, as well as vulnerable to Satan
        (*odd* numbered internal chiasm)

> D' (4:11–17) Don't speak against your brother, be arrogant regarding God's will or fail to do the right thing
> (*odd* numbered internal chiasm)
> C' (5:1–11) The rotting of wealth and the reality of judgment, plus the need for patient enduring in light of the Lord's coming
> (*odd* numbered internal chiasm)
> B' (5:12–18) Relief and healing through the prayer of faith
> (*even* numbered internal chiasm)
> A' (5:19–20) Straying ones, view correction as a means to rescue/forgiveness
> (*even* numbered internal chiasm)

As can be readily seen, the central focus of the above outline is G (3:1–12), which deals with the danger of the abuse of the tongue. The other layer of the structure that emphasizes dangers related to speaking is D/D'. In D (1:22–27), it is stated that people who do not "bridle their tongues" are self-deceived and "their religion is worthless" (1:26). In D' (4:11–17), the audience is admonished not to "speak evil against one another" (4:11). Thus, it is not that much of a stretch to see the problem of sinful speech as a paramount emphasis of the Letter of James.

As far as how the other pairings "work together," A/A' addresses "dispersed ones" (1:2–4) and "wandering ones" (5:19–20); B/B' deals with the prayer of faith in regard to wisdom (1:5–8) and healing (5:12–18); C/C' exposes the temporary nature of wealth, the certainty of judgment on the wicked wealthy, and the great need for patience (1:9–21/5:1–11); E/E' focuses on how others are treated due to partiality (2:1–13) and selfishness (4:1–10), offering the solutions of keeping "the royal law"/"the law of freedom" (2:8, 12) and resisting the devil (4:7) and humility before the Lord (4:10).

Layer G (3:1–12) is the focal point of the Letter of James. Its emphasis on the grave danger of sin while speaking is spotlighted for the Letter's audience to easily understand.

However, that point is not easy to grasp in modern cultures in which our eyes are on the page reading, and in which we expect the main point of a document to be at the beginning or the end. Yet, in oral cultures[63]—which all ancient cultures were—all people (whether they could read or

---

63. In an oral culture, as far as possible, everything was communicated face-to-face, by speaking. The only situations that were exceptions were: 1) if it was impossible for a speaker/author to travel to where the intended audience was for the message to be delivered in a timely manner; and 2) for purposes of permanency (e.g., legal records or historical data). As is obvious, both situations were very much applicable in the composition and reception of the scriptures.

not) learned early to interpret what they *heard*. Due to extensive prior experience in listening, they had mastered hearing various kinds of oral communication patterns, such as the Letter of James. They would have been able to track the inverted parallel structure well, especially after the whole letter had been read in their synagogue (Jas 2:2) multiple times.[64]

Breaking down the sectional structuring of the Letter of James

While it appears not to always be the case, the book-length chiastic structures in both the HB and the New Testament that are most readily recognized and validated also are made up of smaller section-by-section internal chiastic structures. As will be seen in the discussion below, that is the case with the overall inverted parallel outline of the Letter of James presented above.

As with the larger layers of the letter, for the internal parallelism of each section to be considered legitimate, there must be recognizable interaction among the smaller pairs in each section in one of the three ways mentioned in the explanation above about how chiastic structure works by: 1) saying essentially the same; 2) saying the opposite; or 3) creating a larger truth, when both parts of the pair are considered together.

This is precisely the kind of textual interaction that will be seen as each passage in the Letter of James is considered below. It should be noticed that the pairings from the overall outline of James will be considered together (e.g., A [1:2–4], then A' [5:19–20]), instead of moving straight through the letter. (The wording of the text of the Letter of James below is taken from the NRSV. The underlining in the biblical text of James is of the parallel words or ideas that will be discussed below each section of the letter).

Introduction: Author, Audience, and Greeting

> (1:1) James, a servant of God and of the Lord Jesus Christ, To the twelve tribes in the Dispersion: Greetings.

---

64. It must also be remembered that the original manuscripts and their copies for several centuries did not contain chapter and verse divisions. Thus, if, as in this case, a question about the Letter of James was asked after it had been read to the gathering, it would have been necessary to *re*read the entire letter, at least until it had begun to be memorized by members of the audience.

This is the only part of the Letter of James that is not set up in an inverted parallel manner. The reason for that is that 1:1a tells the audience who wrote the letter, while 1:1b describes those who would receive the letter.

(A) Internal inverted parallel structure of James 1:2–4

a (1:2) My brothers and sisters, whenever you face trials of any kind, consider it nothing but joy,
   b (1:3) because you know that the testing of your faith produces endurance;
   b' (1:4a) and let endurance have its full effect,
a' (1:4b) so that you may be mature, lacking in nothing.

The abb'a' structure of A (Jas 1:2–4) is an example of the simplest kind of inverted parallelism. The outside pairing (a [1:2]/a' [1:4b]) is made up of opposites: facing trials (1:2), toward the end of becoming mature (1:4b). Both parts of the inner pairing deal with endurance (1:3/1:4a).

(A') Internal inverted parallel structure of James 5:19–20

a (5:19a) My brothers and sisters, if anyone among you wanders from the truth
   b (5:19b) and is brought back by another,
   b' (5:20a) you should know that whoever brings back a sinner
a' (5:20b) from wandering will save the sinner's soul from death and will cover a multitude of sins.

Again, the abb'a' structure of A (Jas 5:19–20) is simple. The repeating of "wanders" and "wandering" in a (5:19a) and a' (5:20b) is obvious parallel. The same is true of "brought back" in b (5:19b) and "brings back" in b' (5:20a).

(B) Internal inverted parallel structure of James 1:5–8

a (1:5a) If any of you is lacking in wisdom, ask God,
   b (1:5b) who gives to all generously and ungrudgingly, and it will be given you.
     c (1:6a) But ask in faith, never doubting,

c' (1:6b) for the one who <u>doubts</u> is like a wave of the sea, driven and tossed by the wind;
  b' (1:7) for the doubter, being <u>double-minded and unstable</u> in every way,
a' (1:8) must not expect to receive anything from the Lord.

The structure of B (Jas 1:5–8) is slightly more complex than the two in A (1:2–4) and A' (5:19–20). It has a third layer of parallels: abcc'b'a'. The a/a' layer is made up of complementary ideas: "ask God" (1:5a) and "receive" from "the Lord" (1:8). The b/b' layer contrasts the expressed character of God: "generously and ungrudgingly" (1:5b) and those who are "double-minded and unstable" (1:7). The inner layer (c/c') repeats the idea of "doubting" (1:6a) and "doubts" (1:6b).

(B') Internal inverted parallel structure of James 5:12–18

a (5:12) Above all, my beloved, do not swear, either by heaven or earth or by any other oath, but let your "Yes" be yes and your "No" be no, so that you may not fall under condemnation.
  b (5:13) Are any among you suffering? They should <u>pray</u>. Are any cheerful? They should sing songs of praise.
    c (5:14–15) Are any among you sick? They should call for the elders of the church and have them <u>pray</u> over them, anointing them with oil in the name of the Lord. <u>The prayer of faith</u> will <u>save the sick</u>, and the Lord will raise them up; and anyone who has committed sins will be forgiven.
    c' (5:16a) Therefore confess your sins to one another, and <u>pray</u> for one another, so that you may be <u>healed</u>.
  b (5:16b) The <u>prayer</u> of the righteous is powerful and effective.
a' (5:17–18) Elijah was a human being like us, and he prayed fervently that it might not rain, and for three years and six months it did not rain on the earth. Then he prayed again, and the heaven gave rain and the earth yielded its harvest.

The structure of B' (5:12–18) is the same as that of B (1:5–8 [abcc'b'a']), even though B' is a longer passage. The words "heaven" and "earth" is repeated in both a (5:12) and a' (5:17–18). Prayer is found in both parts of the b pairing (5:13/5:16a). In the c layer, prayer is again seen (5:14–15; 5:16a), as well as saving the sick (5:14–15) and healing (5:16a).

(C) Internal inverted parallel structure of James 1:9–21

a (1:9–11) Let the believer who is lowly boast in being raised up, and the rich in being brought low (*tapeinosei*), because the rich will disappear like a flower in the field. For the sun rises with its scorching heat and withers the field; its flower falls, and its beauty perishes. It is the same way with the rich; in the midst of a busy life, they will wither away.

> b (1:12) Blessed is anyone who endures temptation. Such a one has stood the test and will receive <u>the crown of life that the Lord has promised to those who love him</u>.

>> c (1:13–15) No one, when tempted, should say, "I am being tempted by God"; for God cannot be tempted by evil and he himself tempts no one. But one is tempted by one's own desire, being lured and enticed by it; then, when that desire has conceived, it <u>gives birth</u> to sin, and that sin, when it is fully grown, <u>gives birth</u> to death.

>>> *d (1:16–17) Do not be deceived, my beloved. Every generous act of giving, with every perfect gift, is from above, coming down from the Father of lights, with whom there is no variation, or shadow due to change.*

>> c' (1:18a) In fulfillment of his own purpose he <u>gave us birth</u> by the word of truth,

> b' (1:18b) so that we would become <u>a kind of first fruits of his creatures</u>.

a' (1:19–21) You must understand this, my beloved. Let everyone be quick to hear, slow to speak, slow to anger, for your anger does not produce God's righteousness. Therefore, rid yourselves of all sordidness and rank growth of wickedness, and welcome with meekness (*prauteti*) the implanted word that has the power to save your souls.

The C (C/C') layer of the Letter of James (1:9–21/5:1–11) is the first major section of the book that has an odd number of parts: ab*cdc*'b'a'. In the a layer (1:9–11/1:19–21), as seen above, the idea of humility/meekness is found in both parts. In the b layer (b/b'), there are complementary ideas of "the crown of life" and being "a kind of firstfruits of his creatures." The idea of "giving birth" is found in both c/c' (1:13–15/1:18a). The focal point of the C section is the description of the astounding generosity of the Father of Lights: d (1:16–17).

(C') Internal inverted parallel structure of James 5:1–11

a (5:1–3) Come now, you rich people, weep and wail for the miseries that are coming to you. Your riches have rotted, and your clothes are moth-eaten. Your gold and your silver have rusted, and their rust will be evidence against you, and it will eat your flesh like fire.
    b (5:4–6) Listen! The wages of the laborers who mowed your fields, which you kept back by fraud, cry out, and <u>the cries of the harvesters have reached the ears of the Lord of hosts</u>. You have condemned and murdered the righteous one, who does not resist you.
        c (5:7a) Be patient, therefore, beloved, until <u>the coming of the Lord</u>.
            d (5:7b) The farmer waits for the precious crop from the earth, being patient with it until it receives the early and the late rains.
        c' (5:8) You also must be patient. Strengthen your hearts, for <u>the coming of the Lord</u> is near.
    b' (5:9) Beloved, do not grumble against one another, so that you may not be judged. See, <u>the Judge is standing at the doors</u>!
a' (5:10–11) As an example of suffering and patience, beloved, take the prophets who spoke in the name of the Lord. Indeed, we call blessed those who showed endurance. You have heard of the endurance of Job, and you have seen the purpose of the Lord, how the Lord is compassionate and merciful.

The structure of C' (1:9–21) is the same as that of C: abc*d*c'b'a'. In the first internal layer (a/a'), the long-term destiny of the unrighteous rich (5:1–3) is contrasted with the compassionate, merciful purpose of the Lord in regard to Job, a righteous man (5:10–11). The b layer contains the two descriptions of God as "the Lord of Hosts" (5:4–6) and "the Judge" (5:9). Both parts of the c layer (5:7/5:9) contain the wording "the coming of the Lord." The central point of the structure (d) is the example of the farmer's patience in waiting for rain, in comparison to waiting for the coming of the Lord (5:8).

(D) Internal inverted parallel structure of James 1:22–27

a (1:22) But be doers of the word, and not merely hearers who deceive themselves.
    b (1:23–24) For if any are <u>hearers of the word and not doers</u>, they are like those who look at themselves in a mirror; for they look at themselves and, on going away, immediately forget what they are like.

> c (1:25a) But those who look into the perfect law, the law of liberty, and persevere,
>> b' (1:25b) being <u>not hearers who forget but doers who act</u>—they will be blessed in their doing.
>
> a' (1:26–27) If any think they are religious, and do not bridle their tongues but deceive their hearts, their religion is worthless. Religion that is pure and undefiled before God, the Father, is this: to care for orphans and widows in their distress, and to keep oneself unstained by the world.

The internal structure of D is odd-numbered (i.e., like both C and C'), but simpler: abcb'a'. It is also crystal clear in its parallelism. For example, a (1:22) contains "deceive themselves," while a' (1:26–27) has "deceive their hearts." In the b/b' layer, there are practical opposites: "hearers of the word and not doers" (1:23–24) versus "not hearers who forget but doers who act" (1:25b). In the middle (d) is the important wording "those who look into the perfect law, the law of liberty, and persevere" (1:25a).

(D') Internal inverted parallel structure of James 4:11–17

> a (4:11–12) Do not speak evil against one another, brothers and sisters. Whoever speaks evil against another or judges another, speaks evil against the law and judges the law; but if you judge the law, you are not a doer of the law but a judge. There is one lawgiver and judge who is able to save and to destroy. So who, then, are you to judge your neighbor?
>> b (4:13) Come now, you who say, "<u>Today or tomorrow we will go to such and such a town and spend a year there, doing business and making money.</u>"
>>> c (4:14a) Yet you do not even know what <u>tomorrow</u> will bring.
>>>> d (4:14b) *What is your life? For you are a mist that appears for a little while . . .*
>>> c' (4:14c) . . . <u>and then vanishes away</u>.
>> b' (4:15) Instead you ought to say, "<u>If the Lord wishes, we will live and do this or that</u>."
>
> a' (4:16–17) As it is, you boast in your arrogance; all such arrogance is evil. Anyone, then, who knows the right thing to do and fails to do it, commits sin.

The structure of D' is abcdc'b'a'. It is fairly clear as to its internal parallelism: The word "evil" is twice in a (4:11–12), then again in a' (4:16–17). There is a marked contrast in the b/b' layer, between the independent attitude of relocating and making money (4:13) versus the attitude of dependence that says, "If the Lord wills, we will live and do this or that" (4:15). The c/c' layer compares the idea of not knowing "what tomorrow will bring" (4:14a) with mist that "vanishes away" (4:14c). The midpoint (d) asks a hard question: "What is your life" and answers "[Y]ou are a mist that appears for a little while" (4:14b), very humbling wording.

(E) Internal inverted parallel structure of James 2:1–13

> a (2:1–4) My brothers and sisters, do you with your acts of favoritism really believe in our glorious Lord Jesus Chris. For if a person with gold rings and fine clothes comes into your assembly, and if a poor person with dirty clothes also comes in, and if you take notice of the one wearing the fine clothes and say, "Have a seat here, please," while to the one who is poor you say, "Stand there," or "Sit at my feet," have you not made distinctions among yourselves and become judges with evil thoughts?
> > b (2:5–7) Listen, my beloved brothers and sisters. Has not God chosen the poor in the world to be rich in faith and to be heirs of the kingdom that he has promised to those who love him? But <u>you have dishonored the poor</u>. Is it not the rich who oppress you? Is it not they who blaspheme the excellent name that was invoked over you?
> > > c (2:8) You do well if you really fulfill the royal law according to the scripture, "<u>You shall love your neighbor as yourself</u>."
> > > > *d (2:9–10) But if you show partiality, you commit sin and are convicted by the law as transgressors. For whoever keeps the whole law but fails in one point has become accountable for all of it.*
> > > c' (2:11a) For the one who said, "<u>You shall not commit adultery</u>," also said, "<u>You shall not murder</u>."
> > b' (2:11b) Now if you do not commit adultery, but if you murder, <u>you have become a transgressor of the law</u>.
> a' (2:12–13) So speak and so act as those who are to be judged by the law of liberty, for judgment will be without mercy to anyone who has shown no mercy; mercy triumphs over judgment.

The E layer is structured abc*d*c'b'a'. In a (2:1–4), "favoritism" is an act that shows no mercy, making persons with partiality "judges with evil thoughts," while a' (2:12–13) makes it clear that those who have not shown mercy will receive no mercy when they are judged. In b (2:5–7), the utter wrongness of dishonoring the poor is developed, while b' (2:11b) speaks of being "a transgressor of the law." Both parts of the c layer (2:8/2:11a) contain commands from the HB: "Love your neighbor as yourself" in c, and "You shall not commit adultery" and "You shall not murder" in c'. The midpoint (d) underscores the difficulty of trying to keep the Torah: "For whoever keeps the whole law but fails in one point has become accountable for all of it" (2:9–10).

(E') Internal inverted parallel structure of James 4:1–10

a (4:1–3) Those conflicts and disputes among you, where do they come from? Do they not come from your cravings that are at war within you? You want something and do not have it; so you commit murder. And you covet something and cannot obtain it; so you engage in disputes and conflicts. You do not have, because you do not ask. You ask and do not receive, because you ask wrongly, in order to spend what you get on your pleasures.
   b (4:4) Adulterers! Do you not know that friendship with the world is enmity with God? Therefore, whoever wishes to be a friend of the world becomes an enemy of God.
      c (4:5) Or do you suppose that it is for nothing that the scripture says, "God yearns jealously for the spirit that he has made to dwell in us."
         d (4:6a) But he gives all the more grace;
      c' (4:6b) therefore it says, "God opposes the proud, but gives grace to the humble."
   b' (4:7–8a) Submit yourselves therefore to God. Resist the devil, and he will flee from you. Draw near to God, and he will draw near to you.
a' (4:8b–10) Cleanse your hands, you sinners, and purify your hearts, you double-minded. Lament and mourn and weep. Let your laughter be turned into mourning and your joy into dejection. Humble yourselves before the Lord, and he will exalt you.

The internal structure of E' is also abcdc'b'a', as is its counterpart section (i.e., E). In internal layer a/a', several examples of sinful attitudes and behavior are listed (4:1–3), then applications for the guilty parties to deal with their sin are also listed (4:8b–10). Pairing b/b' speaks of friendship with "the world" (4:4), then resisting "the devil" (4:7–8a). Both parts of the c layer (4:5/4:6b) refer to the scripture. The midpoint (d [4:6a]) states that, in the midst of all the sinful thought and behavior described in this section, God "gives all the more grace."

BACKGROUND ISSUES   33

(F) Internal inverted parallel structure of James 2:14-26

> a (2:14-17) *What good is it*, my brothers and sisters, if you say you have faith but do not have works? Can (that) faith save you? If a brother or sister is naked and lacks daily food, and one of you says to them, "Go in peace; keep warm and eat your fill," and yet you do not supply their bodily needs, *what is the good of that*? So faith by itself, if it has no works, is dead.
>
>> b (2:18) But someone will say, "You have faith and I have works." <u>Show me your faith apart from your works, and I by my works will show you my faith</u>.
>>
>>> c (2:19-22) You believe that God is one; you do well. Even the demons believe—and shudder. Do you want to be shown, you senseless person, that faith apart from works is barren? <u>Was not our ancestor Abraham justified by works when he offered his son Isaac on the altar? You see (Greek *blepo*) that faith was active along with his works, and faith was brought to completion (Greek *teleios*) by the works</u>.
>>>
>>>> d' (2:23) *Thus the scripture was fulfilled (Greek pleroo) which says, "<u>Abraham believed God, and it was reckoned to him as righteousness,</u>" and he was called the friend of God.*
>>>
>>> c' (2:24) <u>You see (Greek *orao*) that a person is justified by works, and not by faith alone</u>.
>>
>> b' (2:25) Likewise, was not Rahab the prostitute also justified by works when she welcomed the messengers and sent them out by another road?
>
> a' (2:26) For just as the body without the spirit is dead, so faith without works is also dead.

In the F section (2:14-26), the a layer (a [2:14-17]; a' [2:26]) sets up the whole passage. By reading these four verses, it become clear the issue is not simply faith and all types of works, but faith that is expected to express itself in works that confront the need in front of the believer. Unless faith is expressed in that type of works, it is dead. In parallel, a' (2:26) observes that faith without works is as dead as a body without a spirit, because there is no animating power.

The b layer is made up of b (2:18) and b' (2:25). The main point of 2:18 (b) is that faith *cannot* be demonstrated without works. The b' portion of the pairing (2:25) describes Rahab as a classic example of her faith being demonstrated by her "works" of protecting the two Jewish messengers. (<u>Note</u>: In Josh 2, there is no clear statement of faith on Rahab's part, but she certainly *acts* as if she is a believer in the one true God of

Israel. Also, in Heb 11:31, it says, "By faith Rahab the prostitute did not perish with those who were disobedient, because she had received the spies in peace.")

The c layer is made up of c (2:19–22) and c' (2:24). The largest of the pairings in 2:14–26 is c (2:19–22). The reason all this material is together is because these verses develop the almost comical contrast between the "bare" (i.e., "barren") belief of demons in the existence of God with Abraham's faith expressed in his testing by God in which he was obedient in his "work" to sacrifice Isaac in Gen 22. The explanation of this in 2:22 is crucial: Abraham's faith was active along with his works, which resulted in the maturing (Greek *teleios*) of his faith. It is in that sense that Abraham was "justified by works" (2:24): his faith was unquestionably demonstrated by his "works" in sacrificing Isaac, as God had commanded Abraham, in order to test him.

The central point: d (2:23)—The scripture was "filled full" (the only use of *pleroo* in the Letter of James, meaning that there is no way to compare James's usage of *pleroo* elsewhere) and here it cannot mean "fulfilled *at a point in time*." The reason for that is that there had been some thirty years between God's declaration that Abram was "justified" in Gen 15:6 until the Akedah in Gen 22:1ff. This is a completely different understanding of "justified" from Paul's concept in Galatians and Romans. The scripturally unique way of referring to Abraham—as "the friend of God"—found only in Isa 41:8 and 2 Chr 20:7 is to show that Abraham's relationship with God *matured* to the point where he was unusually close to the Lord.

(F') Internal inverted parallel structure of James 3:13–18

a (3:13) Who is wise and understanding among you? Show by your good life that your works are done with gentleness (*prauteti*) born of wisdom.
  b (3:14) But if you have bitter <u>envy</u> and <u>selfish ambition</u> in your hearts, do not be boastful and false to the truth.
    c (3:15) Such wisdom does not come down from above, but is earthly, unspiritual, devilish.
  b' (3:16) For where there is <u>envy</u> and <u>selfish ambition</u>, there will also be disorder and wickedness of every kind.
a' (3:17–18) But the wisdom from above is first pure, then peaceable, gentle (*epieikeis*), willing to yield, full of mercy and good fruits, without

a trace of partiality or hypocrisy. And a harvest of righteousness is sown in peace for those who make peace.

Section F' has an abcb'a' structure, which is easy to see: two almost interchangeable terms for gentleness are found in both a (3:13) and a' (3:17–18). The b layer repeats "envy and selfish ambition" (3:14/3:16). The midpoint (c [3:15]) clearly states the origin of envy and selfish ambition: it "does not come down from above, but is earthly, unspiritual, devilish."

(G) Internal inverted parallel structure of James 3:1–12

a (3:1) Not many of you should become teachers, my brothers (and sisters), for you know that we who teach will be judged with greater strictness.

  b (3:2) For all of us make many mistakes. Anyone who makes no mistakes in speaking is perfect, able to keep the whole body in check with a bridle.

   c (3:3–4) If we put bits into the mouths of horses to make them obey us, we guide their whole bodies. Or look at ships: though they are so large that it takes strong winds to drive them, yet they are guided by a very small rudder wherever the will of the pilot directs.

    d (3:5) So also the tongue is a small member, but it boasts of great exploits. How great a forest is set ablaze by a small fire!
     e (3:6a) And the tongue is a fire. The world of evil....[65]
    d' (3:6b) The tongue is placed among our members; it stains the whole body, sets on fire the cycle of nature, and is itself set on fire by hell (Greek *geennes* [lit. "Gehenna"]).

   c' (3:7) For every species of beast and bird, of reptile and sea creature, can be tamed and has been tamed by the human species,

  b' (3:8–10a) but no one can tame the tongue—a restless evil, full of deadly poison. With it we bless our Lord and Father, and with it we

---

65. The standard translation being used in this book is the NRSV, which generally offers a reasonably literal rendering. However, in Jas 3:6, a very important phrase, which I have literally translated from the text of the *UBS Greek New Testament* 5th ed. (Revised) as "the world of evil" (Greek *ho kosmos tes adikias*), has been relocated in the NRSV to read "And the tongue is a fire. The tongue is placed among our members as a world of iniquity." The proper order of the wording from the Greek text, which is reflected above in the structural outline of Jas 3:1–12, is followed in, e.g., ESV, NIV, CSB, and NASB 2020. No explanation is given in the NRSV notes for the change from the Greek word order in the translation.

curse those who are made in the likeness of God. From the same <u>mouth</u> come blessing and cursing.

a' (3:10b–12) My brothers (and sisters), this ought not to be so. Does a spring pour forth from the same opening both fresh and brackish water? Can a fig tree, my brothers and sisters, yield olives, or a grapevine figs? No more can salt water yield fresh.

Section G (3:1–12) is the midpoint of the entire Letter of James. Its focus is on the tongue—speaking—and on just how destructive it can be. In the a/a' internal layer, the repeated wording is "brothers (and sisters)" (3:1/ twice in 3:10b–12). It may be noteworthy that section G is the only section of the Letter of James that has "brothers (and sisters)" bracketing both ends of the section. Layer b has "speaking" in 3:2 and "the tongue" and "mouth" in 3:8–10a. Layer c speaks of horses and ships being "guided" by small things (3:3–4) and other animals being "tamed" (3:7). In the d layer, both parts (3:5/3:6b) speak of tongues as members of our body and the tongue setting fires ablaze. The midpoint (e) of not only Section G, but of the entire Letter, is 3:6a: "And the tongue is a fire. The world of evil . . . ." What a direct, incredibly practical point for James to place in the biggest spotlight in his letter!

Because this book is not a biblical commentary, the above structure of the Letter of James will be referenced only when clarifications provided by the structure naturally come into play regarding answering issues related to a supersessionist perspective discussed in the remaining chapters of the book. However, the above overview of the book-length chiastic structure of James should be kept in mind throughout for two reasons: 1) it has offered an initial overview of sorts of the whole Letter of James; and 2) it explains why certain wording or ideas are placed where they are in the various passages throughout the letter.

Conclusion

This chapter has discussed all the major introductory background issues related to the Letter of James, except for its original audience. That issue will be handled next, in chapter 3.

In order, those background issues were: 1) date; 2) authorship; 3) location of the author; 4) literary genre; and 5) the structure of the letter. The date of James was concluded to be in the mid-40 CE. The author is James, the brother of Jesus. The location of James when he wrote his letter was in Jerusalem. The Letter of James is best understood as a type of Jewish literature called an "apostolic diaspora letter," though there are likely other types of literature within the book. Finally, the structure of the Letter of James is a chiasm, an inverted paralleling of the entire text of the letter, except the Introduction in 1:1, that centers on 3:1–12, the danger of abuse of the tongue, specifically on 3:6a: "And the tongue is a fire, a world of unrighteousness."[66]

---

66. Author's lit. translation from the Greek text of Jas 3:6a.

3

"The twelve tribes in the diaspora"[1]

THIS CHAPTER WILL SEEK to answer the question: Who was the original audience of the Letter of James? Beyond the standard supersessionist view of James's audience, there are several possible understandings of the basic Jewish audience view, all of which have implications for the wider understanding of the letter. All the major views of the audience to whom James was written will be discussed in the rest of this chapter: what I call *firm* supersessionism; *soft* supersessionism; *soft* post-supersessionism; and *firm* post-supersessionism. First, however, it will be helpful to survey the meanings of the wording "the twelve tribes" and "the Diaspora" in James's day, as seen in the use of the wording throughout the New Testament. Following that, there will be a historical and hermeneutical survey of the supersessionist position.

The use of "the twelve tribes" in the New Testament

There are only four uses of the phrase "the twelve tribes" (Greek *tais dodeka phylais*) in the entire New Testament: Matt 19:28; Luke 22:30; Jas 1:1; and Rev 21:12. In both Matt 19:28 and Luke 22:30, the twelve apostles are told that, in the end times, they will sit on "thrones, judging the twelve tribes of Israel." In Matt 19:28, that event is part of what is called "the renewal of all things." In Luke 22:30, Jesus calls it "my kingdom." Revelation 21:12 is found in the description of the new heaven and earth in Rev 21–22, and specifically of "the holy city, the New Jerusalem" (21:2). In

---

1. The chapter title is a literal translation of the following Greek wording in Jas 1:1: *tais dodeka phylais tais en te diaspora*.

describing the twelve gates of the holy city, the author states that, "on the gates are inscribed the names of the twelve tribes of the Israelites."

The significance of all three of these uses of "the twelve tribes" refer to events or realities in the end times or the eternal state. *That must mean the twelve tribes of Israel will still be in existence at the end of the age and forever.*

Why is that particular point important to this study regarding the meaning of "the twelve tribes" in Jas 1:1? Its importance is linked to the tendency of supersessionists to try to discredit attempts to take the wording "the twelve tribes" at face value by claiming that there were only *two tribes* left after the Assyrian Empire effectively destroyed the ten tribes of the Northern Kingdom of Israel in 722–721 BCE.[2] On the other hand, if "the twelve tribes" will still be in existence at the end of the age and on into eternity, as seen in the discussions above of Matt 19:28, Luke 22:30, and Rev 21:12—that understanding agrees completely with Ezek 37:19–23:

> This is what the Lord God says, "Behold, I am going to take the stick of Joseph, which is in the hand of Ephraim, and the tribes of Israel, his companions; and I will put them with it, with the stick of Judah, and make them one stick, and they will be one in my hand. (37:19)

Also, while hardly accounting for all the supposed "lost tribes" of the northern kingdom of Israel, it is significant that King Hezekiah of Judah, after restoring the Temple worship in Jerusalem (2 Chr 29), sent messengers to "all Israel and Judah" to come to the Temple "in Jerusalem to the Passover to the Lord God of Israel" (30:1). The most amazing part of this is that the northern kingdom of Israel had been overrun by the Assyrian Empire some years before, during the reign of Hezekiah's predecessor, Ahaz. Thus, Hezekiah did not treat the northern kingdom of Israel as if all ten of its tribes had been destroyed or deported to Assyria.

While many in the northern kingdom laughed at Hezekiah's messengers and "mocked them" (30:10), some from the tribes of "Asher, Manasseh, and Zebulun" humbled themselves and came to Jerusalem" (30:11). Then, at the time of the Passover, "many from Ephraim and

---

2. The actual outcome was that the bulk of the population was killed, some were relocated to the northeastern frontier of the Assyrian Empire, and some fled to the Southern Kingdom of Judah. In all these cases collectively, it is most accurate to say that the nation of Israel was decimated, though not entirely wiped out.

Manasseh, and Issachar and Zebulun" (30:18) showed up to worship. As a result of the wonderful time of worship before the Lord, "all the assembly .. rejoiced .. both the strangers who came from the land of Israel and those living in Judah" (30:25). This glimpse may also imply that many of those of the remainder of the ten tribes of the northern kingdom stayed on in Judah, at least partly to worship YHWH.

Therefore, it is entirely plausible that all "twelve tribes" (Jas 1:1) were in existence at the time of the letter of James.[3] At least, that seems to be the way James viewed the audience of his letter, even if contemporary biblical scholars cannot yet be sure where all the tribes were living at the time. Thus, James quite naturally *would have* addressed "the twelve tribes" in a natural, not a figurative, manner in Jas 1:1.

The use of "Diaspora" in the New Testament

There are but three uses in the New Testament of the Greek term *diaspora,* which means "dispersion," particularly of "dispersion of the Jews among the Gentiles":[4] John 7:35; Jas 1:1; and 1 Pet 1:1. The use in John 7:35 is almost impossible to understand as referring to anything other than the Diaspora of Jews dispersed from Jerusalem or wider Israel. John 7:32 tells of the plot of the Jewish religious leadership to arrest Jesus, in Jerusalem for the Festival of Booths (7:10, 37). In 7:33–34, Jesus tells the crowd that he would not be with them much longer but would return to the one who sent him (i.e., the Father), and that where he was going, they could not find him or go there. Verse 35 represents the confused response by those hearing Jesus: they wondered if he meant he was going to the *diaspora* to teach Greeks. That wording refers to the lands outside Israel where Jews lived among Greek-speaking gentiles.

---

3. Bauckham (*James*, 14) helpfully discusses the improbable nature of arguments that the church, as the presumed "New Israel," would have been addressed by James as either "the twelve tribes" or the Diaspora at that early date.

4. BAGD, *diaspora*, 188.

The meaning of 1 Pet 1:1 is almost equally clear in its wording and context as John 7:35, but has been taken quite differently by supersessionists over the centuries. Verse 1 reads: "To the exiles of the Dispersion (Greek *diasporas*) in Pontus, Galatia, Cappadocia, Asia and Bithynia" (NRSV). The supersessionist position on the meaning of this wording in 1 Pet 1:1 is that it is to be spiritualized to understand the recipients of 1 Peter as either: 1) Christians in general; or 2) a mixed Jewish and gentile audience.[5]

Clear examples of views 1) and 2) are found in the first and second editions of the Tyndale New Testament Commentary (TNTC) series volumes on 1 Peter. A. M. Stibbs, whose work in the first TNTC series was published in 1959, states in his comments on 1 Pet 1:1:

> The word *diaspora*, rendered "Dispersion," was used to denote Jews living outside Palestine (see John vii. 35). It is used here to describe Christians and to suggest that in this world they are not only scattered but away from their true homeland or metropolis in heaven.[6]

Oddly, though Stibbs accurately states the meaning and original Jewish context of "Diaspora," he does not even mention the *possibility* of that same undisputed Jewish historical meaning continuing in 1 Pet 1:1, reflecting a supersessionist viewpoint not even considering any other interpretive option.

Things do change somewhat—but with the same interpretive bottom line—in the expressed view of Wayne Grudem, in his 1988 TNTC replacement volume on 1 Peter. As will be seen below, his view remains supersessionist—though not as scant on historical perspective. Regarding the meaning of Diaspora in 1 Pet 1:1, Grudem writes:

> The Dispersion (*diaspora*) was a term used by Greek-speaking Jews to refer to Jewish people "scattered" throughout the nations, "dispersed" from their homeland, Israel (see Jn 7:35). Here and in James 1:1, "Dispersion" refers to Christians, but this does not imply that Peter was writing only to Jewish Christians. . . . Rather, the term here has a new spiritual sense, referring to Christians

---

5. I would refer to the view that 1 Peter is written to "Christians" in general as *hard* supersessionism and the view that the letter was written to a mixed audience of Jewish and Gentile believers as *soft* supersessionism. However, it should be understood that both understandings still amount to replacement theology.

6. Stibbs, *First Epistle General of Peter* TNTC, 72.

"dispersed throughout the world and living away from their heavenly homeland (yet hoping someday to reach it)."[7]

Grudem at least briefly mentions the most straightforward of the possible meanings of *diaspora* in 1 Pet 1:1—that it *could* be speaking of a scattered audience of Jewish believers in Jesus Messiah—before quickly dismissing the view.

Similar to Grudem's view (but more detailed), D. A. Carson, in speaking of the use of *diaspora* in 1 Pet 1:1, states:

> That one word forces us to reflect on the Diaspora. . . . The word reminds the reader of the impact of the exile under the Assyrian and Babylonian superpowers, with countless thousands of Jews still scattered all over the Mediterranean world and beyond. Through the OT prophets, however, God promised, both before the exile and after the initial return from exile, that he would gather his exiled people and reconstitute the twelve tribes (Isa. 11:11–12; Jer. 31:8–14; Ezek. 37:21–22; Zech. 10:6–12)—promises that lived on in the expectations of later Judaism (e.g., *Pss. Sol.* 17:26–28; *T. Benj.* 9:2). . . . A circumstantial case can be made for the thesis that Christians, both Jews and Gentiles, were among those forcibly sent. If this is correct, then Peter's readers were Christians (both Jews and Gentiles) who had been converted elsewhere, perhaps in Rome, but whose forceful relocation guaranteed their sense of dislocation, setting them up to feel very much like a new generation of exiles in a strange land.[8]

Carson is on target in his understanding of the background of the key term *diaspora*, even tracing the continuing idea forward well into the Second Temple era extrabiblical literature, into which time period he finds that the "gravitational pull" of the return to the promised land for those in the Diaspora was still very much alive. Thus, Carson is to be commended for admitting he is working with but "a circumstantial case" regarding his "thesis" that "both Jews and Gentiles" are the intended audience, having been "forcibly sent" to the five regions of Asia Minor listed in 1 Pet 1:1,[9] especially given that he had already mentioned the ongoing Jewish expectations in that time period to return from the Diaspora to the promised land.

---

7. Grudem, *1 Peter* TNTC, 49.
8. Carson, "1 Peter," 1015–16.
9. Carson, "1 Peter," 1016.

But why would Peter necessarily depart from the standard Jewish understanding of "Diaspora," in favor of the supersessionist view that the church replaced Israel? What evidence in 1 Peter would cause an interpreter to take such a view, other than viewing the text of 1 Peter through a predetermined supersessionist "lens?"

To clarify that a post-supersessionist view of 1 Peter is quite viable, though, I must disagree with the NRSV translation "exiles" for the Greek word *parepidemois* in 1 Pet 1:1—a rendering Carson also uses. It is at least as likely to be accurately rendered as "stranger, sojourner, or resident alien."[10] There is nothing in the historical record stating Christians—Jewish and gentile—were "exiled" from Rome during the period of the likely date of 1 Peter in the mid-60s CE.[11] Instead, it is more likely that such believers fled persecution emanating from Rome, and went to the various provinces in Asia Minor listed in 1 Pet 1:1, making the idea of temporary residency in "sojourner" or "resident alien" more accurate possible translations of *parepidemois* than "exiles."

There are also other reasons for not taking the view that 1 Peter is written to either a gentile audience or a mixed audience of Jews and gentiles: 1) The wording in 1 Pet 2:9, which ideas are taken from Exod 19:5, 6—the first narrative related to God's making of the Mosaic covenant with Israel—cannot easily be taken exegetically as referring to gentile Christians, because the church is not "a chosen *race*"[12] (Greek *genos* [most likely "race" or "nation"]) or "a holy *nation*"[13] (Greek *ethnos* [the singular usage most likely means "nation"). As above, the (presumed) "exegetical" factor[14] that leads to taking a replacement theology perspective on 1 Peter is to view the biblical text through a supersessionist grid; 2) The wording in

---

10. BAGD, "*parepidemos*," 625.

11. According to the latest detailed study of NT chronology (Bernier, *Rethinking the Dates of the New Testament*, 275, 278). The date of the expulsion of Jews from Rome by Emperor Claudius in 49 CE is too early to come into play here. See the helpful discussion of Brian Tucker (*Reading Romans after Supersessionism*, 16–18) on whether Claudius's decree actually dealt with Jesus Messiah or not.

12. Italics mine.

13. Italics mine.

14. What occurs in such cases is more accurately termed *eis*egesis, which means "reading into a text external meaning, then reading it back out as if it is the meaning of the text," as opposed to *ex*egesis, which means "reading out meaning from the text." The difference is that, with *exegesis*, the interpreter allows the text to speak as much as possible to answer the questions raised in the passage, while, with *eisegesis*, at least the contours of the major interpretive decision(s) are already made before approaching the text.

2:12—"Conduct yourselves honorably among the [g]entiles"—is not easily reconciled to the view that 1 Peter is addressed to gentile Christians, or even to a mixed audience; and 3) though Peter ministered in primarily gentile contexts in Corinth (see 1 Cor 1:12) and Rome (see 1 Pet 5:13), it did not make him any less the apostle to the Jews (see Gal 2:7–8), any more than Paul going to Jews on his missionary journeys (e.g., "to the Jew *first* and also to the Greek"[15] [Rom 1:16]) made him any less the apostle to the gentiles. To the extent such logic is correct, it would be expected that Peter wrote 1 Peter to Jewish believers in Jesus Messiah scattered as a sort of "Diaspora" throughout the five Roman provinces in Asia Minor listed in 1:1.

Finally arriving at the use of the Greek *diaspora* in Jas 1:1, it is encouraging to find that D. A. Carson, who also wrote the segment on "James" in the *Commentary on the New Testament Use of the Old Testament,* disengages and re-engages hermeneutically in coming to his following conclusion on the original audience of James:

> If the Epistle of James was written early (in the 40s), then it may well be that James, by these expressions,[16] betrays that he has Jewish Christians in mind—Jewish Christians who have been "scattered" not only as the heirs of the exile but also as a result of persecution (cf. Acts 11:19).[17]

Why did I say that Carson was able to "disengage" and "re-engage" in his conclusion on the original audience of the Letter of James? Because just before his concluding paragraph on this topic (see above), Carson had written the following:

> [D]ebates rage over (1) the extent to which these references refer to empirical, racial Israel or, in typological fashion, to the eschatological Israel of the new covenant; (2) the extent to which the years of the exile ended with Cyrus's decree or continued until the time Jesus as the Davidic king introduced the long-promised kingdom, or continue yet until the consummation.[18]

In other words, Carson virtually admits he seriously considered the replacement view of the audience in Jas 1:1. However, to his credit, in the

---

15. Italics mine.
16. "To the twelve tribes in the Dispersion" (i.e., the *diaspora*).
17. Carson, "James," 998.
18. Carson, "James," 998.

end he realized the textual/contextual evidence in favor of an actual Jewish "Diaspora" audience for the Letter of James was too strong to ignore.

Craig Keener comes to a reasonably clear post-supersessionist view of the meaning of *diasporas* in Jas 1:1, also adding more helpful historical background, though he even-handedly includes the supersessionist view:

> The "dispersion" or Diaspora included Jews in the Parthian as well as the Roman Empire, and James would meet Jews from many nations at the pilgrimage festivals to Jerusalem. Some commentators believe that he means the term symbolically for all Christians as spiritual Israelites . . . , but given the letter's contents, James probably particularly addresses Jewish Christians.[19]

To conclude this discussion of the meanings of "twelve tribes" and *diaspora* in Jas 1:1, it appears that the post-supersessionist view fits well both the exegetical and background data having to do with the wording generally translated "To the twelve tribes in the Dispersion" in the first verse of the Letter of James. Thus, it is worth asking at this point how the supersessionist/replacement theology perspective gained the position of prominence that it continues to have within the academic arena and many Christian groups.

Supersessionist thinking: its historical and hermeneutical roots

The roots of supersessionism in early church history

I recently published a book titled *God's Land Promise to Israel: Its Continuation from Genesis to Revelation*,[20] in which both the Introduction (pp. ix–xxxiii) and much of chapter 1 ("Hermeneutics: How to Interpret Israel's Land Promise" [pp. 1–38]) were focused on the topic of the background (i.e., in the Introduction) and the hermeneutical procedure utilized by those who hold the position of replacement theology—in the case of that book particularly regarding God's land promise to Abraham and his descendants. Much of what was discussed in those chapter portions apply to the subject of the basis for a supersessionist viewpoint on the Letter of James—particularly regarding the wording "To the twelve tribes in the Dispersion" (Jas 1:1).

---

19. Keener, "James," 672.
20. Luter, *God's Land Promise to Israel*.

Historically, it is necessary to begin by recognizing that, from at least the time of the early Christian apologist, Justin Martyr (ca. 100–165 CE), the church has been understood by some as the "true Israel."[21] And, according to his later contemporary, Irenaeus (ca. 145–202 CE), "God has ended his covenant with Israel because he was punishing them for rejecting the Messiah."[22] Though such a view did not nearly approach a unanimous view in the earliest centuries of church history, by the time of Augustine (354–430 CE), it was easily the majority perspective.[23]

That was perhaps the key juncture historically in the development of the supersessionist view, given that, from Augustine forward, that perspective found only rare disagreement for over a thousand years[24] and is still held by a sizeable percentage of Christendom today.[25] The reason for this was largely the consensus that developed around Augustine's approach to interpreting scripture.

By the time of Augustine, there had emerged a great rivalry between exponents of the slightly earlier *allegorical* school of biblical interpretation, centered in Alexandria, Egypt and somewhat later so-called *literal* school of interpretation, centered in Antioch, Syria. The two great thinkers of the allegorical school were, first, Clement of Alexandria (ca. 155–220 CE), then the enormously gifted Origen (ca. 185–254 CE). Major thought leaders related to the school of Antioch were the great preacher, St. John Chrysostom (ca. 347–407 CE), and the noted scriptural interpreter, Theodore of Mopseustia (ca. 350–428 CE).[26]

The Alexandrian school followed the previous interpretive approach of the Jewish community in Alexandria in allegorizing scripture: looking for *deeper* spiritual meaning beyond the straightforward *surface* wording of the Bible. In doing so, Clement believed that, like humanity being made up of body and soul, so there were two dimensions to the

---

21. The wording in quotation marks is Justin Martyr's, from his *Dialogue with Trypho*, 11.5.

22. Cited by Gerald McDermott, in *Israel Matters*, 8–9.

23. See the discussion in Fredriksen, *Secundem Carnem*, 29–30.

24. Until at least the broader Reformation/immediate post-Reformation era(s).

25. To a greater or lesser extent, modern church groups that have Reformation roots, as well as Roman Catholicism and at least some Orthodox groups, are Augustinian in at least this aspect of their theology.

26. See, e.g., the very helpful discussion of the schools of thought in Alexandria and Syrian Antioch in chapter 2 ("The History of Interpretation") of Klein, Blomberg, and Hubbard, *Introduction to Biblical Interpretation*, 37–40.

Bible: literal and spiritual. Origen held that humanity was made up of body, soul, and spirit, and he posited that these were paralleled by the literal, spiritual, and moral levels of biblical interpretation.[27]

The basic problem with the allegorical approach to biblical interpretation—both in earlier church history and when it is utilized today—is that there are no controls regarding what an interpreter might "understand," purportedly from a biblical passage, once that person has gone beyond the surface literal wording. (Interestingly, a later significant Alexandrian thinker, Cyril [ca. 378–444 CE] rejected the allegorical approach due to its "arbitrary tendencies" and assumed a "more grammatical approach" to biblical interpretation.)[28]

The Antiochene school strongly reacted against the excesses of the allegorical method and asserted a largely literal approach to biblical interpretation. However, though their major points of contention with the allegorical school were heard in many quarters, their influence was not powerful enough to stop the period of the Middle Ages (ca. 600–1500 CE) from being dominated by allegorical interpretation.[29]

This brings the present survey to the pivotal role of Augustine.[30] On the one hand, he was the strongest "influencer" in limiting the impact of the allegorical method until the Middle Ages. He did so by emphasizing the straightforward interpretive method of the school of Antioch in *most* areas of theological thinking. On the other hand, Augustine continued to allow what could be called *mild* allegorical interpretation in difficult passages, notably dealing with biblical prophecy, but with a restriction: the interpretation was to conform to the "rule of faith." (In that era, the "rule of faith" was the acknowledged authoritative collection of doctrinal beliefs of the church, functioning much like creeds did in the period of church history just ahead of that era.)[31] According to Kaiser, Augustine's apparent motivation in tying interpretations of difficult passages and

---

27. Klein, Blomberg, and Hubbard, *Introduction to Biblical Interpretation*, 38–39.
28. Klein, Blomberg, and Hubbard, *Introduction to Biblical Interpretation*, 39.
29. Klein, Blomberg, and Hubbard, *Introduction to Biblical Interpretation*, 42–45.
30. Augustine can generally be "grouped with several other theologians such as Hilary, and Jerome, the translator of the Latin Vulgate, as representatives of the Western School of Interpretation" (Luter, *God's Land Promise to Israel*, xxi, note 7) in that era. Of those, as said in the text above, Augustine clearly had the greatest long-term influence.
31. Kaiser, "Short History of Interpretation," in W. Kaiser and M. Silva, *Introduction to Biblical Hermeneutics*, 222–23.

prophecy to the rule of faith was to prevent the improper reading of external interpretations into scripture.[32]

There is, however, a hermeneutical/theological *blind spot* in Augustine's reliance on the rule of faith to guarantee proper interpretive outcomes. That blind spot is revealed in asking and answering the following question: *What if the rule of faith did not have everything right or had not yet worked everything out doctrinally?*[33]

I sought to answer that very question in my article, "'The Holy Catholic Church': A Test Case for the Theological Interpretation of Scripture," in the *Criswell Theological Review* in 2017. I pointed out that, in the various versions of the ancient rule of faith known today, the only wording that deals with the people of God in any real sense is "the holy catholic church."[34] That, of course, says absolutely nothing about Israel.

The significance of that observation is that, in Augustine's interpretive approach of falling back on the rule of faith with difficult or prophetic passages, it was not an option at all to interpret a passage as referring to *ethnic* Israel, even if it directly said so and all exegetical indicators pointed to that conclusion. *And that is the way supersessionist biblical interpretation continued until roughly the beginning of the twenty-first century.*

A shrewd recent adjustment to supersessionist thinking

It is fair to say that, while not all supersessionists hold to covenant theology,[35] many do.[36] The reason I made that connection is because, for many years, the approach of most covenant theologians to interpreting biblical prophecy was called a "dual hermeneutic." By that wording what is meant is that, when such covenant thinkers interpreted the rest of the Bible, they did so in a generally straightforward (i.e., natural or literal) manner. However, when it came to prophecy, they approached things quite differently, employing a "spiritual hermeneutic"[37] in a manner very close to the Augustinian approach.

---

32. Kaiser, *Introduction to Biblical Hermeneutics*, 222–23.
33. Luter, *God's Land Promise to Israel*, xxii–xxiii.
34. Luter, "'Holy Catholic Church,'" 79–88.
35. I *am* well aware there is a newer hybrid view called progressive covenant theology. I am *not*, however, aware at this time of any who hold to progressive covenant theology who are not also supersessionists.
36. I should also hasten to say that, while not all who hold to covenant theology are supersessionists, most are.
37. Although the terminology is currently offensive to some covenant theologians,

In recent decades the tag of "spiritualizing" the interpretation of prophecy appears to have finally reached the point at which covenant theologians tired of the implied criticism, especially since there was no obvious way to answer the charge. Thus it was that another hermeneutical route was found to get to the same destination: interpreting biblical prophecy and related passages in a less than natural manner.

What is this more recent "hermeneutical route"?[38] It's called typological interpretation—but that is not to be confused with "types" or "typology," both of which are indeed biblical concepts. The word "type" is taken from the Greek *typos*, which means "pattern, example." A key NT example of the use of *typos* is found in 1 Cor 10:6: "Now these things occurred as *examples* for us . . . ." The wording "these things" speaks of what happened to Israel in the wilderness (10:1–5), all of which were to be taken as foreshadowings in the Hebrew Bible for Paul's audience in Corinth to learn from.

"Typology" is the study of such "types." R. T. France, citing G. W. H. Lampe, helpfully defines "typology" as "the recognition of a correspondence between New and Old Testament events, based on a conviction of the unchanging character of the principles of God's working."[39]

The most important part of this definition is the latter wording: ". . . based on a conviction of the unchanging character of the principles of God's working." The reason that is the case is, *if* "the principles of God's working" are of an "unchanging character," *then* the meanings of prophecies or other related passages dealing with ethnic Israel would necessarily remain the same in the New Testament as in the Hebrew Bible.

When full-bore typological interpretation has been employed over the centuries of church history, there has been a repeated tendency for it to ooze over into allegorical interpretation. Hence, the beginning of the following definition of "typological interpretation" by Kaiser and Silva is eminently understandable:

---

it has not been many years since it was not uncommon to hear of the covenant approach to interpreting prophecy as "spiritualizing" scripture. It may be that the touchiness regarding that terminology has to do with the fact that such terminology historically has also been used to describe allegorical interpretation.

38. Typological interpretation per se cannot be described as "new," because forms of typological interpretation have existed since the earliest centuries of church history. However, it has been employed much more in the past couple of decades by supersessionists.

39. France, *Gospel according to Matthew*, 40.

> Distinguished from allegorical interpretation, this approach affirms the historical meaning of the text but notes that entities (people, objects, events) mentioned in the text prefigure subsequent and corresponding entities (for example, King David is viewed as a type of Christ).[40]

At this point, regarding the most focal issue concerning the wording "To the twelve tribes in the Diaspora" in Jas 1:1, it is worth stating:

> Nowhere in the New Testament does it ever say in so many words that Israel is a prefiguring of Jesus or the Church. That view is more theological deduction than even-handed exegesis. In fact, over 50 years after its publication, there still has not been a compelling answer to Peter Richardson's volume in the Society of New Testament Studies Monograph Series, *Israel in the Apostolic Church*,[41] in which he asserted that there is no New Testament usage of the name "Israel" that can unequivocally be understood as referring to other than ethnic Israel.[42]

Additionally, it must be remembered that Kaiser's and Silva's definition of "typological interpretation" includes the typological elements of 1) entities that prefigure (i.e., *precede* in time); and 2) subsequent (i.e., *later* in time) and corresponding entities. To use the technical terminology, it is "types" (earlier foreshadowings) and "antitypes"[43] (later fulfillments).

The chronological relationship of types and antitypes (i.e., earlier vs. later) is thus crucial, *if* a later entity is to be considered a legitimate antitype of an earlier entity. That very point is why

> Israel *cannot* be a type for either Jesus or the Church because it continues *alongside* both, unchanged in theological significance throughout the entirety of the New Testament. The existence of an actual type requires prefiguring/foreshadowing, then the receding/ceasing of the type in favor of the ongoing existence of the heightened antitype.[44]

---

40. Kaiser and Silva, *Introduction to Biblical Hermeneutics*, 286.
41. Richardson, *Israel in the Apostolic Church*.
42. Luter, *God's Land Promise to Israel*, 35.
43. The word "antitype" comes from the Greek term *antitypos*, which, according to the first definition offered in BAGD means "corresponding to something that has gone before" (76).
44. Luter, *God's Land Promise to Israel*, 37–38. Italics in cited text.

By contrast, ethnic Israel does not "recede" and certainly does not "cease." Instead, a new spiritual entity, the church, is born and begins to grow up next to Israel. Thus, a recent hermeneutical perspective thought to bolster supersessionism is found to be less certain in its trustworthiness than has been assumed in replacement theology circles.

Firm supersessionist interpretation of "the twelve tribes of the Diaspora" (James 1:1)

It is becoming increasingly difficult to find commentators on the Letter of James today who openly espouse the standard (or, as I am referring to it—*firm*) supersessionist position, because their view has been widely—and rightly—critiqued as "spiritualizing" the text and those who followed earlier supersessionist thinkers became more aware of the predictable—and valid—criticism and thus chose their wording much more carefully. However, the following example from the 1950s, by R. V. G, Tasker, in the first series of Tyndale New Testament Commentaries, minces no words in its supersessionist viewpoint:

> James is not addressing a single group of Christians with whose circumstances he is especially familiar, but various congregations of Christians scattered far and wide throughout the Roman world. Together, these groups constitute the people of God who are continuous with the old Israel but consist of all, regardless of their nationality, who acknowledge Jesus as God's Messiah. The comprehensive term used to describe the old Israel in its totality, *the twelve tribes,* can, not unfittingly, be used as a symbolic description of the new Israel.[45]

Tasker's wording in the last sentence of this quotation is quite telling: "The comprehensive term used to describe the old Israel in its totality, *the twelve tribes,* can . . . be used as a symbolic description of the new Israel." As stated above, there is *no* passage in the New Testament in which the church is actually called "the new Israel." Thus, this is nothing more or less than a classic example of an interpreter—a scholarly interpreter,[46] at that—reading a previously determined hermeneutical/theological

---

45. Tasker, *General Epistle of James*, 39. Italics his. One interesting omission in Taker's introductory section to the commentary is that he does not discuss the recipients of the letter but leaves that to his comments on Jas 1:1.

46. Tasker was, at the time of the writing of his James commentary for the TNTC series, professor of New Testament exegesis, King's College, University of London.

commitment into the biblical text. Tasker essentially presents no evidence to back his conclusion, simply choosing to refer to the phrase "the twelve tribes" as "a symbolic[47] description of the new Israel" (i.e., the church).

Soft supersessionist interpretation of "the twelve tribes of the Diaspora" (James 1:1)

A relatively recent example of what I call a *soft* supersessionist understanding of the address to the original audience in Jas 1:1 is found in David Nystrom's NIV Application Commentary volume on James:[48]

> James addresses his letter to the multiracial church, but the native thought world of the letter is Judaism, the multiform Judaism of the first century, and more particularly messianic Judaism. Finally, James writes with a sensitivity to Jewish monotheism, but desires to make the case the loyalty is due to Jesus Christ, and that this loyalty does not endanger loyalty to God.[49]

In the interest of even-handedness, it must be pointed out Nystrom's conclusion is drawn only after he weighed the evidence for both what we now call the post-supersessionist and the supersessionist views. Interestingly, as will be seen below, Nystrom sets forth five points in favor of the post-supersessionist understanding and only four favoring the supersessionist view.[50]

His points for understanding "the twelve tribes" as meaning Jews or Jewish Christians (i.e., the post-supersessionist view) are:[51]

- This is an obvious way of referring to the Jewish nation.
- Parallels in Qumran literature and Haggadah intend ethnic distinctions.
- *Phyle* ("tribe"), when unmodified, must refer to ethnic Israel.

---

47. "Symbolic" interpretation does not mean precisely the same thing as "spiritual" interpretation (or spiritualizing the text). However, the results in interpretation are almost, if not completely, identical.
48. Nystrom, *James*.
49. Nystrom, *James*, 39.
50. Nystrom, *James*, 38–39.
51. So as not to go on at great length, I summarize Nystrom's longer points in both of his listings.

- While the New Testament does use the term in reference to the church,[52] it can use it to refer to ethnic Israel (e.g., Rev 21:12).
- While a symbolic interpretation of the "twelve tribes" is possible, the addition "scattered among the nations"[53] necessarily limits the referent to Jews, and probably to Jewish Christians . . . .

At this point, it can be said that Nystrom has marshalled five solid pieces of evidence favoring understanding the phrase "the twelve tribes" in Jas 1:1 as referring to ethnic Jews. The sad reality, though, is that he tips his hand as to his predetermined supersessionist preference in point 4 by *leading with* the replacement theology view: "While the New Testament does use the term in reference to the church . . ."—*but this is not true!*

Nystrom then counters with his four points favoring taking the wording "twelve tribes" symbolically (i.e., the supersessionist view):

- If the "twelve tribes" must refer to ethnic Israel, then it is unclear how it can refer only to Jews who happen to be Christians.
- Others argue that while the "twelve tribes" clearly indicates ethnic/geographic Israel, the addition of the "scattered among the nations" opens the possibility of a symbolic meaning, since after the fall of the northern kingdom the ten tribes were "lost."
- "Twelve tribes" stands for the unity and integrity of the nation of Israel/people of God. The church, in the universal view of the New Testament, is the successor to Judaism in this regard.
- The fact that the Greek-speaking Jews in Jerusalem could employ a formula that approximated the traditional Hebrew greeting tends to imply an ethnically mixed audience as the intended recipients of the letter of James.

In answer to each of Nystrom's four points: 1) If the recipients of the Letter of James still met in synagogues (Greek *synagoge* [2:2]), it is unlikely unbelieving Jews would have been excluded.[54] Thus, addressing

---

52. As seen in the section at the beginning of this chapter, this statement is not correct. None of the three other uses of "the twelve tribes" in the NT (Matt 19:28; Luke 22:30; Rev 21:12) refer to the church.

53. The NIV paraphrase—it is not a credible translation—of the Greek *en te diaspora* (lit. "in the Diaspora/dispersion") in Jas 1:1 is highly unfortunate.

54. Keener makes essentially this same point in speaking of the audience of James: "James addresses especially Jewish Christians (and probably any other Jews who would listen) . . . ." (*IVP Bible Background Commentary: New Testament*, 670).

the letter to the "twelve tribes" (1:1) would mean the letter would be read to the entire congregations—Jewish believers in Jesus Messiah and Jewish unbelievers alike—though it was intended more for the edification of the believers in the wider group; 2) As noted earlier in this chapter, the other three NT uses of "twelve tribes" (Matt 19:28; Luke 22:30; Rev 21:12) all speak of the "twelve tribes" as realities present at the end of the age or in the eternal state; 3) There is no statement in all of the NT—much less it being the "universal view of the New Testament"—that remotely resembles this claim by Nystrom: "The church . . . is the successor to Judaism." That wording is nothing more or less than a theological decision without clear exegetical warrant; and 4) It is absolutely no surprise that Jews during the NT era would translate their standard Hebrew greeting into Greek, given that Koine Greek was the *lingua franca* of the entire Roman Empire—much as English is the second language of the world today—and does not at all "imply an ethnically mixed audience" for the Letter of James.

Having considered Nystrom's lists for the post-supersessionist and supersessionist positions regarding the meaning of the "twelve tribes of the Diaspora" in Jas 1:1, it is hard not to think that if he had not been so previously attached to the supersessionist view before he wrote that section, he would have taken the post-supersessionist position. After all, he set forth both more and better arguments for the post-supersessionist view!

Fence-sitting interpretation of "the twelve tribes of the Diaspora" (James 1:1)

The terminology just above in the sectional title is being used to describe an interpreter who does not seem to want to make a decision in choosing between the supersessionist and post-supersessionist positions. As a result, it is unclear as to where he or she stands but, in the end, he or she effectively bends over backwards toward the supersessionist position.

An example of interpretive ambivalence about the audience of James 1:1—leaning metaphorically

Robert Wall has written a significant commentary on the Letter of James.[55] However, I have chosen to draw the citations below from his

---

55. Wall, *Community of the Wise*.

entry "James, Letter of" in the *Dictionary of the Later New Testament and Its Developments,* because of the relative conciseness of Wall's thoughts in that NT dictionary article.[56]

In reference to the wording "the twelve tribes in the Diaspora," Wall comments:

> If this opening phrase is taken at face value, the readers are probably Jewish believers ("twelve tribes") with an address in some Roman territory outside of Palestine ("in the Diaspora"). ... If, however, the phrase is taken metaphorically, the scope of possible meaning and setting is significantly widened. ... In a similar way the audience of James consists of those whose primary identity appears religious and eschatological rather than ethnic and national; that is, they form a spiritual people whose life is guided by God's word and whose destiny is the realization of God's promised blessing.[57]

Unfortunately, "relative conciseness" does not guarantee clarity. Why do I say that? Because most readers who looked only at the top three lines of Wall's quote just above would conclude that he is post-supersessionist in his viewpoint. However, most who read only the last five lines of the quotation would conclude that Wall is a supersessionist.

While it is probably not gracious for one scholar to accuse another scholar of "trying to have his cake and eat it too" on a topic like the audience of the Letter of James, that appears the case with Wall's words. However, to give him the benefit of the doubt, it will be left with simply saying that Wall did not conclude that the evidence he weighed was sufficiently clear to come down on either side of the issue.

The problem such a muddled, "on the fence" discussion causes readers who are trying to make up their minds on a crucial issue like supersessionism vs. post-supersessionism is that it leaves the impression it doesn't matter that much which viewpoint you choose. In truth, it matters greatly where every person comes down in their thinking regarding supersessionism!

---

56. Wall, "James, Letter of," in *Dictionary of the Later New Testament,* 545–61.
57. Wall, "James, Letter of," in *Dictionary of the Later New Testament,* 548.

An example of interpretive ambivalence about the audience of James 1:1—leaning ethnically

In the last sub-section, Rob Wall's words began with a positive discussion of the post-supersessionist view of the wording the "twelve tribes in the Diaspora," then shifted into at least as positive of a discussion of the supersessionist view, without clearly opting for either view. In contrast, Peter Davids begins his discussion by presenting and sifting evidence in a manner that appears to favor the supersessionist view. However, in the latter part of his discussion, his view comes down in favor of the post-supersessionist case. Thus, it must be recognized that some scholars sift things thoroughly and go one way, while others sift things just as thoroughly, but go the other way on this key exegetical/hermeneutical issue.

Peter Davids contributed the volume on *The Epistle of James* in the New International Greek Testament Commentary series.[58] In his comments on the audience of the letter, he writes:

> In using the phrase *hai dodeka phulai,* the author looks on the recipients of the epistle as the true Israel. The church has quite naturally appropriated the title, for it was the work of the Messiah to reestablish the twelve tribes (Je. 3:18; Ezk. 37:19–24; Pss. Sol. 17:28), and Christians recognized themselves as the true heirs of the Jewish faith (Rom. 4; 1 Cor. 10:18; Gal. 4:21–31; Phil. 3:3). . . . The second part of the title, however, produces some controversy; the term *diaspora* was used by Jews to indicate that part of Judaism living outside of Palestine. . . . But what would such a term mean to Christians? On the one hand, it is possible that they adopted the term and used it metaphorically to indicate their state as "strangers and pilgrims" upon the earth (cf. Heb. 11:13; 13:14; and 1 Pet. 1:1, 17; 2:11). . . . On the other hand, if one assumes not only a Palestinian, but also a *Jewish* Christian provenance for the work, it would be unnatural to leap over the literal meaning. . . . As a result, we conclude . . . that although the metaphorical sense is attractive, accepting as we do the Jewish Christian origin of the epistle, the most natural way of reading this phrase is as an address to the true Israel (i.e., Jewish Christians) outside of Palestine (i.e., probably in Syria or Asia Minor).

---

58. Davids, *Epistle of James.*

Firm post-supersessionist interpretation of "the twelve tribes of the Diaspora" (James 1:1)

Blomberg and Kammel concisely state their conclusion on the recipients of the Letter of James: "[T]he twelve tribes in the dispersion" most likely refer to a collection of Jewish-Christian congregations somewhere outside Israel toward the eastern end of the Mediterranean basin, perhaps in Syria.[59] There is no hesitation in the statement of their position. They have done their research, made up their minds, and crisply state their post-supersessionist conclusion on the recipients of the Letter of James.

The second example of the *firm* post-supersessionist position, by Aida Besancon Spencer, is not as succinct, but it is equally clear in affirming that those who received the Letter of James were from ethnic Israel.

> The twelve tribes refer to the twelve sons of Jacob, originally Reuben, Simeon, Levi, Judah, Zebulun, Issachar, Dan, Gad, Asher, Naphtali, Joseph, and Benjamin (Gen. 49). Sometimes the two sons of Joseph are counted (Ephraim and Manasseh), omitting Joseph and Levi (e.g., Josh. 13, 15–19). In Revelation 7:5–8 Dan and Ephraim are omitted,[60] replaced by Manasseh and Joseph. Notwithstanding how the tribes are counted, they are a clear reference to the Jewish people.[61]

Indeed! But, there is another part of the wording in Jas 1:1 describing the original audience of the Letter of James. As Spencer asks:

> [T]o which diaspora (1:1) does James refer? The readers were both Christians and Jews, believers in "our glorious Lord Jesus Christ" (2:1) who were undergoing some kind of "trials" (1:2), ... who left Jerusalem after the stoning of Stephen to avoid the Jewish persecution (Acts 8:1–4). At first, they left for the provinces of Judea and Samaria. Eventually they travelled as far as Phoenicia, Cyprus, and Antioch, preaching at first only to other

---

59. Blomberg and Kammel, *James*, 48.

60. To avoid confusion in regard to the deleting of the tribes of Dan and Ephraim in the listing of the twelve tribes of Israel in Rev 7:5–8, the following is my note on that passage from my "Revelation" segment in the *Christian Standard Bible Study Bible*, 2027: "The tribes of Dan and Ephraim are omitted from the listing, perhaps because of their instances of gross idolatry (Jdg 17–18). They are replaced by Joseph and Levi, neither of which was included in the military encampment of tribes in Nm 2."

61. Spencer, *James*, 57. Bold print is used in the source cited.

Jews (Acts 11:19). These dispersed Jewish believers appear to be James's readership.[62]

It does not seem to be mere coincidence that Blomberg and Kammel conclude "With this short letter, therefore, we have what is probably the first NT document written"[63] and that Spencer asserts that the Letter of James "needs to be set between Acts 8–15"[64] (i.e., between ca. 34 and 48 CE). The apparent point here is that an early dating of the Letter of James fits hand in glove with the conclusion that the intended original audience of James was messianic Jewish, although other Jews being present for the reading of the Letter in each "synagogue" (Jas 2:2) cannot be ruled out.

Conclusion

This chapter has traced the meanings of the wording in the description of those to whom James write his letter in Jas 1:1: "the twelve tribes" and "in the Diaspora." Regarding both of those phrases, it is not possible to make them mean "the church" (i.e., as the supposed "new Israel" or "true Israel") without recourse to spiritual/symbolic or typological interpretation. As seen in the discussion above, the problem with calling such approaches measured "exegesis" of the text of the Letter of James is that the interpretive perspective shaping the meaning comes from a specific preunderstanding regarding the text. Now, it must be admitted that it is impossible to do truly objective exegesis of a biblical text. The reason for that is because preunderstandings exist in any biblical scholar's mind and they color the study and understanding of the text in question. With that reality squarely in mind, however, it does become possible to approach a passage with a greater degree of awareness and discretion that minimizes the danger of simply reading in a theologically comfortable meaning from elsewhere in the Bible or that person's individual theological position.

The latter part of this chapter was eye-opening in that it was demonstrated how representative scholars have expressed their understandings of the wording "to the twelve tribes in the Diaspora" (Jas 1:1). For the sake of setting forth a more nuanced way of categorizing such views, examples were given of a thinker holding a *firm* supersessionist position,

---

62. Spencer, *James*, 58. Bold print in source cited.
63. Blomberg and Kammel, *James*, 35.
64. Spencer, *James*, 32.

of one holding a *soft* supersessionist position, of one holding a *soft* post-supersessionist position, and of two holding *firm* post-supersessionist positions. A final observation also was made that it appears that those scholars holding an early dating of the Letter of James (i.e., early to late 40s) were more likely to also draw a post-supersessionist conclusion on the original audience of the Letter of James.

4

"The perfect law of liberty"

IN GAL 3:10, THE apostle Paul makes the following assertion concerning the law of Moses: "For all who rely on the works of the law are under a curse; for it is written, 'Cursed is everyone who does not observe and obey all the things written in the book of the law.'" Paul's stated perspective there, at least at first glance, seems dramatically different than where James seems to be coming from in referring to "the perfect law of freedom" (Greek *nomon teleion ton tes eleuthrias*) in Jas 1:25.

Both Paul and James were devout messianic Jews. That point is crystal clear in the advice of James and the elders of the Jerusalem church to Paul in Acts 21:17–26 to carry out a vow to show that he was still a Torah-observant Jew. Paul immediately followed that advice—with absolutely no sense in the text that he was compromising any personal convictions in doing so—demonstrating that both men had the greatest respect for, and commitment to, observance of the Torah (i.e., the wording "the law" usually refers to the Torah in the New Testament).

If that was the case, how could their apparent expressed views on the Mosaic law be so different? Or, were they really that far apart? The rest of this chapter will deal with the uses of "law" in Letter of James and their meaning, then the overall view of the law in the letter. By the end of the chapter, it will have become clear why both Paul and James say what they do about the law—and that there actually is no significant discrepancy at all in their views of the Torah.

"THE PERFECT LAW OF LIBERTY" 61

Comparing the amount of discussion about the law by Paul and James

It is initially surprising that, in the thirteen New Testament letters of the apostle Paul, he uses the noun "law" (Greek *nomos*) a total of 123 times. However, the term "law" is only found in six of Paul's letters: Romans, 1 Corinthians, Galatians, Ephesians, Philippians, and 1 Timothy. Of those six, there is only one usage in Ephesians, three in Philippians, and two in 1 Timothy. Thus, there are only three of Paul's letters in which "law" is a significant issue: Romans, 1 Corinthians, and Galatians.

Of Paul's three letters with the most usage of the word "law," 1 Corinthians has nine uses, but Galatians has thirty-two inclusions and Romans has seventy-six! Thus, between the thirty-two uses in Galatians and the seventy-six in Romans, almost 88 percent (i.e., 108 of 123) of Paul's uses of "law" appear in just those two letters. That means, with its six chapters, Galatians averages 5.33 uses of "law" per chapter. Romans, with its sixteen chapters, averages 4.75 uses per chapter.

In stark contrast, James uses the term "law" just ten times. That averages out to just two uses per chapter for the five chapters of the Letter of James. At first reaction, this comparison of the use of "law" in James to its usage in Paul's letters seems quite odd, especially since James is written to a messianic Jewish audience. However, as we will see in moving through this chapter, the reason behind the disparity in the number of uses of "law" by Paul and James is not that unusual.

The ten uses of "law" in the Letter of James

The first use of "law" in James is in 1:25: "But those who look into the perfect *law*, the law of liberty,[1] and persevere, being not hearers who forget but doers who act—they will be blessed in their doing."

The second through sixth uses of "law" in James are found in 2:8, 9, 10, 11, 12:

> You do well if you really fulfill the royal *law* according to the scripture, "You shall love your neighbor as yourself." But if you show partiality, you commit sin and are convicted by the *law* as transgressors. For whoever keeps the whole *law* but fails in

---

1. In the Greek text, there is no second mention of "law" (Greek *nomos*) in Jas 1:25—as in the NRSV portion cited above. Instead, the Greek *nomon teleion ton tes eleutherias* is best translated as "the perfect law of liberty." Italics mine.

one point has become accountable for all of it. For the one who said, "You shall not commit adultery," also said, "You shall not murder." Now if you do not commit adultery but you do murder, you have become a transgressor of the *law*. So speak and so act as those who are to be judged by the *law* of liberty.²

The final four uses of "law" in James are all in one verse—4:11:

> Do not speak evil against one another, brothers and sisters. Whoever speaks evil against another or judges another, speaks evil against the *law* and judges the *law*; but if you judge the *law*, you are not a doer of the *law* but a judge.³

In analyzing the placement of these ten uses of "law" in James, it should first be noted that the ten are found in only three contexts in the letter. In addition, it is important to realize that: 1) Jas 1:25 is in the *middle* of the paragraph 1:22–27, which is D in the chiastic structuring of the book explained at the end of chapter 1; 2) Jas 2:8–12 is in both *the middle and much of the second half* of the section 2:1–13, which is E in the overall chiastic outline of James; 3) Jas 4:11 is found in the a (*outside*) pairing in 4:11–17, which is D' in the book-length chiastic outline.

The meaning of "the perfect law of liberty" in James 1:25a

What insights do such initial observations provide to our understanding of "law" in each of these three passages in the Letter of James? Regarding 1:25a, it is particularly helpful to visualize how it functions within the section 1:22–27, as in the structural diagram just below:

(D) Internal inverted parallel structure of James 1:22–27

a (1:22) But be doers of the word, and not merely hearers who deceive themselves.
   b (1:23–24) For if any are <u>hearers of the word and not doers</u>, they are like those who look at themselves in a mirror; for they look at themselves and, on going away, immediately forget what they are like.

---

2. Italics mine.
3. Italics mine.

> *c (1:25a) But those who look into the perfect law, the law of liberty, and persevere,*
>> *b' (1:25b)* being <u>not hearers who forget but doers who act</u>—they will be blessed in their doing.
>
> *a' (1:26–27)* If any think they are religious, and do not bridle their tongues but deceive their hearts, their religion is worthless. Religion that is pure and undefiled before God, the Father, is this: to care for orphans and widows in their distress, and to keep oneself unstained by the world.

As can be seen from the diagram just above, Jas 1:25a is the central focal point of the section (1:22–27). The repetition in this section functions in urging the hearers/readers of the Letter of James *not* to be hearers of the word only (b/b'), who deceive themselves (a/a'). Instead, James urges them to be those who (c) "look into the perfect law, the law of liberty, and persevere" (i.e., as "doers of the word").

What specifically is meant by "the perfect law of liberty?" To break this consideration down somewhat, first, *why* is the term "perfect" (Greek *teleios*) included as part of the description of what is otherwise "the ... law of liberty?" Because of the previous use of *teleios* in Jas 1:17, Wall is correct in asserting that James's placement of "perfect" in 1:25 "reminds the reader that the law is God's perfect gift for those undergoing testing."[4] Similarly, Johnson states, "God is the source of 'every perfect gift,' and the law, for James, is certainly among them."[5]

McKnight helpfully lists three possible understandings of "the perfect law of liberty":

> First, there is the (supposedly) Hellenistic Judaism view: it refers to a free life in accordance with reason, with "reason" being a way of describing the law of Moses. Second is a nomistic[6] Judaism view: it refers to the Law of Moses as that which brings freedom to the obedient. Third is a Christian Judaism view: it refers to the Law of Moses as understood by and interpreted by Jesus in accordance with the double commandment to love God and others.[7]

---

4. Wall, *Community of the Wise*, 81.
5. Johnson, *Letter of James*, 209.
6. "Nomistic" means, in the simplest terms, law-oriented, in this case the law of Moses.
7. McKnight, *Letter of James*, 155.

McKnight also states at this point that the interpreter must "keep in mind that James is a Torah-observant messianist."[8]

The first two of McKnight's possible understandings of "the perfect law of liberty" can be ruled out quickly. Because James is a "Torah-observant messianist," both "the (supposedly) Hellenistic Judaism view" and "the nomistic Judaism view"[9] would be unlikely to be held by James, the brother of Jesus and head of the Jerusalem church. Because of James's location in Jerusalem, and that he was not from a Hellenistic Jewish background, the first view does not make sense.[10] Because the way James refers to the law of Moses diverges from the perspective of the standard Torah-focused Jew, the nomistic Judaism view also seems to hold little merit.[11] Thus, what McKnight calls "the Christian Judaism view"[12] is the best of the options. To lend some needed specificity to this conclusion, more needs to be said on this conclusion below.

Before that, to briefly demonstrate the breadth of interpretative opinion about this phrase, it is worth noting that both Allison[13] and Luke Johnson[14] discuss the possibility that elements of the Stoic concept of "law" are mixed with the law of Moses, with the result being what James calls "the perfect law of liberty," though Johnson closes his discussion by saying that "any direct dependence on Stoic ideas" is "unnecessary."[15]

From an evangelical perspective, Moo states concerning "the perfect law of liberty":

8. McKnight, *Letter of James*, 155.

9. McKnight, *Letter of James*, 155.

10. Without question, Hellenistic views had penetrated and remained part of the Jewish intellectual world for two centuries at this point. However, what can be known of James' background, as well as what is reflected in his letter, does not mesh with wider Hellenistic influences much beyond his command of the Greek language itself.

11. Though James certainly does take every command of the Mosaic law seriously (Jas 2:10), his balancing emphasis on the importance of the "royal law" (i.e., "Love your neighbor as yourself [2:8]) of Jesus makes it clear that "Torah-observant messianist" is the most accurate category among McKnight's options.

12. By "Christian Judaism" McKnight means messianic Judaism, as demonstrated in his following words on the audience of the Letter of James in his commentary on Jas 1:1: "We conclude then on balance it is more likely that James writes his letter to the messianic Jewish community or communities, which are residing in the Dispersion . . ." (*Letter of James*, 67–68).

13. Allison, *James*, 338.

14. Johnson, *Letter of James*, 209.

15. Johnson, *Letter of James*, 209.

Granted James's background and context, a reference to the law of Moses seems certain. This appears to be confirmed by the fact that James quotes an OT command to exemplify the law in 2:8. The law that God gave to Israel through Moses at Sinai was a center point in OT revelation and absolutely basic to the life of Jews at the time of Christ. For Jews, "law" meant torah, the rules and regulations that God had given his special people to govern their nation, their religion, and their day-to-day conduct. Like James, Jews often described the law of Moses as "perfect" (e.g., Ps. 19:7) and even as liberating (e.g., m. Avot. 6:2).[16]

A straightforward textual and wider biblical contextual interpretation of the phrase "the perfect law of liberty" in Jas 1:25a leads to an understanding that James has the Torah of Moses in mind, at least in the main. However, before pulling this discussion together, it is helpful to consider Moo's further comments on this issue:

> But we must hesitate before simply equating "law" for James with the law of Moses. First, in ch. 2 James's description of the law suggests that he has at least one eye on the "fulfillment" of that law in the teaching of Jesus. . . . Second, James often bases his own commands to his readers on the teaching of Jesus, quoting the OT only rarely.[17]

Using similar reasoning, McKnight concludes his discussion of the meaning of "the perfect law of liberty" in these words:

> James has a Christian hermeneutic of the Torah in mind here. (1) James speaks of a law defined by "liberty" and "perfection." In earliest Christianity both terms are connected to the Torah as taught by Jesus himself (cf. Matt 5:17–20, 48). . . . (2) The notion of "liberty" is not prominent in this letter, but in 2:8–11 James appeals to the Jesus Creed of Mark 12:28–32 (law and love) as how the Torah is to be understood. . . . Thus, in 2:8–12, we see that James understands the "law of liberty" as the Christian reinterpretation of the Torah through the Jesus Creed. The "liberty" of 2:12 must be connected to the "liberty" of 1:25a. . . . James is Torah observant in a Jesus kind of way.[18]

---

16. Moo, *Letter of James*, 2nd ed., 123.
17. Moo, *Letter of James*, 2nd ed., 123.
18. McKnight, *Letter of James*, 158. The "Jesus Creed" is wording McKnight popularized largely through his book, *The Jesus Creed: Loving God, Loving Others*.

To clarify the meaning of "the perfect law of liberty" in Jas 1:25a, I must take exception with aspects of the quotations by both Moo and McKnight about how much James *narrows* his meaning of the term "law" from the Torah in the Tanakh. First, regarding Moo's comments cited above, I make two points: 1) his statement "James's description of the law suggests that he has at least one eye on the 'fulfillment' of that law in the teaching of Jesus" is too inclusive. The only use of "fulfill" (Greek *teleo*) in regard to "law" is in Jas 2:8, where the fulfillment of "the royal law according to the scripture" has to do with the single Torah passage "You shall love your neighbor as yourself" (Lev 19:18). Yes, the immediately succeeding context does speak of "the whole law" (2:10), but not as being fulfilled. It states that a person becomes a "transgressor" of "the whole law" by failing (i.e., sinning) in "one point." Thus, unlike Moo's contention above, James is not arguing for the fulfillment of "the whole law" by loving your neighbor as yourself, but for the realization that a person becomes "a transgressor of the law" by breaking only one law; 2) Moo's statement "James often bases his own commands to his readers on the teaching of Jesus, quoting the OT only rarely" is statistically incorrect.[19] Yes, according to the "Index of Quotations" (i.e., in the New Testament, from the Hebrew Bible) in the United Bible Societies 5th rev. ed. (hereafter UBS5Rev) of *The Greek New Testament*, there are only five quotations of the Hebrew Bible in four passages in the Letter of James: Lev 19:18 (in Jas 2:8); Exod 20:13–14/Deut 5:17–18 (in Jas 2:11); Gen 15:6 (in Jas 2:23); and Prov 3:34 LXX (in Jas 4:6).[20] However, the immediately following "Index of Allusions and Verbal Parallels" in UBS5Rev includes twenty-seven passages in the Hebrew Bible echoed in the Letter of James,[21] making a total of thirty-two HB passages used in James. By contrast, Dale Allison, in by far the longest and most detailed commentary on the Letter of James of this generation,[22] lists only seventeen passages from what he refers to as "the Jesus Tradition" (i.e., Matthew, Mark, and Luke [and Q[23]]) that are clearly cited in the Letter of James (several of which are

---

19. Oddly, in making an assertion of that magnitude, Moo presents no statistical proof for his claim.

20. *The Greek New Testament* 5th ed. rev., 863.

21. *The Greek New Testament* 5th ed. rev., 864–82.

22. Allison's ICC series volume on James contains fifty-one (li) pages of prefaced bibliography and 790 pages of discussion of introductory issues and textual commentary (i.e., about 840 pages total in Allison's treatment of the Letter of James).

23. 'Q' (shorthand for the German *Quelle*, meaning "source") refers to a

parallel passages in the Gospels): Matt 5:3/Luke 6:20 (in Jas 2:5); Matt 5:11–12/Luke 6:22–23 (in Jas 1:2); Matt 7:1–5/Luke 6:37, 41–42 (in Jas 4:11–12); Matt 7:24–27/Luke 6:47–49 (in Jas 1:22–2); Matt 7:7–11/Luke 11:9–13 (in Jas 1:5, 17; 4:3); Matt 6:19–21/Luke 12:33–34 (in Jas 5:1–3); Matt 21:21/Mark 11:23 (in Jas 1:6); Matt 5:33–37 (in Jas 5:12); Luke 6:24 (in Jas 5:1–3); Luke 6:25 (in Jas 4:9; 5:1).[24] Thus, by a proportion of nearly two to one (i.e., thirty-two uses of the Hebrew Bible vs. seventeen widely acknowledged uses of Jesus's words in the Synoptic Gospels),[25] the Letter of James uses the Hebrew Bible (i.e., the wider Torah, in the minds of Jews of that era) more than "the Jesus Tradition," making it clear James was in no way pushing the Hebrew scriptures into the background in favor of a way of viewing the Torah *completely* through the lens of Jesus's interpretation of the greatest (and second) commandment(s) (Matt 22:36–40).

I know Scot McKnight to be a skillful and careful exegete. However, regarding the final citation from his commentary on James referenced above, I respectfully offer three points on which I either: a) differ with him; or b) would prefer he present his thoughts more precisely: 1) McKnight's wording "James has a Christian hermeneutic of the Torah in mind here"[26] is, at best, overly broad. "A Christian hermeneutic of the Torah" could mean many things, not least of which could be a *supersessionist* "Christian hermeneutic of the Torah."[27] I firmly, but respectfully, suggest the alternative wording "A *messianic Jewish* hermeneutic of the Torah."[28] 2) In urging readers to compare "liberty" and "perfection" re-

---

hypothetical document(s) including mainly sayings of Jesus which are found in Matthew and Luke, but not in Mark.

24. Allison, *James*, 56–57.

25. Admittedly, many of the twenty-seven "allusions and verbal parallels" in the Letter of James are not nearly as obvious as the five outright quotations of the HB. However, neither are the echoes of the words of Jesus always immediately obvious. Thus, in James, it is not an "apples and oranges" comparison to put the quotations and the allusion/parallels together to compare with the number of the sayings of Jesus.

26. McKnight, *Letter of James*, 158.

27. A comparison with Acts 15 and 21 clearly indicates that the Jerusalem Council made *no change* regarding whether messianic Jewish believers should keep the Torah, as before. Therefore, it cannot be the case that James, who presided over the Jerusalem Council (Acts 15:13–21) and "reached the decision" as to how gentile believers should relate to Jews and the Torah (15:19–21), in his letter intends to effectively "shrink" the Torah to obedience to the two love commands Jesus referred to in Matt 22:36–40. In other words, from a wider biblical perspective, understanding the wording in Jas 1 and 2 through a supersessionist grid is nonsensical, *though it is often done*.

28. What such a messianic Jewish hermeneutic of the Torah might look like, at least in broad brush strokes, will be addressed at the end of this chapter.

garding the law in Matt 5:17–20, 48 with Jas 1:25a ("the perfect law of liberty"), it turns out there really is no basis for comparison. The Greek term *teleios*, rendered "perfect" in Jas 1:25a, is indeed found in Matt 5:48, but it describes "your heavenly Father," not the law. Also, the Greek *eleutheria*, translated "liberty" in Jas 1:25a, is not found at all in Matt 5—or in any of the Gospels, for that matter. Thus, it is impossible to understand what McKnight had in mind asking for a comparison between Jas 1:25 and Matt 5:17–20, 48. 3) Support for McKnight's contention that James "understands 'the law of liberty'" as the Christian reinterpretation of the Torah through what he calls the Jesus Creed by equating the meaning of "liberty" in 1:25a and 2:12 is valid, but his precise understanding of both of these uses of "liberty" is not. He is correct that the use of "the perfect law of liberty" in 1:25a is in the wider context of being a doer of the word (1:22–24, 25b) and the practical aspects of "pure and undefiled religion" (1:26–27) and that the practical context of 2:12 is a plea for mercy (2:13a). However, neither context expressly reinterprets the Torah through the lens of the love commands, as McKnight asserts. Instead, the passages represent what can be called the positive and negative sides of a messianic Jewish believer in Jesus Messiah's relationship to the Torah. By that I mean Jas 1:25a speaks of the person who looks into (Greek *parakypto*, "to look intently into by stooping over" [i.e., so as to read more carefully][29]) "the perfect law of liberty" and is a persevering doer, who is blessed as a result (1:25b). By contrast, in its context, Jas 2:12 refers to the need to speak and act mercifully, unlike the "transgressor of the law," who will be "judged by the law of liberty" unmercifully (2:13a). Thus, neither 1:25a or 2:12, interpreted in context, argues for the summarizing "reinterpretation" of the Torah in the love commands.

The meaning of "the royal law," "the whole law," and "the law of liberty" in James 2:8–12

As stated above, the five uses of "law" in section E (2:1–13) are all located in the central part and much of the second half of the chiastic structure of that passage, as seen in the structural diagram that follows:

---

29. Moo, *Letter of James*, 2nd ed., 122.

(E) Internal inverted parallel structure of James 2:1–13

> a (2:1–4) My brothers and sisters, do you with your acts of favoritism really believe in our glorious Lord Jesus Chris. For if a person comes with gold rings and fine clothes comes into your assembly, and if a poor person with dirty clothes also comes in, and if you take notice of the one wearing the fine clothes and say, "Have a seat here, please," while to the one who is poor you say, "Stand there," or "Sit at my feet," have you not made distinctions among yourselves and become judges with evil thoughts?
>> b (2:5–7) Listen, my beloved brothers and sisters. Has not God chosen the poor in the world to be rich in faith and to be heirs of the kingdom that he has promised to those who love him? But <u>you have dishonored the poor</u>. Is it not the rich who oppress you? Is it not they who blaspheme the excellent name that was invoked over you?
>>> c (2:8) You do well if you really fulfill the royal law according to the scripture, "<u>You shall love your neighbor as yourself</u>."
>>>> *d (2:9–10) But if you show partiality, you commit sin and are convicted by the law as transgressors. For whoever keeps the whole law but fails in one point has become accountable for all of it.*
>>> c' (2:11a) For the one who said, "<u>You shall not commit adultery</u>," also said, "<u>You shall not murder</u>."
>> b' (2:11b) Now if you do not commit adultery, but if you murder, <u>you have become a transgressor of the law</u>.
> a' (2:12–13) So speak and so act as those who are to be judged by the law of liberty, for judgment will be without mercy to anyone who has shown no mercy; mercy triumphs over judgment.

To offer but a brief comment at this point on this important passage on James's understanding of the "law," the *central* (i.e., most significant) segment d (2:9–10) spotlights the focus of the whole segment (2:1–13): showing partiality against the poor is a transgression of the law, which makes the person who is guilty of such partiality effectively a transgressor of *the entire law*. The rest of the structure makes the related point that, if a person chooses not to take *merciful* action to "love your neighbor as yourself"—which is part of the "royal law" (Lev 19:18)—then he or she must expect to be judged unmercifully by the "law of liberty."

What does James mean by "the royal law" in the following wording: "You do well if you really fulfill *the royal law*[30] according to the scripture: 'You shall love your neighbor as yourself'" (Jas 2:8)? The Greek word

---

30. Italics mine.

rendered "royal" is *basilikos*, used only here in the Letter of James. According to BDAG, in this passage, *basilikos* means "royal, so called . . . because it is given by the king (of the kingdom of God) Js 2:8."[31] The only kindred term to "royal" used in James is in the immediately preceding context: "Has not God chosen the poor in the world to be rich in faith and to be heirs of the kingdom (Greek *basileia*) that he has promised to those who love him?"

Therefore, in Jas 2:1–13, it seems clear the phrase "the royal law" means the *nomos* (i.e., Torah) of God, the king. However, the context—both before and just after the wording "the royal law" in 2:8—is focused on the sin of showing partiality (2:1–7, 9). Thus, James is emphasizing the pressing need for his audience to follow the "royal law" of God, the King, by not showing partiality. His logic in the preceding context seems to be that, since the poor have been chosen by God to be "rich in faith and to be heirs of the kingdom," it makes no sense for James's audience to mistreat them through favoritism (2:5–7), plus such favoritism is as much transgression against the Torah as adultery or murder (2:9–11).

What specifically does James mean by the wording "the whole law" (Greek *holon ton nomon*) in 2:10? Since James contrasts "the whole law" with "one point" (i.e., of the law) in 2:10, then follows in 2:11 by listing two specific "points" of the law (adultery and murder), the obvious contextual answer is that "the whole law" refers to *the entire Torah*.[32] The practical point of 2:10 is that a hypothetical person who almost "keeps" (Greek *tereo*, "keep, observe, fulfill, pay attention to, esp. of law and teaching"[33]) *the whole law* successfully—failing in just "one point"—is still *enoxos* ("liable, answerable, guilty")[34] for "all of it," clearly speaking of "the whole law."

A key point to notice in 2:10 regarding supersessionist thinking is that James does not *discount* guilt regarding not keeping "the whole law." Certainly, the main contextual issue here is whether they speak and act

---

31. BGAD, S.v. "*basilikos*," 136.

32. There is not enough detail in this passage to determine whether "the whole law" means the entirety of the law of Moses or just the Decalogue (i.e., the Ten Words/Commandments). Contextual support for the first option is that "You shall love your neighbor as yourself" comes from Lev 19:18, not the Decalogue. Contextual support for the second option is that both of James's examples—adultery and murder—are found in the Decalogue.

33. BDAG, S.v., *tereo*, 815.5 refers specifically to Jas 2:10.

34. BDAG, S.v. *enoxos*, 267.

with partiality toward the poor (2:1–7). However, nothing is said by James that leads to the conclusion that no other sins against the law count any more except for a lack of love (2:8) or partiality (2:9). The wording here does not in any way support the collapsing of "the whole law" ([2:10] i.e., the Torah) into the law of love (i.e., Lev 19:18), as if James does not have a continuing expectation for messianic Jewish believers to observe "the whole law" (Jas 2:10).[35]

The remaining issue related to "the law" in Jas 2 is the use of "the law of liberty" in 2:12. Unlike 1:25a (i.e., "the perfect law of liberty"), 2:12 does not repeat "perfect." As stated above, while these two references to "the law of liberty" must mean the same thing, the practical contexts are significantly different. In 1:25a, James says the outcome of a person looking intently into "the perfect law of liberty" and persevering as a doer is being blessed (1:25b). In the context of 2:12, James advises the person who realizes he/she is a transgressor of the law (2:11) to "so speak and so act as those who are to be judged by the law of liberty" (2:12).

In other words, the same "law of liberty" that offers blessing to the persevering doer promises judgment "without mercy" to the one who transgresses the law by not showing mercy (2:13a [i.e., the flip side of showing partiality in 2:1–7]). Perhaps the use of the wording "the law of liberty" in 2:12 seems somewhat ironic, given its tone of seeking to turn the transgressor of the law toward the path of showing mercy (2:12b–13a). However, that "the law of liberty" can pronounce judgment on unmerciful transgressors of "the whole law" does not mean that it is any less "the law of liberty." Ultimately, it is up to the response of the persons who "look into" the law (1:25) whether he/she ends up with "liberty" or judgment by virtue of their obedience or transgression.

The meaning of "judging the law" in James 4:11

The remaining four uses of "law" in the Letter of James are all found in 4:11, part of the a/a' pairing (4:11–12/4:16–17) in section D' (4:11–17) of the overall inverted parallel outline of the book. The point made in 4:11 is that speaking *evil* against or judging another is the same as speaking *evil*

---

35. The kind of thinking expressed in the sentence this note is related to—that James is laying out a kind of low-key argument for Torah observance by messianic Jewish believers to give way to keeping only "the love commands"—undermines one of the most central aspects of messianic Jewish identity and is thus part and parcel of a supersessionist mindset.

against or judging "the law"—which is effectively placing yourself in the position of God, who is the lawgiver and only rightful judge. The other part of the a pairing (4:16–17) makes the complementary point that *evil boasting is arrogant*.

(D') Internal inverted parallel structure of James 4:11–17

a (4:11–12) Do not speak evil against one another, brothers and sisters. Whoever speaks evil against another or judges another, speaks evil against the *law* and judges the *law*; but if you judge the *law*, you are not a doer of the *law* but a judge. There is one lawgiver and judge who is able to save and to destroy. So who, then, are you to judge your neighbor?
    b (4:13) Come now, you who say, "Today or tomorrow we will go to such and such a town and spend a year there, doing business and making money."
        c (4:14a) Yet you do not even know what tomorrow will bring.
            d (4:14b) What is your life? For you are a mist that appears for a little while . . .
        c' (4:14c) . . . and then vanishes away.
    b' (4:15) Instead you ought to say, "If the Lord wishes, we will live and do this or that."
a' (4:16–17) As it is, you boast in your arrogance; all such arrogance is evil. Anyone, then, who knows the right thing to do and fails to do it, commits sin.

Why does Jas 4:11 say speaking evil against or judging another person amounts to the same thing as "speaking evil against the law" and "judging the law?" As Johnson writes, "The logic of [James's] conclusion, however, remains obscure unless one grants that James has in mind precisely an allusion to Lev 19:16."[36] That verse, Lev 19:16a, only two verses before the "love command" (i.e., "you shall love your neighbor as yourself"), says, following the Hebrew Bible, "You shall not go around as a slanderer among your people." Of course, "speaking evil against" a person is, practically speaking, the same thing as slander,[37] so both verses deal with the same idea.

    Johnson continues,

---

36. Johnson, *Letter of James*, 293.

37. BAGD, s.v. "katalaleo," 412. *Katalaleo*, used three times in Jas 4:11a, may mean "speak against, speak evil of, defame or slander." Hence, Jas 4:11a is dealing with *the same issue* as Lev 19:16.

> Why is slander against a neighbor also a judging of the law? Because the law of love forbids such slander ... ! To practice slander and judgment against a neighbor is, therefore, to assume not only an arrogant superiority toward the law which forbids such behavior; one assumes the right to decide which laws apply and which ones don't.[38]

The last portion of Johnson's wording above leads seamlessly into Jas 4:12. To summarize 4:11 in its context, to "speak evil against" (i.e., slander) or to "judge" another person is to "judge the law" with an attitude of arrogant superiority to the law and, in effect, elevate oneself into the role held only by God, "the one lawgiver and judge" (4:12).

This insight from Jas 4:11–12 works against a supersessionist perspective in two important ways: 1) It makes it clear again, as argued above, that the concept of "the law" in the Letter of James has not been collapsed into "the law of love" (Lev 19:18; Jas 2:8). The reference to not "speaking evil" against one another (4:11a) clearly echoes Lev 19:16, thus indicating at least that James's approach to "the law" has a somewhat wider scriptural basis than just Lev 19:18;[39] 2) The emphasis on the power of "the one lawgiver and judge" (i.e., God) to "save and destroy" in Jas 4:12a is reminiscent of 2:13a, the end of the second passage on "the law" in the Letter of James: "For judgment will be without mercy to anyone who has shown no mercy."

These two points undermine the supersessionist attempt to say that the coming of the new covenant has brought about the fulfillment of the law in the love command. Not only has the church not become the new Israel, but the broader Torah remains in effect for the Jews, God's covenant people.

As has been seen, all three passages in the Letter of James that include uses of the term "law" have powerful practical messages. The first (1:22–27) is a *positive* message (i.e., seeking to impress those in James's audience to live ["be a doer of the word"] in a certain manner), while the second (2:1–13) and third (4:11–17) passages are *negative* (i.e., seeking to impress the audience to change certain attitudes and actions—from

---

38. Johnson, *Letter of James*, 293.

39. In fact, Johnson makes an excellent case that James cites or echoes Lev 19 numerous times in the Letter of James. See especially his article, Johnson, "The Use of Leviticus 19 in the Letter of James," 391–401. This angle will be discussed at some length in chapter 4.

partiality to mercy [2:1–13] or stay away from specific attitudes and actions—from speaking evil and judging others [4:11–17]).

"The law" and "the word" in the Letter of James

As noted in the previous discussions in this chapter, in Jas 1:25a, the Greek term *nomos* is found in the phrase best rendered as "the perfect law of liberty." However, what has not been considered so far is how *nomos*, at that point in the immediate context (i.e., 1:22–27), picks up the previous interchangeable usage of *logos* (i.e., "word, speaking"),[40] which goes back to 1:18, then to the ensuing verses to 1:25.

First of all, it is helpful to note that, out of five uses of *logos* in the Letter of James,[41] four are found in the close preceding context of James 1:25a: in 1:18, 21, 22; and 23. As will be seen, the wording surrounding the first two uses (1:18; 1:21) serve as explanatory descriptors of "word" and the flow of thought related to the second two uses (1:22; 1:23) describe human reactions to the "word."

The first inclusion, Jas 1:18, reads, "In fulfillment of his own purpose, [God] gave us birth by *the word of truth*,[42] so that we would become a kind of first fruits of his creatures." Clearly, the use of the wording "gave birth" (Greek *apokyo*) in 1:18 is intended as a striking contrast with the wording that sin "gives birth" (also Greek *apokyo*) to death in 1:15b. The agent that brings about the "birth" of the messianic Jewish believers in 1:18[43] is God's "word of truth."

What is meant by "word of truth" in this textual and historical context? The words following are a summary of Allison's much longer—and

---

40. BAGD, S.v., *logos*, 477. "Speaking" is the first category listed in this entry.

41. The fifth (and final) use of *logos* in the Letter of James is found in 3:2b, which is rendered in the NRSV in the following words: "Anyone who makes no mistakes in speaking (Greek *logos*) is perfect, able to keep the whole body in check with a bridle." That use deals with human speech, while the four uses in Jas 1:18, 21, 22, 23 refer to the word of God.

42. There is no article in the Greek before "word of truth." Thus, the literal translation of the phrase is "a word of truth." However, because the immediately preceding wording in Jas 1:18 speaks of God's directly purposeful involvement in "giving birth" to "us" (presumably a group including at least James and his messianic Jewish audience) through "a word of truth," it is virtually impossible to conceive how such a "word of truth" with life-giving power would *not* mean God's word. Italics mine.

43. This conclusion is clear from the wording in 1:18: "[H]e (i.e., God) gave *us* (i.e., originally James's messianic Jewish audience) birth by the word of truth" (italics mine).

very helpful—discussion of the three predominant historical understandings of this phrase in this context:

> [T]he dominant tradition is that our text is about the supernatural begetting of Christians. . . . [But] James speaks of being born, not reborn or born again. . . . In sum, the interpretation in terms of redemption and/or baptism depends upon reading into James ideas found in other early Christian texts. . . . What then of the possibility that the reader should think of creation rather than redemption? . . . Elsewhere God creates the world by the divine word, so one can construe James' *logo aletheias* to refer to the speech by which God created the world, including human beings. . . . As attractive as [this option is], it fails to explain why James speaks specifically of the "word of truth." There does not appear to have been any traditional link between "truth" and the creation of the world. Furthermore, the use of *logos* in the verses immediately following has nothing to do with creation (1.21, 22, 23). . . . We come, then, to the third possibility. . . . It has much to be said for it. (i) James ostensibly addresses itself to the twelve tribes in the diaspora (1.1) and to those who meet in synagogues (2.2) . . . [thus] it is altogether natural to identify *hemas* [i.e., "us" in 1:18] with the Jewish people. (ii) God gives birth to Israel in Deut 32.18. . . . (iii) Israel is called "first fruits" in Jer 2.3. . . . (iv) The "word of truth" is the Torah or divine revelation in several texts, above all in Ps 119. . . . (v) The *logos* of 1.22 is the same as "the law of freedom" in 1.25, and the latter . . . is the Torah.[44]

McKnight explains well the possible meanings of the final phrase in 1:18, translated "of his creatures" in the NRSV:

> There are three possible ideas connected to this: it could refer to created matter in distinction to humans, to created matter including humans, or more narrowly to the global ecclesial community or the future ecclesial community as distinguished from the messianic community. . . . I suspect James is referring here to the messianic community as a harbinger of a universal ecclesial community—perhaps even the kingdom of God. This would include all of creation.[45]

I tend to agree with McKnight's conclusion above, but with one important exegetical/theological clarification: McKnight did not state that

---

44. Allison, *James*, 280–85.
45. McKnight, *Letter of James*, 130.

"all of creation" refers to the new heavens and earth in Rev 21–22, not the current creation. In other words, the "first fruits" are in this age, but "all of creation" (i.e., the new creation)—if that indeed is the correct understanding of *ktisma* ("that which is created, creature")[46] in 1:18—will not be until the eternal state.

The analogy changes from "birth" to agriculture in the second contextual use of *logos* in 1:21: "[W]elcome with meekness the implanted word, which has the power to save your souls." This wording appears to pick up the end of 1:18, which says that (spiritual) "birth by the word of truth" is intended to result in James's messianic Jewish audience becoming "a kind of first fruits of his creatures" (Greek *ktisma*, meaning either "what is created" or "creature") with "first fruits" also being an obvious agricultural figure of speech.[47]

What is the contextual meaning and implications of the phrase "the implanted word"? The term translated "implanted" (Greek *emphytos*) is used only here in 1:21 in the entire Greek New Testament.[48] According to BAGD, *emphytos* simply means "implanted."[49] But, what "word" is "implanted," and how?

In this context, "the implanted word" in 1:21 is "the word of truth" in 1:18, but it is also "the perfect law of liberty" in 1:25. Yet, that still does not explain what is meant by "implanted" or how that "word" is implanted.

Allison offers three plausible understandings of the idea of "implanted" here. First, "'implanted' refers ... to that which has become implanted through acceptance of the Christian message ...."[50] Second, he states "Jer 31.33 could then be in the background: 'This is the covenant I will then make with the house of Israel after those days, says the Lord: I will put My law within them and write it on their hearts.' ..."[51] "One

---

46. BAGD, S.v. "*ktisma*," 456.

47. BAGD, S.v. "*aparche*," 81, generally groups both sacrificial animals and agricultural produce (e.g., grain, fruit of the vineyard) under the concept of "first fruits," but also includes its use for believers.

48. Such a single use in the entire NT is called a *hapax legomenon*, which means "one word" (or use [i.e., in an entire corpus]).

49. BAGD, S.v "*emphutos*," 258.

50. Allison, *James*, 311.

51. Allison, *James*, 311.

might also (third) compare Jesus' parable of the sower, which the Synoptics interpret as being about 'the word'...."[52]

In the considered opinion of this writer, the most likely understanding of "the implanted word" in Jas 1:21 is a blend of Allison's three stated options. It refers to "the Christian message," if by that is meant "the word" preached by Jewish apostolic leaders in the early chapters of Acts, which derives its "gospel" content from the Torah, such as "Everyone who calls on the name of the Lord shall be saved" (Acts 2:21, citing Joel 2:32), or, from Gen 15:6, the classic verse about "salvation" in the Torah, as cited in Jas 2:23, "Abram believed God, and it was reckoned to him as righteousness." However, the "implanting" can just as readily refer to the new covenant in which God's "law" is written on the hearts of "the house of Israel" (Jer 31:33). Also, the parable of the sower (e.g., Matt 13:1-9, 18-23) must be taken seriously as background for "the implanted word" because of the closing words of Jesus's explanation of the parable of the sower in Matt 13:23: "But as for what was sown on good soil (i.e., which penetrated the soil—was truly "implanted"), this is the one who hears *the word* and understands it, who indeed bears fruit . . . ."[53] This is precisely what James is urging his audience to be in this context in Jas 1: "doers of the word" (1:22); "doers who act" (1:25).

To summarize this discussion: a) a message taken from the Torah, which suggests how to be "saved" (see the final words of 1:21, which will be discussed immediately below) is very likely at least a part of the meaning of "the implanted word" in 1:21; b) so is the fulfillment of the new covenant prophecy in Jer 31:33 of "the law" being written on the hearts of "the house of Israel"; c) and so is the fulfillment of the parable of the sower in Matt 13. These three aspects combine for a beautiful wider sense of what needed to take place theologically with the messianic Jewish audience of the Letter of James.

One more issue remains regarding the contextual meaning of "the implanted word" in Jas 1:21. What is the meaning of the remainder of the verse after "the implanted word" (i.e., "that has the power to save your souls")?

Besides 1:21, there are four other uses of "save" (Greek *sozo*) in the Letter of James: 2:14; 4:12; and 5:15, 20. Of the four additional uses, two appear to have to do with eternal salvation: the use of "save" in 2:14, at

---

52. Allison, *James*, 311-12.
53. Italics mine.

the beginning of James's discussion about whether "faith" or "faith and works" saves a person; and 4:12 calls God "the lawgiver who is able to save and to destroy" (i.e., opposite human destinies).

The other two uses appear to deal with some sort of "saving" having to do with *this life*: 5:15 relates to "the prayer of faith" saving "the sick" (i.e., free from disease);[54] 5:20 says that bringing back a wandering sinner "will save the sinner's soul from death." Note that the wording here does not speak of eternal judgment, but (physical) "death."

It is this latter verse that is the closest in wording to the end of 1:21—which, in the Greek, reads *sosai tas psychas hymon* ("to save your souls"). Quite similarly, 5:20 reads *sosei psychen autou ek thanatou* ("will save his soul from death"). It appears that the relationship between the content of these two verses is that, in 1:21, the focus is on what takes place initially in the messianic believer's life—"the implanted word has the power to save [their] souls," while, in 5:20, a person who has been a believer in Yeshua Messiah for some time has strayed, but has repented and been brought back into the messianic Jewish community and, in the process of that restoration, "saved" from "death," perhaps in a theologically similar situation to the man in 1 Cor 5:1–5,[55] (who appears to be the repentant man of 2 Cor 2:6–11).[56] Further, the process of restoration outlined in Jas 5:19–20 may have been the initial basis behind Paul's advice[57] in dealing with "anyone [who] is detected in a transgression" in Gal 6:1.

The Greek word rendered "power" in Jas 1:21 (*dynamai*) is the final puzzle piece in understanding the wording "the implanted word that has the power to save your souls." The structure of that phrase in 1:21 in the Greek (*ton emphyton logon ton dynamenon sosai tas psyxas*) is almost

---

54. BAGD, S.v. "*sozo*," 798. Meaning 1.c. specifically cites Jas 5:15.

55. In 1 Cor 5:5a, handing the man "over to Satan for the destruction of his flesh" means death. In 5:5b, "so that his spirit may be saved (Gk. *sozo*) in the day of the Lord" means that this sinning man is a believer in Yeshua Messiah and would be "saved" for eternity, if he died and did not repent of his sin. See the thought-provoking brief discussion of these passage by Bruce, *I & II Corinthians*, 55.

56 Bruce, *I & II Corinthians*, 184–86 is not certain that 2 Cor 2:6–11 is speaking of the same man as 1 Cor 5:1–5, because of the harshness of the wording "hand this man over to Satan for the destruction of the flesh" in 5:5a, which he seems to take to refer to certain death without the possibility of repentance.

57. For this to be the case (i.e., Paul following Jas 5:20), the Letter of James would necessarily have been written before Paul wrote Galatians. As argued in chapter 1, I believe James was written in the mid-40s CE. I believe Galatians was written in 48–49 CE.

exactly parallel to 4:12 ("the lawgiver and judge, who has the power to save and to destroy"[58] [*ho nomothetes kai krites ho dynamenos sosai kai apolesai*]).

The apparent intention of this parallelism between "the implanted word that has the power to save your souls" (1:21) and "lawgiver and judge who has the power to save and to destroy" (4:12) works this way: The "implanted word"—which is also paralleled by "the law of liberty" in 1:25 (which, as argued above, is the Torah)—is powerful to *specifically* save souls. The lawgiver/judge (i.e., God) has the power to both "save" and "destroy" in 4:12—*overarching categories for the power of God*. Thus, in this context, "the implanted word"/the Torah is one of the good and perfect gifts that the Father—who is also the lawgiver/judge who is powerful to "save and destroy"—bestows (1:17) on those to whom he "gave . . . birth by the word of truth" (1:18).

To succinctly summarize this lengthy discussion about the relationship between "the law" and "the word" in the Letter of James: the *spoken* "word" in Jas 1:18, 21, 22, 23 is the message that gives spiritual birth by "the word of truth" (1:21), that is "implanted" by God, the giver of every perfect gift—including his *spoken* (1:18) and *written* "word"/his Torah (1:21, 25). To persevere in doing God's written Torah results in spiritual freedom and blessing (1:25). It is particularly important to persevere in "the royal law"—loving your neighbor (2:8)—because to fail to keep even that single law of the Torah makes a person a transgressor of the whole law. That is because judgment will be on the basis of the whole law—which is a "law of liberty" for the obedient, but a law of merciless judgment for the unmerciful lawbreaker (2:13).

Conclusion: making peace between James and Paul on "the law"

As stated at the beginning of this chapter, there does *appear* to be considerable tension between Paul's statement in Gal 3:10 and James's perspective in 1:25. On first consideration, it almost seems that there is a great gulf fixed between James's wording about "the perfect law of liberty" and Paul's citation of Deut 27:26: "Cursed is everyone who does not observe and obey all the things written in the book of the law." However, as will be seen, those difference are readily explicable in the light of the historical

---

58. Lit. translation of the Greek by the author.

background of the two letters and the hermeneutical approaches employed, as well as the contextual argument of each book.

As far as the *historical background* of the Letter of James, it is written to messianic Jewish believers (1:1), probably in the mid-40s CE, who continue in their observance of the Torah, as a part of their faith in Yeshua Messiah. Paul's audience in the Letter of Galatians, probably written in 48–49 CE,[59] is "the churches of Galatia" (Gal 1:2), which apparently were largely gentile ethnically.[60]

Since James was likely written before Galatians, it is misguided to attempt to read James through a grid made up of the teaching of Paul in Galatians—but that is precisely the kind of *hermeneutical* (i.e., interpretive) approach many people bring to the Letter of James: whether consciously or not, they "overlay" what was meant for a later gentile audience onto what was meant for an earlier messianic Jewish audience. Simply put, this is illicit both hermeneutically and theologically.

In addition, as seen above, James strongly argues for the continuation of the Torah, which he calls "the law of liberty" (1:25; 2:12) and "the royal law" (2:8), in the lives of his messianic Jewish audience. By contrast, Paul is making his impassioned case against gentiles trying to be saved "by the works of the law" (Gal 3:10a).[61] Even though the Jerusalem Council of Acts 15 (which took place in 49 or 50 CE) had not yet occurred, both James and Paul articulate in their letters exactly what became the formal findings for the two ethnic groups at the end of the Council: gentiles do not have to proselytize to Judaism (Acts 15:28–29) and, because nothing was stated related to the Council that needed to be changed by the messianic Jews, their lives in regard to the Torah essentially continued as before (see the closely related later passage in which the practical findings of the Jerusalem Council are referred to in Acts 21:17–26).

---

59. Moo, *Galatians*, discusses the date of Galatians in considerable detail, finally concluding it was written in 48 CE (8–18).

60. In discussing the "Occasion and Purpose" of Galatians, Moo (*Galatians*, 19–21) covers several possibilities for the audience and situation to which the letter was written, all of which see those receiving Galatians as (at least predominately) gentile.

61. It is most helpful to realize that there are no uses of the phrase "works of the law" in the Letter of James, though there are six uses of that exact wording in Galatians (2:16 [3 uses]; 3:2, 5, 10). The significance of that observation is that, while trying to be saved by "works of the law" was a major issue Paul addressed with the gentile audience of Galatians, it was not at all the same kind of issue with James's messianic Jewish audience, who were still Torah observant.

Often overlooked—or at least wrongly understood—is that there has been no other such proceeding like the Jerusalem Council in history in which binding findings regarding faith and practice came forth from "the Holy Spirit and *us*" (i.e., "the apostles and elders, with the consent of the whole church" [15:22]). The importance of that point is not just what happened in Acts 15, but the fact that, by the inspiration of the Holy Spirit (2 Tim 3:16), those findings have been deposited permanently in the new covenant scriptures. That is not the case with any other human council. Thus, it is the "counsel" of the Jerusalem Council that is still, to this day, the scriptural guide for messianic Jewish and gentile believers in Yeshua Messiah regarding the Torah.

5

"Pure and undefiled religion"

DALE ALLISON MAKES TWO striking observations about typical Christian responses to Jas 1:26–27, which verses read as follows:

> If any think they are religious, and do not bridle their tongues, but deceive their hearts, their religion is worthless. Religion that is pure and undefiled before God, the Father, is this: to care for widows and orphans in their distress, and to keep oneself unstained by the world.

The first of Allison's observations is:

> Like so much of the rest of James, our verses have occasioned hostile generalizations about Jews. . . . Among the Jews the godly and pure person is someone who has not touched a dead body or someone who has washed in a running stream. In God's view the one who helps orphans and widows in their afflictions or raises up an oppressed brother or aids the needy with money is godly and pure. To a Jew whoever eats pork is impure. To God anyone is impure whose soul has been tainted and sullied by the passions of this world. These words are sadly representative.[1]

Allison's second observation about 1:26–27 is this:

> Although nothing about 1.26–27 is explicitly Christian, commentators have constantly read Christian ideas and themes into the text. They have done this by, among other things, citing NT texts to illustrate every word and phrase, by equating *threskeia* with Christianity . . . by appealing to the imitation of Christ, by stressing the Christian content of "Father," by asserting that

1. Allison, *James*, 349.

visitation of the needy is of little or no value unless rooted in "Christian love," by equating "the world" with the non-Christian world, and even by opining that the widows and orphans of v. 27 belong to the Christian community.[2]

The first type of reaction Allison describes to Jas 1:26–27 can be rightly described as *overzealous anti-Semitic criticism*. This type of criticism is manifestly unfair to Jewish people in general, but especially to messianic Jews, who were James's audience (1:1).

Yes, Yeshua Messiah does adopt a similar critical tone in a verse like Matt 23:25b: "[F]or you clean the outside of the cup and of the plate, but inside they are full of greed and self-indulgence." However, it should be noticed that, in these words, Yeshua is specifically addressing the "scribes" and "Pharisees" as "hypocrites" (23:25b). Seldom, if ever, do Yeshua's criticisms of this type extend elsewhere beyond the religious and political leaders to rank-and-file members of the Jewish population. Thus, for anyone to say that he or she is simply doing what Jesus did in criticizing Jewish hypocrisy is very close to what would be the case if someone saw another person do something wrong or "two-faced" and assumed everybody else would do the same thing. While that may be a broad generalization, sadly, there are many people today, even in a post-Holocaust world, who universalize every negative thing they hear about Jewish people, religious and otherwise.

The practical implication here regarding the topic of this chapter is that non-Jewish readers of the Letter of James must make sure that they are not falling prey to unfair stereotypes about the Jewish purity standards of James's day, at the least, with the altogether too real possibility of adopting very harmful anti-Semitic attitudes, at the worst. After all, it was, among many other factors, such distorted stereotypes that eventually led to the Nazis' attempted genocide of the Jewish people remembered as the Holocaust.

Allison's second type of reaction can be called accurately *overzealous misapplication*. If the tragic bias of anti-Semitism discussed above is at least partly due to not really understanding Jewish people and their Torah-based religious standards, the problem of "overzealous misapplication" comes about largely from not really understanding how to correctly move from interpreting to applying the Bible.

---

2. Allison, *James*, 350.

In my remarks below, I will give the benefit of the doubt to many readers of the present volume, who do have some awareness of what is involved in properly interpreting and applying scripture.[3] By that, I mean he or she can "correctly interpret passages in their literary and historical contexts...."[4] However, in spite of that (at least basic) knowledge of how to interpret biblical passages, they bring such generally valid interpretations "to bear on situations where they simply do not apply."[5] Every example listed by Allison in the second quotation at the beginning of this chapter represents errors of this type.

According to Klein, Blomberg, and Hubbard, the current evangelical consensus on how to determine legitimate application is a process usually called "principlizing,"[6] which means "an attempt to discover in a narrative [i.e., a biblical text] the spiritual, moral, or theological principles that have relevance for the contemporary believer."[7] Klein, Blomberg, and Hubbard offer the following helpful four-stage model[8] for carrying out such a "principlizing" process in regard to a biblical passage:

1. Determine the original application(s) intended by the passage.

2. Evaluate the level of specificity of those applications to their original historical situations. If the original specific applications are transferable across time and space to other audiences, apply them in culturally appropriate ways.

3. If the original applications are not transferable, identify one or more broader cross-cultural principles that the specific elements of the text reflect.

4. Find appropriate applications for today that implement those principles.

Regarding Stage 1, *everything* having to do with proper application *must* begin with understanding God's intended practical application for

---

3. If it is *not* the case that the reader already has some background in how to interpret and apply the Bible, it is suggested that he or she acquire a copy of Duvall and Hays, *Grasping God's Word: A Hands-on Approach to Reading, Interpreting, and Applying the Bible*, 4th ed. It is an excellent resource for almost all significant interpretive and applicational issues related to the scriptures.

4. Klein, Blomberg, and Hubbard, *Introduction to Biblical Interpretation*, rev. ed., 482.

5. Klein, Blomberg, and Hubbard, *Introduction to Biblical Interpretation*, rev. ed., 482.

6. Klein, Blomberg, and Hubbard, *Introduction to Biblical Interpretation*, rev. ed., 483.

7. Virkler, *Hermeneutics*, 212.

8. Klein, Blomberg, and Hubbard, *Introduction to Biblical Interpretation*, rev. ed., 483.

the original audience. In the case of Jas 1:26–27, that intended audience is messianic Jews of the mid-first century CE who were the first readers and hearers of the Letter of James. Thus, the concept of "pure and undefiled religion" must be initially interpreted and applied specifically *in that cultural context*.

In Stage 2, the issue becomes determining how closely tied the original first-century CE applications are to their original first-century CE setting. If those applicational principles can be applied to other audiences across space and time, however, that should be done with care. In this case, Jas 1:26–27, because it was intended for a messianic Jewish audience—albeit a first-century messianic Jewish audience—can legitimately be applied "across space and time," but that fairly direct application is limited to *a contemporary Messianic Jewish audience*.

In Stage 3, the original application(s) can be transferred reasonably directly to a contemporary Messianic Jewish audience but can also be more broadly applied to a wider audience today. This is the applicational significance of 2 Tim 3:16 for contemporary readers when it says: "All scripture is inspired by God and is useful for teaching, for reproof, for correction, and for training in righteousness." The significance of "all scripture" today is the entire Bible.[9] The point Paul is making is that *any biblical portion*[10] has some applicational value (i.e., teaching, reproof, correction, training) *for every reader*, though some of those applications may be quite broad. In the case of Jas 1:26–27, it is thus possible to apply the idea of "pure and undefiled religion," as well as the associated concepts of bridling the tongue, caring for orphans and widows, and remaining "unstained by the world" outside a theological context whose backdrop is the Jewish Torah. However, to attempt to apply Jas 1:26–27 as if those verses somehow undercut the Torah is to make the all too common interpretive/applicational mistake referred to in the last chapter: *to wrongly read the Letter of James through the lens of Paul's Letter to the Galatians.*

In Stage 4, the specific areas disattached from the Torah theological setting in Stage 3 are pursued by specifying, then acting upon, such specific applicational points.[11]

---

9. In the first century CE, when Paul wrote 2 Timothy, "all scripture" was limited to the Hebrew Bible and whatever part of the New Testament had been written and widely recognized within the communities of believers in Yeshua as Messiah as scriptural.

10. I.e., of Scripture that existed at the time Paul wrote 2 Timothy.

11. In the opinion of this writer, the best source for help in learning how to frame—for action—legitimate applications of the biblical text is (though it is slightly

Having now staked out the two extreme positions and offered an overview and a short discussion of a balanced approach to determining biblical significance and application, the remainder of chapter 4 will seek to discuss the relevant facets of the issue of what James calls "pure and undefiled religion" (1:27). This will be handled in the following order: 1) understanding Jas 1:26–27 in its close structural context; 2) understanding the role of 1:26–27 in introducing important issues to be dealt with throughout the rest of the Letter of James; 3) determining what James means by an unbridled tongue being "worthless religion"; 4) demonstrating that "purity" was a primary Jewish identity marker; 5) attempting to grasp the meaning and implications of the wording "pure and undefiled religion before God the Father"; 6) and 7) exploring the significance of "caring for orphans and widows in their distress" and "keeping oneself unstained by the world."

The importance of the structural context of James 1:26–27

Jas 1:26–27 is part of the last paragraph of the first chapter of James (i.e., 1:22–27). The inverted parallel structure of that paragraph (as seen just below [and as developed in chapter 1 above]) is D in the overall structure chiastic structure of the Letter of James:

> a (1:22) But be doers of the word, and not merely hearers who deceive themselves.
> > b (1:23–24) For if any are <u>hearers of the word and not doers</u>, they are like those who look at themselves in a mirror; for they look at themselves and, on going away, immediately forget what they are like.
> > > c *(1:25a) But those who look into the perfect law, the law of liberty, and persevere,*
> > b' (1:25b) being <u>not hearers who forget but doers who act</u>—they will be blessed in their doing.
> a' (1:26–27) If any think they are religious, and do not bridle their tongues but deceive their hearts, their religion is worthless. Religion that is pure and undefiled before God, the Father, is this: to care for orphans and widows in their distress, and to keep oneself unstained by the world.

---

dated) Kuhatschek, *Applying the Bible*. Regarding Stage 4 in the current discussion, his material on "Applying General Principles Today" (chapter 5 [pp. 65–77]) and "The Limits of Application" (chapter 10 [pp. 145–54]) is particularly helpful.

It is quite clear in layer a/a' that the problem is self-deceit ("deceiving themselves [1:22]/ "deceive their hearts" [1:26]). This self-deceit is expressed by being merely a hearer of the word (1:22), by not bridling the tongue (1:26), not caring for orphans and widows in their distress, and being stained by the world (1:27).

Layer b/b' contrasts those who are "hearers of the word but not doers" (1:23-24) with those who are "not hearers who forget but doers who act," the outcome of whose lives is blessing (1:25b). Layer c (i.e., the midpoint of the structure) ties the focus of the entire paragraph to the desired end of "seeing" and persevering in doing "the perfect law of liberty."

The reason for this structural analysis of Jas 1:22-27 at this point in the chapter is to clarify that "pure and undefiled religion" in 1:27 must be understood against the backdrop of the Jewish Torah. However, as stated in the last chapter, that law, approached properly, is "the perfect law of liberty" (1:25a).

James 1:26-27 and the remainder of the Letter of James

Think about what happens with themes in 1:26-27 moving forward in the Letter of James:

- The immense problem of the unbridled tongue (1:26) effectively sets up the discussion of the tongue in 3:1-12, where James employs the analogy of being able to bridle the whole body, *if* the tongue were to make no mistakes in speaking (3:2).
- "Religion that is pure" (Greek *katharos*, "clean, pure")[12] in 1:27 sets the stage for "purify your hands (Greek *katharizo*, the kindred verb to *katharos*) in 4:8.
- "Religion that is pure and undefiled before God, the Father" (1:27) fits hand in glove with "the wisdom from above is first pure" (3:17).
- "To care for orphans and widows in their distress" (1:27), who must be considered among the poor, is directly related to not showing favoritism to the rich over the poor (2:1-13) and not unjustly holding back wages from the poor field workers (5:4) as parts of the overall category of the needy in the Letter of James.

---

12. BAGD, S.v. "*katharos*," 388.

- The wording "to keep oneself unstained (Greek *aspilos*) by the world (Greek *kosmos*) is stated positively, while two passages later in James deal with the negative side of the issue: "the tongue is placed among our members as a world (Greek *kosmos*); it stains (Greek *spiloo*) the whole body" (3:6); and "Do you not know that friendship with the world (Greek *kosmos*) is enmity with God? Therefore, whoever wishes to be a friend of the world (Greek *kosmos*) becomes an enemy of God" (4:4).[13]

Thus, it becomes clear that Jas 1:26–27 plays an important role in previewing themes developed throughout the rest of the letter. That "role" appears to be a major reason why a number of recent commentaries on the Letter of James have, to one degree or another, viewed Jas 1:26–27 as a part of the "preview" (i.e., which they all view as part, or all, of Jas 1) to the remainder of the letter.[14] Most notable among the contributions of such commentaries are the conclusions of: 1) Spencer, who sees 1:19–27 as what she calls the "thesis paragraph"[15] of the Letter of James; 2) Davids, who views 1:26–27 as the "Summary and Transition" between Jas 1—which he terms James's "Opening Statement"—and the rest of the letter;[16] 3) Francis, who similarly understands 1:26–27 as the "hinge"[17] between Jas 1 and the content of the rest of the book; and 4) Moo, who goes so far as to say about 1:26–27: "[T]he simple point of these verses . . . becomes the leitmotif[18] of the next four chapters. To some extent, then, these verses set the agenda for the rest of the letter."[19]

---

13. Moo (*Letter of James*, 2nd ed., 125) offers a slightly shorter, but similar, list of themes in 1:26–27 previewing the rest of the Letter of James than the one above and organizes it strictly around "controlling the tongue," "concern for the helpless," and "avoidance of worldliness."

14. See Blomberg and Kamell, *James*, 23–27; McKnight, *Letter of James*, 47–55; and Moo, *Letter of James*, 2nd ed., 58–64.

15. Spencer, *Commentary on James*, 47.

16. Davids, *Epistle of James*, 22–28.

17. Francis, "Form and Function of the Opening and Closing Paragraphs of James and 1 John," 118–24.

18. "*Leitmotif*" is an English derivation of the German *leitmotiv*, meaning "leading motive."

19. Moo, *Letter of James*, 2nd ed., 125.

"Worthless" religion: the unbridled tongue

According to James in 1:26, it is the very height of self-deception to presume (Greek *dokeo*, "think, believe, suppose, consider")[20] yourself "religious" if you have no self-control over your speech. That means whatever "religion" is understood to be practiced by the self-deceived person is absolutely "worthless."

So far, so easy to *understand in generalities*. However, to fully grasp what James is seeking to get across to his audience, three major concepts need to be clearly understood: "religious"; not bridling the tongue; and "worthless."

The first concept comes from the Greek word *threskos*, which is rendered "religious" in the NRSV, NIV, ESV, CSB, and NASB. Because it is a *hapax legomenon* (i.e., a word used only once in the New Testament), it would have been somewhat slippery to nail down meaning-wise, except that its cognate (i.e., closely related) term *threskeia* ("religion") is used at the end of Jas 1:26, then again in 1:27, as well as in Acts 26:5 and Col 2:18.

In Acts 26:5, Paul refers to Judaism as his "religion," with the Pharisees as "the strictest sect" of Judaism. However, Col 2:18, translated literally, says the "religion of angels," though it is probably best understood as referring to "worship of angels."[21] The wording "worship of angels" can be understood within the mode of Judaism, given that the veneration of angels was well known in the Judaism of the first century CE, as likely reflected in Heb 1:5–18.

These examples, unfortunately, in and of themselves, do not help much in *specifying* the meaning of *threskos* beyond "religious," with an element of "worship." Helpfully, Luke Timothy Johnson offers a definition of *threskos* worthy of consideration: "it denotes a relationship with the divine."[22] That is the case even when the relationship is not according to correct understanding or practice, because it is based on the assumption of relationship.

Regarding the specific meaning of "not bridle their tongues"—as well as how one can bridle the tongue, Allison also makes two very helpful practical points: 1) he[23] cites Donald Burdick's probing, yet obvious,

---

20. BAGD, S.v., "*dokeo*," 201.
21. Pao, *Colossians and Philemon*, 188–90.
22. Johnson, *Letter of James*, 210.
23. Allison, *James*, 346.

observation: "Exactly how his speech offends is not indicated...";[24] and 2) "James is also mute regarding how one gains the ability to bridle the tongue."[25]

Looking ahead to the central part of the Letter of James in 3:1–12 (see the structural argument in chapter 1), at issue there is also the tongue, with the use of the same "bridle" illustration in view in 3:2. Because it seems likely that 1:26a is previewing 3:1–12 (please see the section of this chapter just above for the argument about that point), and 3:1–12 apparently is dealing with the speech of "teachers" (3:1 [i.e., leaders]), McKnight is likely right in making the following observations:

> Contextually, I suggest that we look back to 1:19–20 and infer from those verses that James is concerned in 1:26a with the control of the *volatile* tongue.... If a case can be made ... for 3:1–12 being about divisive teachers, a stronger case can be made for James worrying about verbal speech patterns that are connected to anger or violent outbursts by leaders. His willingness to reduce moral exhortations to bridling the tongue is best understood in a specific rather than general context: this control is needed by hotheads who are tempted to indulge their desires with angry verbal abuse.[26]

In the view of this writer, McKnight is correct about the problem in view both in 1:26 and 3:1–12 not being about leaders teaching false doctrine, but instead verbal abuse—particularly by at least some teachers/leaders in the messianic Jewish community. James says that those who "do not bridle their tongues" are deceiving themselves (1:26), which effectively echoes his earlier warning to his audience about being "deceived" (1:16) concerning the too often subtle process of sin developing in the life of a person who has been tempted (1:14–15). In addition, James's exhortation in the preceding context in 1:19 to be "quick to listen, slow to speak, slow to anger" could easily be part of what is meant about self-deception in not bridling the tongue (1:26).

James's conclusion at the end of 1:26—that the religion of the person who does not bridle his/her tongue "is worthless" seems to point to just such sin perhaps riding beneath the surface, except when it comes to controlling the tongue. In such cases, the sin that has been covered up by

---

24. Burdick, "James," 176.
25. Allison, *James*, 347.
26. McKnight, *Letter of James*, 164.

a "religious outer layer" makes itself apparent through unwise, uncaring, and possibly ungodly words.

In what sense is this kind of "religious" person who cannot—or will not—control his/her speech judged as "worthless" by James? The word translated "worthless" in 1:26 is the Greek *mataios*, which can mean in various contexts "idle, empty, fruitless, useless, powerless, lacking truth."[27] BAGD believes that "lacking truth" is the correct nuance of meaning in Jas 1:26, although the literal translation offered there also renders *mataios* as "worthless."[28] The implication of such an understanding is that anyone who claims to be "religious," but is not truthful—especially in his/her words—is practicing *worthless religion*. Not being truthful also includes "shading the truth" (or "coloring the truth") by exaggeration, minimizing or failing to tell the whole truth.

Now, this is not to say that there are not many other types of "worthless" religion. However, James has chosen to focus on the kind that is *lacking in worth* before God because it is *lacking in truth (or perhaps does not speak the truth in love)*,[29] whether that be lack of verbal integrity or anger or harshness in the way the verbal content is presented is not stated. Whatever is the case, though, James's statement in 1:26 is strong and apparently pointed toward a particularly influential grouping within his audience: leaders, including teachers.

It is also not to say that James is ignoring—and especially not in any way discounting—Torah-prescribed ritual related to purity/cleanness. Relatedly, Allison is correct in saying the following about Jas 1:26-27:

> That James uses cultic language without reference to cultic practices says nothing about his religious observance or his understanding of Torah. Christian commentators, reading themselves into our text, sometimes affirm that our author could not have been an observant Jew. . . . This is a tenuous argument from silence. Law-abiding Jews could use purity language in a figurative or moral fashion, and the status of Gentiles might not be relevant in an epistle ostensibly addressed wholly to Jews (1.1). There is, moreover, no antithesis here between external ritual and internal purity, nothing to indicate that maintenance of the latter requires jettison of the former.[30]

27. BAGD, S.v., "*mataios*," 495.
28. BAGD, 495.
29. See Eph 4:15.
30. Allison, *James*, 253-54.

"Purity" as an identity marker for Judaism (and messianic Judaism)

A listing of eight Jewish identity markers[31] during the Second Temple period—which includes the first century CE—offered by Maurice Casey has been well-accepted. Those eight markers are: "ethnicity, scripture, monotheism, circumcision, Sabbath observance, dietary laws, purity laws, and major festivals."[32]

As far as the Torah is concerned, the "purity laws" are found in Lev 11–15 and Num 19.[33] Leviticus 11 deals with clean and unclean foods and unclean animals. Leviticus 12 explains the purification of women after childbirth. Chapters 13 and 14 relate to leprosy and its purification. Chapter 15 has to do with bodily emissions and the related purification process. Numbers 19 focuses on the purification of a person after touching a corpse.

To fully understand the Jewish concepts of "purity" and "purification," though, it is necessary to grasp the broader concepts of "clean and unclean" and "holy and unholy." Allen Ross explains these ideas clearly, and in enough detail to be helpful:

> Under the law everything was classified according to the categories of holy and unholy, with only the holy being permitted in the presence of God. What was not holy (i.e., what was common) included two subcategories: clean and unclean. The normal state or condition of most people and things was clean; what was clean could be elevated to holy through sacrificial ritual; but it could also be degraded to unclean by pollution or sinfulness. Accordingly, the Levitical ritual was designed to cleanse and sanctify: something that was unclean could be made clean by purification, and then what was clean needed the blood ritual to make it holy. . . . [We] must distinguish clearly between unclean (*tame*) and clean (*tahor*) within Israel's laws. Sins were certainly classified as unclean; and when sin was the reason, the ritual necessarily required confession and forgiveness as part of the purification process. But *tame* commonly described what was

---

31. This is not to say that there have not been other listings of Jewish identity markers of that period set forth that have found favor with certain scholars, but it is to say that Casey's list has been accepted and has the advantage of not being so long as to strain credibility.

32. Casey, *From Jewish Prophet to Gentile God*, 12.

33. See Hartley, "Holy and Holiness, Clean and Unclean," 426, for a helpful concise treatment in this area.

contaminated, diseased, or impure; and when defilement was the reason for someone being unclean, then no sin was involved and so no forgiveness was required. The only thing needed was washing for cleansing and the sanctifying ritual for reentry into the sanctuary.... The impurity had to be dealt with before any further participation in the sanctuary....[34]

For Jewish readers of this work, this lengthy citation may have been little more than restating the obvious. However, for gentile readers, the concepts explained above are necessary if they are to have much hope of understanding the material to be dealt with in the reminder of this chapter.

By now, it is obvious that "purity"/"cleanness" was God's expectation for his unique covenant people, so that they might be sanctified through the prescribed rituals of the Torah. Thus, it is easy to see why Carey included "purity laws" among his list of eight identity markers for Second Temple Judaism. The only ways set up according to the Torah for Jews to relate to their holy God were through the prescribed purification rites and sacrifices.

However, there are different aspects of "purity" that need to be understood and how—if they do—relate to the Letter of James. The best recent work available in this area is that of Darian Lockett, in his volume *Purity and Worldview in the Epistle of James*.[35] Lockett has done two major services for scholars working in James: 1) he surveys at some length the opinions of commentators regarding the meaning of Jas 1:26–27 about "purity";[36] and 2) he also does an excellent job of documenting five different types of "purity"/"impurity" terminology that existed in the first century CE (even if one or more were not commonly used understandings in that period).

Those five kinds of "purity/impurity" are:

- *Natural purity and impurity* (i.e., dross): this category does not relate to the issue at hand.
- *Ritual purity and impurity*: there were different degrees of ritual impurity.
- *Moral purity and impurity*: this involves willful action.

---

34. Ross, *Holiness to the Lord*, 243–44.
35. Lockett, *Purity and Worldview in the Epistle of James*.
36. Lockett, *Purity and Worldview in the Epistle of James*, 6–20.

- *Figurative or spiritual purity and impurity:* this is internal (i.e., thought-based) impurity.

- *Ritual impurity as the occasion for intentional moral impurity:* I have largely relied on Dale Allison's summary of Lockett's explanation of these five areas related to purity/impurity,[37] but he offers no explanation of "ritual impurity as the occasion for intentional moral impurity," other than referring to Lev 7:20–21. The apparent significance of the reference for this discussion of categories of purity/impurity is the progression from what appears to be a *previously known* state of "uncleanness" to *intentionally* eating a "peace offering meal" while unclean, an offense that was to result in (at the least) excommunication from the people of Israel (Lev 7:20–21).[38]

What the Letter of James is referring to in 1:26–27 is *figurative* purity/impurity. Thus, as Allison accurately observes, "James uses cultic language without reference to cultic practices," which, because the usage is figurative, "says nothing about his religious observance or his understanding of Torah."[39]

The implication to be drawn here is that James apparently was not aware of issues related to *ritual* or *moral* impurity among his messianic Jewish audience in the Diaspora (1:1), but he appears to have been very much aware of—and strongly concerned about—issues among them of *figurative* or *spiritual* impurity, such as those listed in 1:26–27: not bridling the tongue, not caring for the helpless who were in distress, and being "stained" by the (unbelieving) world. Verbally depicting these issues in terms of figurative impurity succeeds in making James's appeal to his audience just that much stronger.

"Pure and undefiled religion before God the Father"

As discussed above, regarding ritual and moral purity, it was necessary for the individual Jew to be highly vigilant to be "pure and undefiled" before God. However, James has shifted the expected focus when discussing "purity" and "defilement" from the realm of cultic ritual to internal purity that produces practical action in 1:26–27.

---

37. Allison, *James*, 352–53.
38. Ross, *Holiness to the Lord*, 183.
39. Allison, *James*, 353.

In doing so, James is following consistently the same practical path he has set forth in the previous context (i.e., to be "doers of the word and not merely hearers who deceive themselves" [1:22] and "not hearers who forget but doers who act" [1:25]). The primary difference from the paragraph before is that James has moved from a *general* call to persevering action (1:22–25) to *specifically stated* actions[40] in 1:26–27, actions that demonstrate a person is indeed a "doer of the word" who acts in such a way that he/she will be "blessed" (1:25).

It must be understood that there is thus no hard "split" between the kind of *spiritual* purity spoken of figuratively above and the cultic purity of the Torah. McKnight is correct in his description of this kind of purity:

> For James, to be pure means to be marked off in worldview from those who are unjust, oppressive, and worldly, and the marking off was more internal-moral versus external-moral. But being marked off is not just separation: it is the devotion to compassion and Torah observance that determines the separation.[41]

Allison makes essentially the same point, as well as an additional significant observation, in these words:

> [P]urity language in James constructs a firm value boundary between sympathetic readers and the larger culture. At the same time, the social boundaries are not so fixed as to imply that our letter represents what we might call a sectarian community. . . . He rather seeks common cause with diaspora Judaism.[42]

In other words, the primary reason for the wording of Darian Lockett's monograph, *Purity and Worldview in the Epistle of James,* is that James was indeed imparting a "worldview" to his audience in the Diaspora, a worldview that argued that, while the external moral purity required by the Torah retained its importance, the internal moral purity being described in Jas 1:26–27 was of the essence of the previous context's exhortation to "be doers of the word and not merely hearers" (1:22). In both 1:22 and 1:26, to not be "doers" *practically* is to be self-deceived. In 1:26, the net result of such self-deception is worthless "religion."

There is no obvious reason for the wording "before God, the Father" (1:27), other than perhaps as an allusion to Ps 68:5: "Father of orphans

---

40. McKnight, *Letter of James*, 167.
41. McKnight, *Letter of James*, 167.
42. Allison, *James*, 353.

and protector of widows is God . . . ." This likely scriptural echo will be discussed in the next section of this chapter.

"Caring for orphans and widows in their distress"

Among the first set of "ordinances" (Exod 21:1) that the Lord gave Israel through Moses after the Ten Commandments (20:1–17) was "You shall not abuse any widow or orphan" (22:22). The Lord then immediately stated that, if such abuse did take place at the hands of the people of Israel, his wrath would burn against them (22:23–24). Deuteronomy 10:18 clearly states God "executes justice for the orphan and widow."

In addition, the Lord built into the Torah specific ways in which the needs of "orphans and widows" were to be provided for. "Gleaning" during the harvest seasons was one means of meeting their physical needs (Deut 24:19–21) and another was through the tithe given every third year (14:28–29; 26:12–13).[43]

The natural question arising out of Jas 1:27 is why would caring "for orphans and widows in their distress" rise to the level of inclusion in such a *very short* list describing what is meant here by "[r]eligion that is pure and undefiled before God, the Father"? The most obvious answer is two-fold: 1) As stated at the end of the section just above, God is "the father of orphans and the protector of widows" (Ps 68:5)—his divine heart intended to safeguard them and meet their needs; 2) James had become aware that, among his messianic Jewish audience in the Diaspora (Jas 1:1), the "orphans" and "widows" were being overlooked and perhaps even horribly mistreated.

Two terms used in 1:27 help clarify the circumstances of the specific "orphans" and "widows" to which James is referring. The translation "care for" renders the Greek *episkeptomai*, which BAGD, definition 2., specifically citing Jas 1:27 as an example, takes as meaning "go to see, visit" in the sense of "look after orphans and widows in their distress."[44] In other words, James is directly informing the other members of his audience (i.e., who are not "orphans" or "widows") that, for them to be "pure and undefiled before God," they must go out of their ways to attend to the needs of the least fortunate, and most helpless, among them: the

---

43. Christopher Church, "Fatherless," *Holman Illustrated Bible Dictionary*, 560–61; David Stabnow, "Widow," 1671.

44. BAGD, s.v. "*episkeptomai*," 298.

"orphans" and "widows" in his wording in 1:27. In addition, the phrase "in their distress" is ominous, because it implies strongly that whatever the "distress" spoken of is, it exists already as a present reality. Further, the level of intensity of the "distress" is not clear but could be considerable. The Greek word *thlipsis*, translated by the NRSV in 1:27 as "distress," may just as easily be rendered "oppression, affliction, tribulation."[45] And, all three of these nuances infer a highly difficult, and possibly even violent, situation among the "orphans" and "widows" being spoken of among James's messianic Jewish audience in the Diaspora.

In concluding this discussion, it appears the wording in Jas 1:27 fits into a troubling pattern of behavior that emerges in moving through the rest of the letter after 1:26–27, a pattern "that is all too typical of James's readers."[46] Three examples make this point. First, those who are guilty of "partiality" against and "dishonoring" of the poor (2:1–7)—and of favoritism toward the rich—are said in no uncertain terms to be transgressors of the law (2:8–12), who should expect to be judged unmercifully themselves (2:13). Secondly, if a person claims to have faith, but no help is provided to meet the obvious bodily needs of "a brother or sister"[47]—certainly (a) fellow Jew(s), and most likely also (a) fellow believer(s) in Yeshua Messiah—that person's faith is said to be alone and dead (2:14–17). Third, the wages of harvesters—some of whom may well have been "orphans" who had reached the age to be field workers—were being fraudulently withheld by wealthy landowners (5:4) and, in some cases, such field workers who were believers in Yeshua Messiah (lit., "the righteous"), had been murdered by the rich (5:6).

Thus, despite the fact there are few, if any, indications in the Letter of James of doctrinal problems or even typical issues of Jewish purity/impurity among James's audience, that does not mean all is well among these messianic Jewish believers in the Diaspora (1:1). If anything, this is one of several points in the letter at which the view that James's audience was made up of potentially numerous groups of messianic Jewish

---

45. BAGD, s.v., "*thlipsis*," 362.

46. Moo, *Letter of James*, 2nd ed., 157.

47. According to Blomberg and Kamell (*James*, 130), James in 2:15 "intentionally includes the words for both 'brother' (*adelphos*) and 'sister' (*adelphe*). Probably he highlighted the 'sister' because women often comprised the more desperately needy and were the more easily overlooked in his society, especially when they lacked provision by a father or husband."

believers in the Diaspora who continued to worship within wider regular Jewish synagogues makes the most sense.

"Keep oneself unstained by the world"

As stated in the section of this chapter dealing with how Jas 1:26–27 previews numerous major themes in the remainder of the letter (i.e., chapters 2–5), the wording "to keep oneself unstained (Greek *aspilos*) by the world (Greek *kosmos*) in 1:27 fits perfectly. Two passages found later in James also use the words related to "unstained" and/or "world": 1) "the tongue is placed among our members as a world (Greek *kosmos*) of iniquity; it stains (Greek *spiloo*) the whole body" (3:6); and 2) "Do you not know that friendship with the world (Greek *kosmos*) is enmity with God? Therefore, whoever wishes to be a friend of the world (Greek *kosmos*) becomes an enemy of God" (4:4). Both passages help in understanding what James is seeking to get across in 1:27.

Before considering each passage in turn, though, it is insightful to probe the overlap in meaning between the Greek words *amiantos* (rendered "undefiled" in 1:27 by the NRSV) and *aspilos* (translated as "unstained" in 1:27 [NRSV]). BAGD defines *amiantos* as "undefiled, pure"[48] and *aspilos* as "spotless, without blemish."[49] In 2 Pet 3:14, *aspilos* is paired with a word that is cognate to *amiantos*: *amometos*, which means "blameless, unblemished."[50]

What is the significance of James's use of two terms with such close meanings in Jas 1:27? It seems quite possible James is emphasizing that, as important as it is to bridle their tongues" (1:26) and "to care for widows and orphans in their distress" (1:27), the heart of "religion that is pure and undefiled before God the Father" (1:27) is "to keep oneself unstained by the world" (1:27). In other words, the use of the near synonym *aspilos* ("spotless, without blemish") at the end of 1:27 is pointing back to *amiantos* ("undefiled, pure") in the early part of the verse, suggesting that "to keep oneself unstained by the world" may be the most important part—or at least the spiritual core—of a "pure and undefiled life."

This understanding appears to be borne out in the two passages mentioned above: 3:6 and 4:4. In 3:6, the verbal form of the mirror

---

48. BAGD, S.v. "*amiantos*," 46.
49. BAGD, S.v., "*aspilos*," 117.
50. BAGD, S.v., "*amometos*," 47.

opposite of *aspilos* ("spotless, without blemish"), that is, *spiloo* ("to stain, defile")[51] is used to describe the tongue: "it stains the whole body." In addition, the immediately preceding phrase in 3:6 contains *kosmos*: "The tongue is . . . a world of iniquity."

Before further explaining the connection of 3:6 to 1:27, it is necessary to consider the meaning of *kosmos*—usually translated "world"—in the Letter of James. Besides 1:27 and 3:6, there are three additional uses of *kosmos* in James. It is found once in 2:5 and twice in 4:4.

There is some controversy among scholars as to the precise significance of the Greek phrase *to kosmo* in 2:5: "Has not God chosen the poor in the world to be rich in faith and to be heirs of the kingdom that he has promised to those who love him?" According to Blomberg and Kammel, there are basically three options:

> [A] locative dative of place ("in the world"), a dative of respect or reference ("with respect to worldly goods"), or an ethical dative ("in the eyes of the world"). Of these three, the last seems the clearest, coming directly after a passage in which judgment was passed on the poor because of their looks.[52] . . . Bauckham appears to combine the second and third options, paraphrasing the term as "poor with respect to those material goods which the world considers wealth."[53]

Not only does Bauckham's understanding makes the most sense in this context in Jas 2, but it also helps clarify the wider meaning of *kosmos* ("world") in the Letter of James. The shadow of the "world system" is in the backdrop of the use of *kosmos* in 2:5. This theological coloring is also seen in relation to 3:6, when one necessary correction is made to the NRSV rendering of the first part of that verse: "The tongue is placed among our members as a world of iniquity . . . ." The verb translated "is placed" in 3:6 is *kathistatai*, with same verb (and form) also used in 4:4, where it is usually rendered "becomes" (e.g., NRSV, CSB, NIV). However, the preferred translation is "makes himself" (ESV, NASB), reflecting the middle, instead of the passive, because James presents becoming "a friend of the world" in 4:4 as a personal choice (or choices; the Greek term is *boulomai*, "to wish, want, desire," with the implication of decision(s) being made).[54]

---

51. BAGD, S.v., "*spiloo*," 762.
52. I.e., Jas 2:1–4.
53. Blomberg and Kammel, *James*, 112–13.
54. BAGD, S.v., "*boulomai*," 146.

If this line of reasoning is correct, it is quite likely that the better rendering of *kathistatai* is Jas 3:6 is "makes itself." Such a translation clarifies the meaning of 3:6 significantly, that is, as "The tongue *makes itself a world of iniquity among our members.*"[55] This rendering also brings forward an important aspect of the concept of the *kosmos* in the Letter of James: that worldliness is internal (i.e., thoughts, attitudes, feelings) to a believer in Yeshua Messiah every bit as much as external (i.e., actions).

Certainly, James's assertion in 1:26 that failure to bridle the tongue is a—perhaps *the*—sign that one's "religion is worthless" fits in here. Words originate in internal thoughts, which, when released out of the mouth, are a source of great defilement (Matt 15:10, 16–20). From this perspective, it becomes even clearer that James is presenting his category "religion that is pure and undefiled before God" (1:27) as being the exact opposite of what he means by "the world." This meshes well with Lockett's major conclusion that "purity language in James constructs a firm value boundary between sympathetic readers and the larger culture."[56]

The portion of the Letter of James from the section on the abuse of the tongue (3:1–12) until the two final uses of *kosmos* in 4:4 prove insightful regarding the concept of "the world" in the letter. For example, the person who boasts out of a heart full of "bitter envy" and "selfish ambition" (3:14) is guilty of the abuse of tongue and the ultimate source of such attitudes and related speech is, according to Jas 3:15, "earthly, unspiritual, demonic."[57] In fact, such "envy" and "selfish ambition" causes "disorder and wickedness of every kind" (3:16). And all this external "disorder and wickedness" emerges from the internal *kosmos* of unrighteousness, which is closely related to the tongue (3:6).

These types of attitudes and behavior—many of which have verbal aspects—discussed in Jas 4:1–3 also clearly emerge from the internal *kosmos* "of iniquity" (3:6). Then, James levels two accusations at his audience, one direct and the other implied. First, he openly calls them "adulteresses,"[58] echoing the way the prophets in the Tanak often figuratively referred to the result of the Israel's spiritual unfaithfulness toward

---

55. The author's personal translation. Italics also mine.

56. As summarized by Allison (*James*, 353).

57. It is no coincidence that, just a few verses after 3:14–16, James's command to his audience to "Resist the devil, and he will flee from you" (4:7b) is found. It is, of course, ultimately the devil who is behind such demonic "wisdom" (3:15).

58. This is the correct translation of the *feminine* vocative form.

God[59] and possibly the discussion of "the adulterous woman" in Proverbs.[60] Second—and closely related to the first accusation—James, even though he leads with a question and then offers a clarifying statement, effectively calls them friends of the *kosmos*. (It is difficult to understand James's words otherwise immediately after he lambasted them with the term "adulteresses.")

Conclusion

The lengthy route through this chapter has added up to an understanding of messianic Jewish "religion" that is "pure and undefiled" as being what Darian Lockett refers to as a "worldview"[61] related to purity that James fervently sought to impart to his audience. He explains that this "worldview" is the opposite of that which comes from "the world" (*kosmos*) and ultimately from the realm of the demonic (i.e., as controlled by the devil).[62] However, it was to also be realized that there is an equally dangerous internal source that opposes the godly worldview concerning purity: the tongue, which, when out of control, is a *kosmos* of iniquity in its own right and "stains the whole body" (3:6).

---

59. Moo, *Letter of James*, 2nd ed., 233.
60. As held by, e.g., Schmitt, "You Adulteresses," 327–37.
61. Lockett, *Purity and Worldview in the Epistle of James*.
62. It is also worth noting that the listing of the characteristics of "the wisdom from above" begins with "pure" (3:17). That statement strongly infers purity is among the good and perfect gifts which come from the Father of lights (1:17).

6

"Your synagoge" and "the elders of the ekklesia"

As stated previously (see the discussion in chapter 1), most modern English translations render the Greek term *synagoge* in Jas 2:2 as "assembly"[1] or "meeting,"[2] obscuring a quite clear reference to the fact that the members of James's audience in the Diaspora (1:1) almost surely were involved in either traditional Jewish synagogues or newly organized messianic synagogues.[3]

Regarding the use of the Greek *ekklesia* in Jas 5:14, all the major modern translations in English have chosen "church" as the best rendering.[4] Once again, though, the TLV opts for a different translation: the somewhat paraphrased "Messiah's community."

What is the significance of these differences between translating *synagoge* in Jas 2:2 as "assembly" or "meeting" on the one hand, versus "synagogue" on the other hand? Similarly, what is the significance of rendering *ekklesia* as "church" on the one hand versus something like (Messiah's) "community" on the other?

The remainder of this chapter will explore the reasoning behind these differences and the implications of those differences for understanding the background circumstances of the Letter of James. First, the

---

1. E.g., NRSV, ESV, NASB, NET, NKJV.
2. E.g., NIV, CSB.
3. The only modern translation of which this writer is aware rendering *synagoge* in Jas 2:2 as "synagogue" is the messianic Jewish *Tree of Life Version* (TLV).
4. So NRSV, NIV, ESV, CSB, NASB, NET, NKJV.

usage of *synagoge* and *ekklesia* in the standard Greek translation[5] of the Hebrew Bible, usually abbreviated as LXX, will be briefly surveyed. Second, the overall usage of *synagoge* in the New Testament will be surveyed. Third, the overall usage of *ekklesia* in the New Testament will be surveyed. Fourth, the New Testament passages in which *synagoge* and *ekklesia* are found in the text, and where "elders" are mentioned, as in Jas 5:14, will be probed. Fifth, the possible significance of the recent historical construct known as "the parting of the ways" (i.e., between Judaism [notably messianic Judaism] and the church) will be discussed. Sixth, how the data viewed in these chapter sections fits together with Yeshua's declaration in Matt 16:18—"I will build my *ekklesia*"—and the other Gospels inclusion in Matt 18:17, will be explored. Finally, the chapter will conclude by answering this overarching question: How did James and his audience understand his usage of *synagoge* and *ekklesia* in his letter?

A brief sketch of the usage of *synagoge* and *ekklesia* in the LXX

Neither *synagoge* or *ekklesia* were recently coined terms in the first century CE, when the Letter of James was written. Both had lengthy prior histories and wide use within the broader Jewish culture. Ralph Korner underscores this point with the following statistics: "In total, *ekklesia* occurs 103 times in the LXX and *synagoge* 221 times."[6] In addition, Korner offers the recent research perspective that *ekklesia* could be a "synagogue" term and, thus, Christ-follower *ekklesai* (i.e., the pl. of *ekklesia*) could be what is normally called "synagogues."[7] This angle will be discussed in the latter part of this chapter.

The following is a brief, but helpful, overview by Edwin Yamauchi of the meaning and usage of *synagoge* prior to the New Testament era:

> "Synagogue" is a word derived from the Greek *sunagoge*, which meant originally an assembly such as of the Jews meeting for worship. In the Septuagint it is used, for example, in Exodus 12:3 of the whole congregation of Israel. It came to mean local

---

5. There were other translations of the Hebrew Bible into Greek besides the LXX—some in part, some in entirety—but no other version(s) had the geographical coverage and the long-lasting impact of the LXX.

6. Korner, *Origin and Meaning of* Ekklesia, 93.

7. Korner, *Origin and Meaning of* Ekklesia, 263.

gatherings of Jews and then the building where Jewish congregations met.... Though a few scholars ... have stressed the pre-exilic roots of the synagogue, most would ascribe its rise to the postexilic period. Many would place this development in the Jewish exilic community in Mesopotamia.[8]

Peter O'Brien similarly crisply overviews the usage of *ekklesia* prior to the New Testament era:

> In the LXX, *ekklesia* frequently was a translation of the Hebrew *qahal*, a term which could describe assemblies of a less specifically nonreligious kind, such as the gathering of an army in preparation for war (1 Sam 17:47; 2 Chron 28:14) or the "coming together" of an unruly and potentially dangerous crowd (Ps 26[LXX 25:]5). (*Ekklesia* never renders *edah*, "congregation," which represented the people as a national unit.) Of particular significance are those instances of *ekklesia* (rendering *qahal*) which denote the congregation of Israel when it is assembled to hear the Word of God on Mt. Sinai, or later on Mt. Zion, where all Israel was required to assemble three times a year.[9]

Therefore, when James chose to use *synagoge* in 2:2 and *ekklesia* in 5:14, there is every reason to conclude that he had made his decisions on terminology from a background knowledge that not only meant he used the words correctly, but also that his audience would have shared his sense of precisely what both words meant to James.

The overall usage of *synagoge* in the New Testament

There are fifty-six uses of the noun *synagoge* in the New Testament. Thirty-four of those uses are in the Gospels, nineteen are in Acts, one is in the Letters, and two are in Revelation.

The thirty-four uses in the Gospels can be helpfully categorized regarding: 1) singular versus plural uses; and 2) whether the uses are articular (i.e., having a definite article) or anarthrous (i.e., not having an article):

- Singular uses (15): Matt 12:9; 13:54; Mark 1:21, 29; 3:1; 6:2; Luke 4:16, 20, 28, 33, 38; 6:6; 7:5; 8:41; John 6:59

---

8. Yamauchi, "Synagogue," 782.
9. O'Brien, "Church," 124.

- Plural uses (19): Matt 4:23; 6:2, 5; 9:35; 10:17; 23:6, 34; Mark 1:23, 39; 12:39; 13:9; Luke 4:15, 44; 11:43; 12:11; 13:10; 20:46; 21:12; John 18:20
- Anarthrous uses (3): Mark 13:9; John 6:59; 18:20
- Articular uses (31): Matt 4:23; 6:2, 5; 9:35; 10:17; 12:9; 13:54; 23:6, 34; Mark 1:21, 23, 29, 39; 3:1; 6:2; 12:39; Luke 4:15, 16, 20, 28, 33, 38, 44; 6:6; 7:5; 8:41; 11:43; 12:11; 13:10; 20:46; 21:12

By comparison, the lone use of *synagoge* in the Letter of James (and in all the New Testament letters, for that matter) is singular, anarthrous, and with the possessive pronoun "your" (Greek *synagogen hymon*). Interestingly, of all thirty-four uses of *synagoge* in the Gospels surveyed above, *none* is constructed of all three of these factors. The closest is Matt 23:34, which does include the possessive pronoun "your,"[10] but is plural and articular (*tais synagogais hymon*).

However, the aspect of the thirty-four Gospels inclusions of *synagoge* that is both helpful and on which there is no dispute is how the word should be translated. To pull this part of the discussion together with the opening discussion above, all thirty-four uses are agreed as meaning "synagogue," with no attempt to render *synagoge* as "assembly" or "meeting," as was noted above is often the case with *synagoge* in Jas 2:2.

The point just made may seem completely obvious. However, it should still be carefully considered that, though the Letter of James is essentially as Jewish in background as the Gospels, the tendency to translate *synagoge* as other than the natural rendering of "synagogue" still persists. More will be said about this later in this chapter.

The nineteen uses of *synagoge* in Acts are best analyzed as: 1) singular versus plural; and 2) where the "synagogue" or "synagogues" is/are located geographically[11]:

- Singular uses (12): Acts 6:9; 13:14, 43; 14:1; 17:1, 10, 17; 18:4, 7, 19, 26; 19:8
- Plural uses (7): 9:2, 20; 13:5; 15:21; 22:19; 24:12; 26:11

---

10. Matt 23:34 is the only one of the thirty-four passages in the Gospels where *synagoge* is found that includes the possessive "your."

11. This second category was not used above, regarding the usage of *synagoge* in the Gospels, because all uses were of Jewish synagogues in Palestine and no more specific geography would be helpful.

The twelve singular uses of *synagoge* in Acts are found in eight places in the eastern and northern Mediterranean Basin:

- Jerusalem (6:9 ["the Synagogue of the Freedmen"])
- Pisidian Antioch (13:14, 19)
- Iconium (14:1)
- Thessalonica (17:1)
- Berea (17:10)
- Athens (17:17)
- Corinth (18:4, 7)
- Ephesus (18:19, 26; 19:8)

The seven plural uses in Acts of *synagoge* refer to two major cities, one island, and, as stated by James at the key moment of the Jerusalem Council, "every city" (i.e., wherever there were synagogues in the Roman Empire or elsewhere):

- Damascus (9:2, 20)
- Cyprus (13:5)
- "In every city" (15:21)
- Jerusalem (22:19; 24:12; 26:11)

The main thing the listings of singular[12] and plural uses of *synagoge* in Acts have in common with the listing of uses in the Gospels is that, much as Jesus attended, preached, and taught in the synagogues almost everywhere he travelled in his public ministry in the Gospels, the same is true with the singular and plural uses of *synagoge* in Acts regarding the ministry of the apostle Paul. In fact, the local synagogue was almost always where Paul started his ministry upon arriving in a new area (e.g., Cyprus [13:5]; Pisidian Antioch [Acts 13:14]; Iconium [14:1]; Thessalonica [17:1]; Berea [17:10]; Athens [17:17]; Corinth [18:4]; and Ephesus [18:19]).

Also, the list of singular uses of *synagoge* in Acts above is even more relevant to the circumstances related to the Letter of James than is the Gospels list. The reason is that those locations—as well as the plural uses

---

12. The lone exception is the reference to the "Synagogue of the Freedmen" in Acts 6:9, where Stephen argued with some Hellenistic Jews, leading to his being brought before the Sanhedrin in Acts 7.

of *synagoge* in Acts 9:20 (in Damascus) and 13:5 (on the island of Cyprus), are all located in the wider Diaspora, as was James's audience (Jas 1:1). However, if Aida Spencer is correct in her conclusion, which follows immediately below, only part of the nearer area populated by Diaspora Jews is in view:

> James refers to Jewish Messianic believers . . . who left Jerusalem after the stoning of Stephen to avoid the Jewish persecution (Acts 8:1, 4). At first, they left for the provinces of Judea and Samaria. Eventually they travelled as far as Phoenicia, Cyprus, and Antioch, preaching at first only to other Jews (Acts 11:19). These dispersed Jewish believers appear to be James's readership.[13]

Before leaving this analysis of the usage of *synagoge* in the Book of Acts, the same point must be made as regarding all the uses of *synagoge* in the Gospels: there is not even any mild conjecture that *synagoge* should be translated in any other way than as "synagogue." Again, the clear reason is that the uses are each in obvious Jewish contexts, where it is natural to render *synagoge* as "synagogue."

However, as stated above, this same understanding is quite likely to be the case with Jas 2:2: *that the verse is referring to a specifically Jewish place of worship*. After the survey offered above, what compelling exegetical basis can be offered that *synagoge* in Jas 2:2 is *not* speaking of a synagogue?

Evidence is lacking as far as both background and measured exegesis is concerned. Basically, the two primary reasons for choosing to render *synagoge* in Jas 2:2 as "assembly" or "meeting" appear to be: 1) the late-dating of the Letter of James, so as to suggest that James is a "general Christian Epistle"[14] (i.e., to a *general* audience of believers, because it was written at a time too late for a strictly Jewish audience) that happens to contain a number of Jewish elements, which may well be based in 2) conscious or subconscious supersessionist thinking/theology.

As stated above, besides the thirty-four instances of *synagoge* in the Gospels and nineteen in Acts, there are only three other New Testament uses: two in Revelation (2:9; 3:9)—and, of course, the focal passage in Jas 2:2. Both passages in Revelation contain the same immediate

---

13. Spencer, *A Commentary on James*, 58.

14. This is part of what is meant when James is placed within the category of "The General Epistles" in the NT. The other thing intended is to clearly separate the other NT letters from "the Pauline Epistles."

wording, but in mirroring (i.e., reverse) order. Revelation 2:9 speaks of "those who say that they are Jews, but are not, but are a synagogue of Satan" while 3:9 reads "those of the synagogue of Satan who say they are Jews and are not."[15]

These two unusual verses in the Apocalypse have been understood in numerous ways. However, the key general question for a study such as this is whether both descriptions are referring to ethnic Jews or gentiles (assuming, obviously, that the overwhelming similarity in wording between Rev 2:9 and 3:9 is referring to the same people). The other assumption is that *synagoge* is being used there with its normal New Testament meaning (i.e., as a Jewish "synagogue").

Most scholars understand that the "synagogue of Satan" is referring to ethnic Jews in Smyrna, the location of the *ekklesia* receiving Messiah's mini-letter in 2:8–11, and in Philadelphia, the location of the *ekklesia* receiving Messiah's mini-letter in 3:7–13.[16] By contrast, Ramsey Michaels takes the gentile perspective, as stated in the following words:

> A better interpretation is that the synagogue of Satan consisted of Gentile Christians who had "Judaized," that is, who adopted Jewish ways, or even converted to Judaism, perhaps in order to avoid persecution by the Romans. . . . Judaism was an ancient religion, largely tolerated in Roman Asia, while Christianity, being relatively new, was regarded with suspicion by many Romans as an erratic and possibly subversive cult.[17]

While Michaels' view makes sense from a background standpoint, it is more likely that the meaning of "synagogue of Satan" in 2:9 (and 3:9) is that whatever suffering had been taking place—and would soon be taking place—within the Christian community had Satan behind it as its ultimate origin (2:10). What that would mean is that the Jewish synagogues in Smyrna and Philadelphia were, without understanding

---

15. Though the wider significance of the wording that is obviously reversed between Rev 2:9 and 3:9 is not relevant to the discussion of the meaning of *synagoge* across all NT uses, it is worth mentioning here what may a plausible reason for the reversal. It could be that, in 3:9, in contrast with the soon coming "ten days" of *thlipsis* ("affliction, tribulation") in 2:10 on the believers in Smyrna, the promise in 3:10 is, instead, that the believers in Philadelphia would be kept from the "hour of trial that is coming on the whole world."

16. E.g., The discussion of Keener, *Revelation*, 115–16, 150, is particularly helpful, especially his succinct treatment of the "local Jewish repudiation of Christians" (115) even into the early second century CE in that part of Asia Minor.

17. Michaels, *Revelation*, 74.

what they were doing, serving as the tools of Satan through persecuting the Christian assemblies in each city.

If this understanding is correct, the uses of *synagoge* in Rev 2:9 and 3:9 both refer to Jewish synagogues. That conclusion adds to the same conclusions regarding the uses of *synagoge* in the Gospels, Acts, and the Epistles: that the other fifty-five uses of *synagoge* refer to a Jewish "synagogue" (or "synagogues"). What that means is that there would have to be a wealth of data favoring the understanding and translation of *synagoge* in Jas 2:2 as other than "synagogue" to justify a rendering such as "assembly" or "meeting." However, that does not appear to be the case—especially if the early dating of 45 CE for the Letter of James championed in chapter 1 is anywhere close to accurate.

The overall usage of *ekklesia* in the New Testament

There are a total of 114 uses of *ekklesia* in the New Testament. Only three are in the Gospels, all in Matthew (16:18; 18:17 [twice]). Twenty-three inclusions are found in Acts, sixty-two in Paul's letters, and twenty-six are in the messianic Jewish letters,[18] John's letters, and Revelation.[19]

The three inclusions in Matthew will be treated in a later part of this chapter. The twenty-three uses in Acts can be categorized helpfully in the following way, while generally following the movement of the narrative of Acts:

- The *ekklesia* in Jerusalem (9): 5:11; 8:1, 3; 11:22; 12:1, 5; 15:4, 22; 18:22
- The *ekklesia* "in the wilderness" (1): 7:38
- The *ekklesia* "throughout Judea, Galilee, and Samaria" (1): 9:31
- The *ekklesia* in Syrian Antioch (4): 11:26; 13:1; 14:27; 15:3
- Every *ekklesia* in the region of Lystra, Derbe, Iconium, and Pisidian Antioch (2): 14:23; 16:5
- The *ekklesiai* (pl.) in Syria and Cilicia (1): 15:41

---

18. This category of NT letters includes Hebrews, James, 1–2 Peter, and Jude. The rationale behind this category is that these five letters are not accurately categorized as "General Epistles" or "Catholic Epistles," and each have significant Jewish backgrounds and reflect messianic Jewish perspectives and theology.

19. See the similar breakdown of O'Brien, "Church," 124.

- A secular *ekklesia* in Ephesus (3): 19:32, 39, 41
- The *ekklesia* in Ephesus (2): 20:17, 28

The various gatherings of messianic Jewish believers in Yeshua seen in Acts (i.e., 5:11; 8:1, 3; 9:31; 11:22; 12:1, 5; 15:4, 22; 18:22) are all called *ekklesia*. This appears to be: 1) to differentiate messianic Jews from Jews who did not believe in Yeshua and their place of worship (e.g., see "the Synagogue of the Freedmen" [6:9]); and 2) in remembrance of Yeshua's proclamation "I will build my *ekklesia*" [Matt 16:18, which will be discussed later]). The bulk of the remaining uses of *ekklesia* in Acts refer to either mixed (i.e., Jew and gentile together [11:26; 13:1; 14:23, 27; 15:3, 41; 16:5; 20:17, 28]) congregations of believers in Yeshua or almost completely gentile congregations.

The remaining four uses of *ekklesia* in Acts are also significant, however, because they provide insight regarding the earlier background of the term in both the Jewish and Greek cultures. Those four uses are in two different passages: 1) in Stephen's sermon, in 7:38; and 2) in the description of the Greek group involved in the riot in Ephesus, in 19:32, 39, 41.

In Acts 7:38 ("the congregation in the wilderness" at "Mount Sinai"), *ekklesia* represents the Heb *qahal*, usually translated "congregation" in both the Hebrew Bible and LXX. This is also the case in most of the nearly eighty uses of *ekklesia* in the LXX. Thus, it can be seen from even this single verse in Acts that there is present significant Jewish background for the term *ekklesia*.

The three uses of *ekklesia* in Acts 19 all have the definite article (i.e., "the assembly").[20] This kind of "assembly" was the primary meaning of *ekklesia* in the secular Greek culture. Thus, since the gospel of Yeshua was spreading throughout the largely Greek culture of the Mediterranean Basin in the Book of Acts, it is not at all unexpected that the Greek coloring of *ekklesia* would come into play.

The sixty-two passages in which *ekklesia* is used in Paul's Letters break down book by book as follows:

- In Romans (5 times)
- In 1 Corinthians (22 times)
- In 2 Corinthians (9 times)

---

20. The use of *ekklesia* in Acts 19:39 reads *te ennomo ekklesia* (lit. "the lawful assembly").

- In Galatians (3 times)
- In Ephesians (9 times)
- In Philippians (2 times)
- In Colossians (4 times)
- In 1 Thessalonians (2 times)
- In 2 Thessalonians (2 times)
- In 1 Timothy (3 times)
- In Philemon (1 time)

Paul uses *ekklesia* at least once in each of his letters except 2 Timothy and Titus. According to O'Brien, all these uses refer to either: 1) "a local assembly or congregations of Christians" (i.e., believers in Yeshua as Messiah); 2) "a house church"; or 3) "a heavenly gathering" (i.e., what is often referred to as "the universal church").[21] Thus, although terms like participial forms of *pisteuo* ("believers") and *agioi* ("saints") were sometimes utilized to refer to the same people in Paul's Letters, *ekklesia* was the primary way Paul referred to those who had believed in Yeshua as Messiah and their assembling.

Of the twenty-six instances of *ekklesia* in the messianic Jewish letters, John's letters, and Revelation, two are found in Hebrews, three in 3 John, twenty in the Apocalypse, and the focal use in Jas 5:14. The simplest of these usages of *ekklesia* to understand are in 3 John 6, 9, 10. All three refer to a particular local church.

Of the two inclusions in Hebrews, one is in a quotation from Ps 22:22 in Heb 2:12, which is speaking of a Jewish assembly for worship. The other speaks of "the assembly (*ekklesia*) of the firstborn (*prototokon*) who are enrolled in heaven" (Heb 12:23). In this case, the plural "firstborn"[22] is referring to believers who have already been *permanently* "enrolled" (Greek perfect tense of *apogegegrammenon*).[23] It is not obvious whether this wording should be taken to refer to what O'Brien spoke of (see above) as "a heavenly gathering" in his summary of Paul's usage or to the "cloud of witnesses" (12:1), looking back to the exemplary people

---

21. O'Brien, "Church," 124–26.

22. Because the form of "firstborn" is plural, it cannot be referring to Yeshua Messiah as firstborn.

23. Rogers and Rogers, *New Linguistic and Exegetical Key to the New Testament*, 548.

of faith in Heb 11.[24] Because of the immediately preceding wording (i.e., "you have come to Mount Zion and to the city of the living God, the heavenly Jerusalem"), it is certainly possible that *ekklesia* in Heb 12:23 is referring to a specifically Jewish deceased group of believers in the Hebrew Bible or all deceased messianic Jewish believers in all ages.[25]

The twenty instances of *ekkesia* found in Revelation are straightforward to categorize:

- "the seven churches" (4 times): 1:4, 11, 20 [twice]
- "the churches" (8 times): 2:7, 11, 17, 29; 3:6, 13, 22; 22:16
- "the church in Ephesus" (1 time): 2:1
- "the church in Smyrna" (1 time): 2:8
- "the church in Pergamum" (1 time): 2:12
- "the church in Thyatira" (1 time): 2:18
- "the church in Sardis" (1 time): 3:1
- "the church in Philadelphia" (1 time): 3:7
- "the church in Laodicea" (1 time): 3:14
- "all the churches" (1 time): 2:23

As clearly seen just above, thirteen of the twenty uses refer to all seven of the churches (1:4, 11, 20 [twice], 2:7, 11,17, 23, 29; 3:6, 13, 22; 22:16), listed together in the latter part of Rev 1:11. The other seven instances refer to each of the seven local churches individually (2:1, 8, 12, 18; 3:1, 7, 14). All twenty refer to local churches in seven cities (or significant towns) in the first-century CE Roman province of Asia. It is likely that the other six local churches had been planted during the apostle Paul's prolonged ministry[26] in Ephesus in Acts 19.[27]

---

24. Bruce, *Epistle to the Hebrews*, rev. ed., 333; Allen, *Hebrews*, 572.

25. It is the view of this writer that the wording in Rev 21:12 ("the names of the twelve tribes of the Israelites") and 21:14 ("the twelve names of the twelve apostles of the Lamb") cinches the theological point that, though there is an aspect of overarching unity in the people of God, there is, and *eternally* will be (i.e., Rev 21–22 is speaking of the new heavens and earth, the eternal state), everlasting distinction between Israel and the church.

26. After his two- to three-year ministry in Ephesus, the next longest period of ministry in one place mentioned in Acts is in Corinth: "a year and six months" (18:11).

27. Because there is no textual indication that Paul ever left Ephesus during the two- to three-year period of his ministry there (Acts 19:8, 10; 20:31), it seems best to

The only instance of *ekklesia* in the New Testament yet to be studied is in Jas 5:14, the lone usage in the Letter of James. Because of the wording there, "the elders of the church" (Greek *ekklesia*), that discussion will be in the next section of this chapter.

The relevance of the "elders" of the *ekklesia* for understanding the audience of the Letter of James

One of the striking realizations upon arriving at this point in this study is that there are no other passages in the New Testament besides in the Letter of James in which *synagoge* and *ekklesia* are: 1) found in reasonably close textual proximity; and 2) referring to the same people. From that standpoint, there are no obvious "apples and apples" comparisons to be made regarding the basic usage of the two terms.

However, when the wording is expanded to "the elders (*presbyterous*) of the church (*ekklesia*)" (5:14), it becomes a somewhat different matter. There are a small number of passages—two quite significant— that offer insight.

The Greek term *presbyteros* ("older, elder, presbyter")[28] is used sixty-seven times in the New Testament. Twenty-five of those are in the Gospels, eighteen in Acts, eleven in the New Testament Letters, and twelve in Revelation.

In the Gospels, twenty-four of the twenty-five inclusions refer to Jewish leaders called "elders,"[29] who are usually in open conflict with, or plotting against, Yeshua. The only exception is the reference in what is generally known as the parable of the prodigal son to the "elder" (i.e., older) son (Luke 15:25).

In Acts, of the eighteen uses of *presbyteros*, one speaks of "old men" (2:17), and seven speak of Jewish leaders in much the same way as do the Gospels (4:5, 8, 23; 6:12; 23:14; 24:1; 25:15). Six refer to the grouping of "apostles and elders" in the leadership of the church in Jerusalem related to the Jerusalem Council (15:2, 4, 6, 22, 23; 16:4).

---

understand that the work in planting the other churches surrounding Ephesus was done by various ministry associates of Paul's.

28. BAGD, S.v., "*presbuteros*," 699–700.

29. The position of "elder" in Jewish leadership recognized by God goes back to at least as far as the wilderness near Mount Sinai when the (Holy) Spirit on Moses was placed on "the seventy elders" in Num 11:16–30.

As will be seen, the remaining four instances of *presbyteros* in Acts are the most helpful for understanding the relationship between *synagoge* and *ekklesia* in the Letter of James. The first speaks of "the elders"—clearly in the Jerusalem church (see Acts 11:27)—to whom Barnabas and Saul (Paul) deliver the relief funds from the church in Syrian Antioch (11:30). The second usage occurs at the end of Paul's first missionary journey, summarizing the apparently necessary appointment of "elders" in "each church" (14:23). The third passage deals with "the elders of the church" in Ephesus (20:17), whom Paul meets in Miletus. The final example describes "James and all the elders" (i.e., of the Jerusalem church [21:18]) in a meeting with Paul upon his return to Jerusalem after the third missionary journey.

Of these four passages, the first (11:30) helps only by indicating an event by which time there were "elders" already functioning in the Jerusalem church. The final passage (21:18) indicates that James, the author of the Letter of James, was working closely with "the elders" of the Jerusalem church. Thus, since it undoubtedly had been a sizeable span of time[30] since "elders" had been put in leadership roles in the Jerusalem church (i.e., at least by 11:30, and perhaps before that), James would have understood well the role that such "elders" were to play in the local congregation.

Regarding the second passage, even though the appointment of "elders" there was in primarily gentile congregations established on the first missionary journey of Barnabas and Saul, Polhill is surely correct as to where the idea of appointing elders originated: "For these early churches, there was no professional clergy to assume their leadership. Consequently, the pattern of the Jewish synagogues seems to have been followed by appointing a group of lay elders to shepherd the flock."[31]

The third passage is the most helpful of the four for this study for the simple reason that the immediate phraseology in Acts 20:17 is identical to that in Jas 5:14, as seen below:

- Acts 20:17-*tous presbyterous tes ekklesiais* ("the elders of the church")
- Jas 5:14-*tous presbyterous tes ekklesiais* ("the elders of the church")

---

30. The most common dating of Acts 21 is 57 CE. Acts 11:30 can be dated as early as 42 CE. If those figures are reasonably accurate, James's experience working with "elders" may have been going on for a decade and a half.

31. Polhill, *Acts*, 319.

The intriguing aspects of the comparison of these two passages in Acts are: 1) Acts 20:17 focuses on an almost entirely gentile church, while Jas 5:14 gives all indications of speaking of a completely Jewish congregation; and 2) the Letter of James may well be the earliest book of the New Testament, having been written between 42 and 45 CE (see the discussion of the dating of the Letter of James in chapter 1), while the events of Acts 20 took place toward the end of the third missionary journey, likely in 57 CE.[32]

Of the eleven uses of *presbyteros* in the New Testament Epistles, five are in Paul's Letters, one is in Hebrews, two in 1 Peter, and one each in 2 John and 3 John. The other inclusion is in Jas 5:14, the focal passage in this study.

Of the five uses in Paul's letters, two are of "old(er) men" (1 Tim 5:2; Titus 2:2). The other three uses all refer to the leadership role of "elder" (1 Tim 5:17, 18; Titus 1:5). The mention of *presbyteros* in Hebrews is in 11:2, being best rendered as "ancestors," as in NRSV, looking back to the people of faith in earlier times in the Hebrew Bible. Both appearances in 1 Peter refer to the office of "elder" (1 Pet 5:1, 5). The uses in 2 John 1 and 3 John 1 refer to "the elder," most likely a self-designation of the apostle John.[33]

Of the thirteen inclusions of *presbyteros* in Revelation, none refer to leaders in the church, at least not on earth. Five passages speak of "twenty-four elders" in the heavenly throne room (4:4, 10; 5:8; 11:16; 19:4). Five shorten the wording referring to the same heavenly group to "the elders" (5:6, 11, 14; 7:11; 14:3). The final two uses refer to "one of the elders" (5:5; 7:13).

At the end of this survey of the presence of *presbyteros* in the New Testament, two things seem clear regarding the unusual presence of *synagoge* and *ekklesia*, with *presbyteros* alongside it, in the Letter of James: 1) the origin of the leadership position of "elder" (*presbyteros*) was Jewish, with "elder" being a standard role not only in national leadership, as in most Jewish examples in the Gospels and Acts, but also in the

---

32. Loveday Alexander ("Chronology of Paul," 122–23) concludes her longer entry (115–23) by offering three somewhat different chronologies of Paul's post-conversion life until his imprisonment in Rome. However, each places the end of the third missionary journey and transition to travel to Jerusalem in 56–57 CE.

33. It is not clear whether *presbyteros* in 2 John 1 and 3 John 1 are referring to the apostle John as an "old man" or as an "elder" in the church, or both. For a recent discussion weighing whether the wording "the elder" could be referring to someone other than the apostle John, see Bernier, *Rethinking the Dates of the New Testament*, 113–18.

local synagogue (*synagoge*)³⁴; and 2) "elders" were active in the church in Jerusalem at least as early as Acts 11:30 (likely ca. 42–44 CE), so there appears to be no compelling reason, from either a Jewish or Christian perspective, why the mention of "elders" in Jas 5:14 cannot reflect the same government of the *ekklesia* as in the mother church from which James's audience departed due to persecution (Acts 11:19).

The major question that remains has to do with how to understand the nature of the "coexistence" of *synagogue* and *ekklesia* in the Letter of James. Both terms can, in proper contexts, be translated "assembly," so the issue is what precisely is being referred to when "synagogue" is employed in 2:2 and "church" is used in 5:14.³⁵

The final two sections of this chapter will provide perspective on that question, first from a historical standpoint, then from the standpoint of what Yeshua meant when he proclaimed he would build his *ekklesia*.

"The parting of the ways" and the Letter of James

The separation of Christianity from Judaism in postbiblical times famously has been referred to as "the parting of the ways."³⁶ Although it is virtually unquestionable such a split took place, it has, however, proven much more difficult to determine the specific dynamics at work and the exact timing of the "parting."

The best known of the contemporary approaches to explaining "the parting of the ways" came from James D. G. Dunn. According to Craig Evans:

> Dunn identifies four important pillars of Second Temple Jewish faith: (1) monotheism (the affirmation that God is one), (2) election (the affirmation of Israel as the chosen people of God), (3) covenant (as affirmed and described in Torah), and (4) the land

---

34. Though the term *presbyteros* is not used regarding a local synagogue in the Gospel or Acts, the terms *archon* ("leader" [Luke 9:41]) and *archisynagogos* ("head of the synagogue" [9:49]) are both applied to Jairus. Yamauchi states: "A group of elders would direct the activities of the synagogue. The *archisunagogos* was probably chosen from among them" (Yamauchi, "Synagogue," 782).

35. An excellent brief discussion of this very tension is found in Campbell, "Church as Israel, People of God," 204–5.

36. This wording is taken from the title of James D. G. Dunn's important, but controversial, work, *The Parting of the Ways: Between Christianity and Judaism and Their Significance for the Character of Christianity*.

of Israel (including Jerusalem and the temple). Dunn explores in what ways Jews and Christians understood these pillars and finds in their differing understandings the seeds of separation.[37]

Although Dunn's viewpoint has been highly influential in wider New Testament scholarship over the past three decades, his biblical and theological analysis is suspect in multiple areas. However, for the purposes of this study, it is Dunn's conclusion that is most relevant. A helpful, measured summary of Dunn's overall conclusion is offered by McKnight: "[T]he parting of the ways took place over time, in different ways and with different results—but, still by the middle of the second century C.E., there were two faiths: Christianity and the foundations of formative, or rabbinic, Judaism."[38]

What does this have to do with understanding the relationship between *synagoge* and *ekklesia* in the Letter of James? The answer to that question is two-fold. First, McKnight's further thoughts on what he calls "a parting within the way" are worthy of careful consideration:

> It is James who may well represent the movement that did not, in social shape, part from Judaism or, put differently, with James we must find a parting within the way of Judaism and thus find another form of Judaism, a "Christian Judaism." James, I believe, was a Jew, a faithful Jew, who both embraced the vision of his brother, Jesus, as well as the faith of his ancestors, what we now call Judaism.[39]

To bring McKnight's point closer to the discussion in this chapter—and from its publication in 1999 to the present, what he calls "Christian Judaism" is well known today as "messianic Judaism." That is precisely what is seen in James: an emerging type of Judaism in which there is no tension involved when James employs *synagoge* and *ekklesia* to refer to the same people in his letter.

However, there is one additional "checkpoint" that needs to be considered before drawing a final conclusion: what Yeshua meant when he promised "I will build my *ekklesia*" in Matt 16:18.

---

37. Evans, "Christianity and Judaism: Parting of the Ways," 161.
38. McKnight, "A Parting within the Way," 83.
39. McKnight, "A Parting within the Way," 84.

Yeshua's words "I will build my *ekklesia*" and the Letter of James

An additional relevant element has been added to this consideration of Matt 16 recently with the publication of Jonathan Bernier's paradigm-shaking volume, *Rethinking the Dates of the New Testament: The Evidence for Early Composition*.[40] Bernier's 2022 work is the first book-length treatment of New Testament dating since John A. T. Robinson's groundbreaking—and controversial—study, *Redating the New Testament*, which was originally published in 1976, a span of close to half a century between the two volumes.

The key point for this study is that Bernier dates the Gospel of Matthew in the range between 45 and 59 CE.[41] This conclusion is not taken lightly, though. Bernier has carefully surveyed the "synchronization" of the Synoptic Gospels,[42] as well as their "Contextualization and Authorial Biography."[43] In addition, Bernier's argumentation throughout is sensitized to be free from "fallacy," to the "quantity of data," and the level of (over)complication of the hypothesis—what he calls "parsimony."[44]

Therefore, it can be said Bernier's hypothesis that the First Gospel was written in 45–59 CE is carefully argued and deserves serious consideration, whether it changes any particular scholar's conclusions on the dating of Matthew or not. As far as this study is concerned, if Matthew can credibly be dated before 48 CE, it would predate the Jerusalem Council in Acts 15.[45] If that were to be the case, James (working from the dating range of 42–45 CE argued earlier in this study) and Matthew would be two of the three earliest New Testament books.[46]

---

40. Bernier, *Rethinking the Dates of the New Testament*. Significantly, all six of the endorsement blurbs on the back cover of the book refer to its future impact on the study of Christian origins in very strong terms, such as: "must read," "major contribution," "bold," "disruptive," "to be reckoned with," or "promises to shake up the scholarly study of the New Testament and some extracanonical Christian works."

41. Bernier, *Rethinking the Dates of the New Testament*, 84.

42. Bernier, *Rethinking the Dates of the New Testament*, 35–67.

43. Bernier, *Rethinking the Dates of the New Testament*, 80–84.

44. Bernier, *Rethinking the Dates of the New Testament*, 28–29.

45. Which is best dated in 48 or 49 CE (see Alexander, "Chronology of Paul," 122–23; Maier, "Chronology," 193.

46. Numerous NT scholars have also dated Paul's Letter to the Galatians in 48 or 49 CE.

What difference would the comparatively early dating of the Letter of James and the Gospel of Matthew make regarding how *synagoge* and *ekklesia* are used in James?[47] Potentially, quite a bit. Consider the following plausible angles:

- Matthew and the "brothers" of Jesus (i.e., including James) were in the Upper Room (Acts 1:13–14) before the Day of Pentecost and Matthew and James would have had the opportunity to get to know one another and work together for well over a decade as leaders in the Jerusalem church.

- As a "tax collector" (Matt 9:9; 10:3), Matthew would have been perhaps the most literate of the apostles[48] and may have helped the leadership of the Jerusalem church regarding financial matters and other leadership/administrative issues.

- If James wrote his letter somewhere between 42 and 45 CE, Matthew may have been a "consultant" and even possibly James's amanuensis (i.e., secretary), if he used one. The idea of being a "consultant" is based on the common usage of wording in both the Letter of James and the Gospel of Matthew, as will be discussed in the next chapter.

- The apparent *ongoing* mission to "the lost sheep of the house of Israel" (Matt 10:5–6) fits well with the single-minded perspective of the Letter of James.[49]

---

47. With little question, it is still a minority view in most scholarly circles that the apostle Matthew wrote the First Gospel and, probably yet more uncommon that the Gospel of Matthew was written in the 40s CE. Yet those views have not been without capable defenders in recent decades. For example: 1) John Wenham (*Redating Matthew, Mark & Luke*, 243) concludes the First Gospel was written around 40; 2) David Alan Black (*Why Four Gospels?*, 73) argues that Matthew was published in 42. Most recently, 3) Jonathan Bernier (*Rethinking the Dates of the New Testament*, 277) places Matthew in a dating range of 45–59. All of these views allow for the idea that James and Matthew could have, to some greater or lesser extent, worked alongside each other in Jerusalem leading up to the publication of the Epistle of James and the Gospel of Matthew.

48. Of the traditional authors of the Gospels, Matthew would likely have been the most skilled writer, given his background as a tax collector. The apostle John did become a prolific writer (i.e., the Fourth Gospel, the three Johannine Letters, and Revelation), but not until decades later. There is no evidence that Mark or Luke were among the apostles and leadership of the Jerusalem church early, as was Matthew since from Pentecost forward.

49. For the development of this understanding, see Konradt, *Israel, Church, and the Gentiles*, 74–85.

- The emphases in the Letter of James on the coming of the Lord (5:3, 7, 8) and eschatological judgment (e.g., 2:13; 4:12; 5:1–3, 5) are notably similar to those themes in Matthew (e.g., 10:23; 13:40–42, 49–50; 25:46).

- With word of the expansion of ethnic outreach to the gentiles, as well as the Jews (e.g., Cornelius, the Roman centurion, and his household [Acts 10]; and the founding and rapid growth of the church in Syrian Antioch [11:19–26]) arriving in Jerusalem (see 11:1–18 [Cornelius]; 11:22 [Syrian Antioch]), the realization of the great significance of Yeshua's climactic post-resurrection command to "go and make disciples of all the nations" (Matt 28:19–20) clicked, perhaps especially with Matthew, who concluded his soon-to-be-completed book on the life and ministry of Yeshua (i.e., the Gospel of Matthew) with that "Great Commission."

Having considered all these angles, as well as Korner's observation above that *ekklesia* could be a "synagogue" term and Christ-follower *ekklesiai* (i.e., the pl. of *ekklesia*) could be what is normally called "synagogues," it is time to bring Matt 16:18 into the discussion. In doing so, it must be noticed initially that Yeshua did not promise to build "an *ekklesia*." Instead, Yeshua's promise was to build "**my** *ekklesia*."

The difference between these two expressions is considerable. If Yeshua had said "an *ekklesia*," it would have meant he was going to erect a completely different kind of *ekklesia* than the *ekklesia* of Israel that had existed previously and was recorded in the LXX. In other words, he would have been stating there would be complete *dis*continuity with the *ekklesia* of Israel that had existed before. However, by saying he would build "my *ekklesia*," Yeshua indicates but three changes: 1) primarily, that the new *ekklesia* he would build would be focused on him as Messiah. If context is a reliable guide—and it always is with narrative literature like the Gospels, the verses just before 16:18 (16:15–16) contain Yeshua's question "Who do you say that I am?" (16:15) and Peter's answer: "You are the Messiah, the Son of the living God" (16:16 CSB);[50] and 2) that Yeshua's *ekklesia* would be closely related to "the kingdom of heaven" (16:19a)—which Yeshua and his closest disciples had been preaching throughout

50. In the view of this writer, the "rock" (Greek *petra*) that Messiah would build his *ekklesia* on is not Simon Peter—who is nicknamed *petros*, which means "little rock" (being *contrasted* with *petra*, that is, not saying the same thing in different terms). Rather, the "rock" in that passage is Peter's correct answer to Yeshua's question in 16:16: "You are the Messiah, the Son of the living God."

his public ministry (e.g., 5:3, 10; 10:7); and 3) that Peter would have the "keys of the kingdom of heaven" (16:19a) and would share the authority of "binding and loosing" with the new *ekklesia* (16:19b; 18:18).

Beyond those three items, no further changes from the previously existing *ekklesia* (i.e., Israel) are stated in Matt 16 as about to take place. In that light, it seems fair to say that the apparent "tension" in the Letter of James between the presence of both *synagoge* (2:2) and *ekklesia* (5:14) may be overblown. The answer to how the seemingly odd co-existence of those two terms is best explained will be given in the final section of this chapter.

Conclusion: How did James and his audience understand his use of *synagoge* and *ekklesia*?

After proceeding through much of this chapter with the generally assumed differences between *synagoge* and *ekklesia* uppermost in focus, there was no apparent answer to how James could have used both terms in his letter, applying both to the same people. However, shifting the focus to comparing the similarities between the *synagoge* and *ekklesia* proved to be a more productive approach. From that angle, the terms can be seen to be complementary, not (apparently) contradictory. In other words, *synagogue* can be (accurately) translated "synagogue" in Jas 2:2 and *ekklesia* can be (just as correctly!) rendered "church" in 5:14.

In the opinion of this writer, the best orientation regarding how to emerge from this challenging study of *synagoge* and *ekklesia* is the following quotation from the insightful article "Boundaries, Intersections, and the Parting of the Ways in the Letter of James," by Kathleen Elkins and Thomas Bolin:[51]

> We see James as a text that sits on the precarious and obscure border between the groups that eventually became Judaism and Christianity. . . . James gives us information about the context of the community: they meet in a synagogue and/or feel comfortable calling their assembly a synagogue. . . . This use of "synagogue" *(sunagoge)* as a straightforward description of their community is but one example of the messy and perhaps nonexistent border we are discussing.[52]

---

51. Elkins and Bolin, "Boundaries, Intersections, and the Parting of the Ways in the Letter of James," 335–43.

52. Elkins and Bolin, "Boundaries, Intersections, and the Parting of the Ways in the Letter of James," 338–39.

Their conclusion can also serve admirably as the last word for this chapter:

> Rather than seeing James as a Christian letter in a community that cannot figure out which side of the border it belongs on, we propose reading James as a Jewish letter in a community that sees Jesus as the Jewish Messiah; that is, this letter exists before any border between Judaism and Christianity exists.[53]

If the Letter of James was written in the mid 40s CE, whatever took place in a so-called "parting of the ways" between Judaism and Christianity was still some half a century away. Thus, it was not just possible, but it was normal, for James's audience to be referred to as both *sunagoge* and *ekklesia*, without any inconsistency whatsoever.

---

53. Elkins and Bolin, "Boundaries, Intersections, and the Parting of the Ways in the Letter of James," 339.

7

Echoes of the Tanakh and the teaching of Jesus in James

AFTER THE SOMEWHAT LENGTHY discussion of the uses of the Greek term *nomos* ("law") in chapter 3, it would be expected that the Letter of James would extensively cite the Hebrew Bible. However, that is not the case. There are generally considered to be only four (five—if you count as two passages the parallel verses from the Ten Commandments in Exod 20 and Deut 5) true quotations from the Hebrew Bible in James.

That does not mean, though, that James does not utilize the Hebrew Bible more heavily in his letter. Instead, there are at least twenty-seven widely acknowledged "echoes" (allusions) to the Hebrew Bible in James. In addition, there are several other possible allusions, which may expand the breadth of the way James employs his allusions.

In addition, there are twenty-three parallels to Yeshua's words between James and Matthew, as well as a total of fourteen such parallels to Yeshua's words between James and the other three Gospels (Mark, Luke, and John). Further—and worth exploring in this chapter—there are fifteen parallels between James and 1 Peter.[1]

This chapter will begin with a straightforward survey of the undoubted citations of the Hebrew Bible in the Letter of James (and one other possible quotation). Next, the widely acknowledged allusions to the Tanakh in James will also be surveyed. At that point, things become

---

1. All statistics utilized in this chapter represent this writer's personal counts from the following features in the *UBS Greek New Testament*, Fifth Revised Ed.: "Index of Quotations," 863; "Index of Allusions and Verbal Parallels," 864–83; and the footnotes to the Greek text of the Letter of James, 750–60.

somewhat more speculative, because there is not wide agreement among scholars regarding the additional purported allusions discussed in the next section of the chapter.

After that, the agreed-upon phenomenon of the words of Yeshua in the Letter of James will be focused upon. Finally, to be thorough regarding the various currents flowing back and forth in the scriptures between the Letter of James and other books, an example will be offered of the extensive common wording between James and 1 Peter and its possible significance.

Before proceeding further, though, it is necessary to ask how this chapter fits in with the overall focus of this volume of reading James in a post-supersessionist way, "within Judaism." In other words, what could be "supersessionist"—whether obviously or not—about how the citations, allusions, and parallels found in the Letter of James are viewed?

To answer that question from an overall perspective: *if* the Letter of James is "late-dated" (i.e., potentially any time significantly after the Jerusalem Council [i.e., after 48–49 CE], but certainly in the 60s CE), the argument that James is more "Christian" than Jewish gains force, specifically that James is a "general epistle"[2] (i.e., written generally to the entire church), which simply employs extensive Jewish imagery used figuratively.

To break things down into the various major foci of this chapter, another potential way that supersessionism could be argued is to note that the small number of (i.e., five likely, and no more than six) citations of the Hebrew Bible calls into question how "Jewish" James really was in his outlook reflected in the Letter of James. Similarly, the numerous apparent allusions to the words of Yeshua could also be used to question James's "Jewishness"—with the idea being that Yeshua's primary (if not exclusive) mission was to found "Christianity," as opposed to Yeshua being the Jewish Messiah who was sent "to the lost sheep of the house of Israel" (Matt 15:24).[3] Finally, if the explanation of the common wording in James and

---

2. Besides the older traditional title for the last section of the New Testament (i.e., the "Catholic Epistles"), the "General Epistles" is the most widely used alternative title. Sadly, it ignores the very strong Jewish feel of at least Hebrews, James, 1 and 2 Peter, Jude, and Revelation, if not 1, 2, and 3 John.

3. This statement should not be taken at all as denying that the "church" is majority gentile, only that when Yeshua began to build his *ekklesia* (normally translated in English as "church") in Acts, it was almost entirely Jewish and in at least one respect remains majority Jewish: the fact that nearly seventy percent of the Christian Bible is the Hebrew Bible/Old Testament.

1 Peter was taken to reflect that 1 Peter was written first, then the Letter of James would be effectively "late-dated"—and thus more susceptible to supersessionist reasoning—given that it is extremely difficult to find a basis on which to date 1 Peter any earlier than 60 CE.[4]

The quotations from the Hebrew Bible in the Letter of James

In the order they are found in the Hebrew Bible (and with the citations taken from the Old Testament portion of the NRSV), the following five passages are cited in the Letter of James, according to the *UBS Greek New Testament* (5th rev. ed.):[5]

- Gen 15:6 (quoted in Jas 2:23): "And [Abram] believed the Lord, and the Lord reckoned it to him as righteousness."
- Exodus 20:13, 14 (quoted in Jas 2:11): "You shall not murder. You shall not commit adultery."
- Lev 19:18 (quoted in Jas 2:8): "You shall not take vengeance or bear a grudge against any of your people, but you shall love your neighbor as yourself: I am the Lord."
- Deut 5:17–18 (quoted in Jas 2:11): "You shall not murder. Neither shall you commit adultery."
- Prov 3:34 (quoted in Jas 4:6): "Toward the scorner he is scornful, but to the humble he shows favor." See the discussion of Jas 4:6 for the LXX translation of Prov 3:34, which is what James uses in 4:6.

(In addition, if it is the case that Jas 4:5 is citing [or at least alluding to] Num 11:24–30, there is a sixth "quotation" (or at least a significant additional allusion) from the Hebrew Bible. That possibility will be elaborated in the next section below.)

The following discussion will move in the order in which the citations are found in the Letter of James. Up front, it is worth noting that, according to D. A. Carson, "In almost all quotations from the OT, the text quoted is the LXX":[6]

---

4. Jonathan Bernier, *Rethinking the Dates of the New Testament*, 213–23.
5. Page 863.
6. Carson, "James," 997.

- **Lev 19:18, cited in Jas 2:8:** Carson states that it is "initially surprising that James quoted Lev 19:18 instead of 19:15, which on first reading is more pertinent to his topic: 'Do not pervert justice; do not show partiality to the poor or favoritism to the great.'"[7] That is true, given the focus on partiality toward the rich man and against the poor man in Jas 2:1–7. However, as argued in chapter 3 above, the immediate context of 2:8 is important for understanding why James employs Lev 19:18 at this point in his letter. The wording "royal law" refers to the law of God, the King, who has spoken in scripture as to the importance of loving your neighbor as yourself (Lev 19:18). After the description of the mistreatment of the poor by the rich in Jas 2:1–7, the ultimate divine answer is to "love your neighbor as yourself."

    It is also quite significant that, in Matt 22:36–40,[8] Yeshua selects Lev 19:18 as the second commandment, which is like the first (i.e., "You shall love the Lord your God with all your heart, and with all your soul, and with all your mind.") It may well be that Yeshua's choice of Lev 19:18 as recorded in Matt 22:36–40 is the reason why James cites Lev 19:18 in Jas 2:8. However, if the Letter of James was written before the Gospel of Matthew—or the Gospel of Mark—as is the viewpoint of this writer, James's citation would be from Lev 19:18, but as guided by the teaching of Yeshua, perhaps recorded by the apostle Matthew, in preparation for the writing of the First Gospel.

- **Exod 20:13, 14 and/or Deut 5:17–18, cited in Jas 2:11:** The reason for listing these verses from both versions of the Ten Commandments (i.e., Exod 20 and Deut 5) is that it cannot be known for sure from which of the two passages James quoted. The reason is that there is no *meaningful* difference in the wording of the two commands in Exod 20:13, 14 and Deut 5:17–18. The only difference of any type is that the Hebrew *waw* is added to Deut 5:18,[9] resulting in a literal translation of the Hebrew text being, "*And* you shall not commit adultery."[10]

---

7. Carson, "James," 999.

8. Matt 22:36–40 is closely paralleled in Mark 10:28–31.

9. This is the structure of the Heb text found in the standard Hebrew text, *Biblia Hebraica Stuttgartensia,* 122 (Exod 20:13, 14) and 295 (Deut 5:19, 20).

10. Italics mine. In other words, Exod 20:14 translates as "You shall not commit adultery," without the preceding "and," which is present in Deut 5:18. Otherwise, the two passages are identical in the Hebrew text.

The oddity of the quotation of these two commandments in Jas 2:11 is that they are cited in reverse order to that found in Exod 20 or Deut 5. However, when Yeshua refers to these same two commandments in the Matthean Sermon on the Mount,[11] it is in the order found in Exod 20 and Deut 5: "You shall not murder" being expanded in accordance with "the love command" (i.e., Lev 19:18) in Matt 5:21–26, and "you shall not commit adultery" similarly expanded in 5:27–30.

Although not explaining the puzzling reversal of order between the commands not to commit adultery and to murder from the Torah to Jas 2:8, a plausible reason for James's choice of which commands he would cite may be found in the wider content of the Letter of James. In Yeshua's discussion of the command not to murder in Matt 5:21–26, he points to the internal cause of "anger" (5:22), which, of course, is also behind bitterness and conflicts/disputes—all of which are obviously problems among the audience of the Letter of James (see Jas 1:19–20; 3:14–16; 4:1–2). The same is true regarding the command not to commit adultery in Matt 5:27–30, which Yeshua pushes back to its origin in "lust" in 5:28. In the Letter of James, "lust" is spotlighted in 1:14, 15 and 4:2.

- **Gen 15:6, cited in Jas 2:23:** The argument utilizing Gen 15:6 in Jas 2 (see the lengthy discussion on Jas 2:14–26 in chapter 8) is, at first, puzzling. That is because it closely connects Abram's faith in Gen 15:6, at a point when Abram was about eighty-five years old,[12] with his "work" of obedience before the Lord in the Akedah,[13] in Gen 22, when Abraham was somewhere around 115 years old[14]—mean-

---

11. Carson accurately notes, "Both the examples of law that James cites are also referred to by Jesus in the Sermon on Mount, a passage with which James has numerous affinities" ("James," 1002). More will be said on this topic in the section of the chapter having to do with allusions.

12. Abram was eighty-six years old "when Hagar bore him Ishmael" (Gen 16:16). Hagar's pregnancy would have been for nine months prior to that, and some additional time had passed between Gen 15 and the events of the beginning of Gen 16. Therefore, Abram was about eighty-five at the time when he believed God and it was reckoned to him as righteousness (Gen 15:6).

13. "The Akedah" is the traditional Jewish term describing God's testing of Abraham in Gen 22:1–19.

14. Genesis 20:5 states, "Abraham was a hundred years old when his son Isaac was born to him." In Gen 22:12, the angel of the Lord (22:11) further instructs Abraham—who had ascended to the top of a mount in the land of Moriah—to sacrifice Isaac (22:2): "Do not lay your hand on *the boy* to do anything to him; for now I know that you fear God, since you have not withheld your son, your only son, from me" (22:12).

ing about thirty years passed from the time of the quotation about Abraham's "faith" in Gen 15:6 until the time of the Akedah in Gen 22. The other factor about the citation of Gen 15:6 in Jas 2:23 worth discussing here is differing readings (resulting in different English translations) in the Hebrew text of Gen 15:6 and the Greek text of Jas 2:23 in one key aspect. A literal rendering of Gen 15:6 from the Hebrew text reads, "And [Abram] believed in the LORD; and [the LORD] credited it to him as righteousness." A literal translation of the Greek behind Jas 2:23 reads, "And Abraham believed God, and it was credited to him as righteousness." The difference between the two translations is that Gen 15:6 speaks of the Lord's action as active (i.e., "credited"), while Jas 2:23 presents it as passive ("was credited"). While there may not be a major difference here in meaning, given the category often called "the divine passive,"[15] it may be part of James's broader contextual argument, which Carson describes in the following words:

> James reads Gen 15:6 within the cycle of the Abrahamic narrative and carefully observes how the kind of faith displayed in that verse is "completed" by the kind of obedience displayed in Gen 22, thereby demonstrating that genuine faith is never alone.[16]

That is, James is apparently arguing in the context of Jas 2:23 that genuine faith *will act*, which action(s) demonstrate(s) its presence and reality. He is not, however, arguing that Abraham's faith spoken of in Gen 15:6 is a meritorious act in and of itself.[17]

Significant evidence for that perspective is found in Heb, another messianic Jewish letter. In 11:8–19, the phrase "by faith" is attributed to Abraham's actions three times (11:8, 9, 17), but none of those three instances are directly related to Gen 15:6. In other words, if God's "crediting" of Abram's faith in 15:6 was intended to

---

The italicized wording "the boy" indicates that Isaac was still a teenager, though it is speculative to try to be more specific.

15. See Carson's comment on this grammatical possibility (Carson, "James," 1004).

16. Carson, "James," 1005.

17. A common question among Jews—and some Christian readers—over the centuries has been whether Abraham obeyed Torah *before* Torah was revealed, which question is based on the following wording in Gen 26:5—looking back to the Akedah in Gen 22: "Abraham obeyed my voice and kept my charge, my commandments, my statutes and my laws."

be understood as a particularly meritorious action on his part, why would it be overlooked in the exemplary listing of the people in the Hebrew Bible whose faith and acts of faith were being recounted as those who had "gained approval through their faith" (Heb 11:39)?

- **Prov 3:34, cited in Jas 4:6:** The LXX version of Prov 3:34 is close to identical to the wording cited in Jas 4:6. A literal translation of the LXX reading of Prov 3:34 reads "[The] Lord resists the proud, but gives grace to the humble." The only difference between that reading and Jas 4:6 is that the latter begins with "God," not "Lord."

  There is one obvious question related to the citation in Jas 4:6 ("But [God] gives all the more grace; therefore it says, 'God opposes the proud, but gives grace to the humble'"). To what does the wording "it says," found just before the citation of Prov 3:34, refer? The answer is that "it says" points back to the phrase "the scripture says" in 4:5. Simply put, that means the noun "scripture" in 4:5 is replaced by the pronoun "it" in 4:6.

  The apparent reason why James chose to quote Prov 3:34 is that, although the terms "arrogant" or "proud" are not used by James in 4:1–4, that clearly is the motivation behind the conflicts (internal and interpersonal) referred to in those verses. The wording employed in 4:7 ("Submit yourselves therefore to God") and 4:10 ("Humble yourselves before the Lord") clarify what was only implied in 4:1–4.

An additional possible quotation from the Hebrew Bible in the Letter of James

Each of the five quotations from the Hebrew Bible employed in the Letter of James that were discussed just above also shared an important introductory feature. The lead-in wording to each citation marked them off as scripture or as the word of God.

Note the distinctive authoritative ways in which the five citations are described by James:

- Jas 2:8   "according to the scripture"
- Jas 2:11a   "for the One who said" (i.e., God)
- Jas 2:11b   "also said" (i.e., playing off Jas 2:11a)
- Jas 2:23   "the scripture says"

- Jas 4:6 "it says" (as noted above, "it" points back to "the scripture says" in 4:5)

If not already noted from the discussion in the last section of this chapter, or in the parenthetical wording related to Jas 4:6 just above, there is an additional occurrence of "the scripture says" in the Letter of James (in 4:5) that has not been accounted for. The reason for that is that it is thought by the bulk of scholars that there is no passage in the Hebrew Bible that reads like Jas 4:5.[18]

That general conclusion, however, does not mean that other explanations have not been forthcoming. For example, it could have been that what is stated in Jas 4:5 represents the theme of "God's jealous love" in the preceding verses of Jas 4.[19] Such an explanation is equally hard to justify or falsify, but the fact that the other five citations from the Hebrew Bible cited in the Letter of James are specific passages makes it quite unlikely.[20]

It also could have been that James was citing "a noncanonical Jewish text."[21] The two problems with that explanation are that: 1) Jewish respect for scripture likely would not allow citation from a nonbiblical book with the lead-in wording "the scripture says"; and 2) No such wording that is clearly close to that of Jas 4:5 has been found in any extant noncanonical Jewish work.[22]

That does lead to another angle on this explanation, though. There is reference in the extracanonical book, *The Shepherd of Hermas*, to Eldad and Modad,[23] biblical figures mentioned only in Num 11:26, 27 (i.e., as two of the seventy elders of Israel chosen to receive a portion of "the Spirit" on Moses) and the lost *Book of Eldad and Modab*.

---

18. Johnson, *Letter of James*, 280.
19. McKnight, *Letter of James*, 336–37.
20. Davids, *Epistle of James*, 162.
21. Moo, *Letter of James*, 2nd ed., 239.
22. The word "extant" in this sentence is crucial. The significance is that the existence of a source that cannot be viewed makes that source *indirect*, at best. Thus, reliance on such an indirect source requires the assumption that the direct source reporting the existence and content of the indirect source be trusted completely, which is a calculated risk, to say the least.
23. It catches the reader's attention that the MT gives the name of the second of these figures as "Medad," which reading is followed by the NRSV, NIV, ESV, CSB, NASB, and NET translations. The spelling "Modab" comes from the LXX. This makes it clear that the writer of the Shepherd of Hermas, and whoever wrote the Book of Eldad and Modad, used the LXX, not the Hebrew Bible.

The larger significance for the discussion here is not regarding the lost Book of Eldad and Modad, though.[24] Rather, it is their role in the biblical passage, Num 11:24–30, and the possibility that it is the passage James had in mind in using the wording "the scripture says" in Jas 4:5.

The first aspect of this wider issue that needs to be clarified is the proper translation of Jas 4:5. The most obvious issue involved is whether *to pneuma* should be taken to refer to the "human spirit" or the "Holy Spirit." This is the key dividing point among interpreters as to whether Num 11:24–30 *might be* related to Jas 4:5. The reason is that, if the wording in Jas 4:5 is taken as referring to the *human* spirit, Num 11:24–30 becomes irrelevant to the discussion of Jas 4:5, because there would be no obvious connection between the two passages. Numbers 11:24–30 only make sense as a possible source for the wording in Jas 4:5 if it is *the Holy Spirit* to whom James is referring.[25]

Many scholars take it that is *the human spirit* in view in Jas 4:5.[26] Luke Timothy Johnson goes so far as to say: "There is no reason to suppose that James is thinking of the Holy Spirit."[27]

Those who hold that it is the Holy Spirit being referred to may or may not think that Num 11:24–30 is the passage in mind in the wording "the scripture says." However, both Allison[28] and Bauckham[29] do see Num 11 in the background of Jas 4:5.

The NASB is the only major English translation to include the view that *to pneuma* (i.e., "the spirit [or Spirit]") in Jas 4:5 refers to the Holy Spirit: "Or do you think that the scripture says to no purpose, 'He jealously desires the Spirit whom he has made to dwell in us.'" Richard Bauckham renders the latter part of 4:5 in this way: "The Spirit of God in us loathes envy."[30]

---

24. This is the case, even though Dale Allison has pursued this angle at length in an article entitled, "Eldad and Modad," 99–131.

25. Normally careful interpreter Scot McKnight is incorrect in saying the following: "'Spirit' (*pneuma*) is not used in the LXX" of Num 11:25–30 and to claim "*psuche* is used" (*Letter of James*, 337 and footnote 288). Instead, *pneuma* is used in the LXX version of Num 11:25, 26, and 29.

26. Among reputable recent commentators who support the view that Jas 4:5 refers to the human spirit are Blomberg and Kamell, Davids, Johnson, McKnight, Moo, and Spencer.

27. Johnson, *Letter of James*, 280.

28. Allison, *James*, 617–21.

29. Bauckham, "Spirit of God."

30. Bauckham, "Spirit of God."

With these points in mind, this writer offers the following literal translation of Jas 4:5, with several explanatory points about the translation to follow: *"Or do you think that in vain the scripture says, 'Against envy he [God] earnestly desires the Spirit, the one he caused to dwell in us."*[31]

- The contextual explanation of this rendering is that God deeply desires his Spirit within believers to triumph over the natural human envy that manifests itself in conflicts (4:1–3) and friendship with the *kosmos* (4:4).

- The above translation is purposely somewhat "wooden" to maintain the Greek word order as much as possible, with its intended natural emphasis.

- The Greek *pros* (at the beginning of the quotation in 4:5), is rendered "against," in keeping with BAGD, p. 710 (meaning III.4., which states that *pros* should be rendered "against" to denote "a hostile or friendly relationship," with the subcategory a. "after verbs of disputing."[32] Although the verb *strateuomai* ("to wage war") in Jas 4:1 may not qualify among "verbs of disputing" (i.e., since it portrays an internal conflict), to go no further than the next verse (4:2), *phoneuo* ("to murder"), *zeloo* ("to be jealous or envious of"), *machomai* ("to quarrel, fight"), and *polemeo* ("to wage war, fight") are all clearly "verbs of disputing," therefore supporting the rendering of *pros* as "against."

- In the above translation, *phthonos* ("envy, jealousy") retains its dark, negative sense[33] and is not mistakenly paired in a positive sense with *epipotheo* ("to long for, desire, yearn over"), as in such translations as NRSV and ESV.

- The logic of the flow between Jas 4:4 and 4:5 may turn on two similar-sounding Greek verbs: *kathistemi* (4:4) and *katoikizo* (4:5). In 4:4, the present passive form of *kathistemi* ("to be constituted, to prove to be") pictures a progressive process in which anyone in James's audience could prove to be an enemy of God by cultivating friendship with the world (*kosmos*). In 4:5, the aorist active of *katoikizo*

---

31. The transliterated Greek text of Jas 4:5 (UBS, 5th rev. ed.) reads: *he dokeite hoti kenos he graphe legei, Pros phthonon epipothei to pneuma ho katokisen en hymin.*

32. BAGD, S.v., "*pros*," 709–10.

33. Allison (*James*, 611) strongly states, "Everywhere else in the Greek Bible, *phthonos* . . . means '(malevolent) envy': its connotation is negative."

("to place, put") speaks of what God has already accomplished by placing his Spirit within the believer, in order that the indwelling Spirit might combat the strong pull of the *kosmos* referred to in 4:4.

- The fact that the Holy Spirit is not mentioned elsewhere in the Letter of James is not a good enough reason to deny that he is mentioned in 4:5, given the analysis provided here and regarding the discussion of Num 11:24–30 just below. There is one additional inclusion of *pneuma* in James, in 3:26, which clearly means *human* spirit. However, a lone example is hardly enough to establish a pattern of usage in favor of translating "(human) spirit" in Jas 4:5.

The following diagram reflects the "shape" of the narrative in Num 11:24–30. As with the Letter of James (i.e., its overall outline and section by section internal structures), this section of Numbers is an inverted parallel structure.

> a (11:24) So Moses went out and told the people the words of the Lord, and he gathered seventy elders of the people, and placed them all around the tent.
>
> b (11:25) Then the Lord came down in the cloud and spoke to [Moses] and took some of the Spirit that was on him and put it on the seventy elders, and when the Spirit rested upon them, they prophesied. But they did not do it again.
>
> c (11:26) Two men remained in the camp, one named Eldad and the other named Medad, and the Spirit rested on them; they were among those registered, but they had not gone out to the tent, and so they prophesied in the camp.
>
> c' (11:27–28) And a young man ran and told Moses, "Eldad and Medad are prophesying in the camp." And Joshua, son of Nun, the assistant of Moses, one of his chosen men, said, "My lord Moses, stop them!"
>
> b' (11:29) But Moses said to him, "Are you jealous for my sake? Would that all of the Lord's people were prophets, and the Lord would put his Spirit on them."
>
> a' (11:30) And Moses and the elders of Israel returned to the camp.

The presence of a chiastic structure in this section of Num 11 is quite clear. There is simply too much present in the first and second halves of the passage of a mirroring nature to deny that it is intentionally paralleled. For example, in the a/a' layer, 11:24 (a) and 11:30 (a') share the parallel presence of the words "Moses" and "elders," but also the opposed wording "went out" (11:24)/"returned" (11:30) and "around the tent" (11:24)/"to the camp" (11:30). Then, in the b/b' layer (11:25, 29), the following parallels and opposites are found: "Moses"; "the Lord"; "the (or his) Spirit"; "the seventy elders" vs. "all the Lord's people"; and "prophesied" vs. "prophets." Finally, the c/c' layer (11:26, 28–29) repeats "Eldad" and "Medad" and "prophesied in the camp"/"prophesying in the camp."

Having noted the strong case for a chiastic structure in Num 11:24–30, the two key questions are: 1) What is the meaning of the structure within this context in Num 11; and 2) Why did James choose to quote from Num 11 and in what sense is it a "citation?"

In answer to Question 1, upon reflection, it appears the obvious mirroring in Num 11:24–30 points to two angles, both important for the people of Israel in the wilderness to understand: 1) The Lord was trustworthy to fulfill exactly what he had promised in 11:16–17: to empower seventy of the elders of Israel by his Spirit to help Moses in bearing the burden of the nation of Israel; and 2) That empowerment also unexpectedly—but graciously—extended to two of the seventy "registered" elders (11:26)—Eldad and Medad—who had not gone to "the tent of meeting" (11:16)—as had been ordered by the Lord, prompting two varied responses: jealousy by Joshua on behalf of Moses (11:28)—versus the gracious expressed desire of Moses that "all the Lord's people were prophets" and that "the Lord would put his Spirit on them" (11:29). Moses' desire for the people of Israel was thus greater than what the Lord had promised to do *at that time*.

However, the time would come when "all of the Lord's people" would not only have "his Spirit" *on them*—as happened on the Day of Pentecost (Acts 2)—but *within them*. Yet, though the Lord has "caused" his Spirit to "dwell in" (Jas 4:5) believers in Yeshua, that does not mean the Spirit will simply overpower attitudes and actions that provoke "disputes and conflicts" (4:1, 2), which reflect jealous selfishness and friendship with the *kosmos* (4:3, 4).

The above explanation appears to be the primary reason James paraphrases Num 11:28–29 in Jas 4:5. Yet, there could be another more subtle angle in play: the Letter of James is written to "the twelve tribes in the Diaspora" (1:1). And, if the letter is dated as early as the mid-40s CE—as argued earlier in this book—and the audience had fled persecution in Jerusalem (Acts 8:1; 11:19)—also as argued earlier in this volume, it might have been the case that the Diaspora audience had seen early on the presence and power of the Holy Spirit while in Jerusalem but wondered about his working away from Jerusalem.

If so, their attention being called to consider Num 11:24-30 and its lessons could make a considerable difference in this very area. Think about it: if Eldad and Medad could experience the presence of the Holy Spirit away from the "tent of meeting"—which would be parallel to the Temple in the day of James and his audience—so could these Jewish believers in Yeshua in the Diaspora in the mid-40s of the first century CE.

At this point, it is worth giving an initial answer to the question of whether any supersessionist thinking has crept in unnoticed to this discussion of the quotations—or, in the case, of Jas 4:5, "paraphrase"—of scripture. The answer is No. Although the Letter of James does not employ a lot of such citations, what it does cite is clearly marked off by wording indicating what it is (e.g., "according to the scripture" [2:8] or "the scripture says" [4:5] or 'it says' [4:6]) or its divine origin (e.g., "the One who said" [2:11]).

The consensus allusions to the Hebrew Bible in the Letter of James

According to the "Index of Allusions and Verbal Parallels" in the *UBS Greek New Testament* (5th rev. ed.),[34] there are twenty-seven allusions to the Hebrew Bible in the Letter of James, as well as three more to two apocryphal Jewish works: The Book of Judith and the Psalms of Solomon.[35] Only the twenty-seven canonical allusions will be treated in this chapter.[36]

The listed allusions in the Letter of James come from fourteen books in the Hebrew Bible. The books are listed in the order of the English

---

34. *UBS Greek New Testament*, 5th rev. ed., 864-83.

35. UBS lists the allusion to Judith as being in Jas 5:3 and the two allusions to the Psalms of Solomon as being in Jas 1:13 and 1:19. If those allusions are legitimate, they represent no evidence for the later dating of the Letter of James (i.e., and thus some type of at least subconscious supersessionist implication of positing a general "Christian" audience for the Letter). In line with common scholarly consensus, Carey Moore dates Judith "sometime after 107 B.C" ("Judith, Book of," 1123) and Joseph Trafton dates the Psalms of Solomon as "from the first century B.C.E." ("Solomon, Psalms of," 115). Thus, both documents would have originated well before the mid-40s CE dating of the Letter of James argued for in this work.

36. Allison posits only twenty-two quotations and allusions from the Hebrew Bible in the Letter of James (*James*, 51), but also sees three allusions to the Apocaypha from Wisdom (1) and Ecclesiasticus (2). (He further lists an "unknown source" for the "citation" related to Eldad and Medad discussed above.)

canon,[37] and the understood number of allusions from each books with be in parentheses after the name of the book: Genesis (1); Exodus (2); Leviticus (1); Deuteronomy (1); Joshua (1); 1 Kings (2); Job (1); Psalms (5); Proverbs (1); Ecclesiastes (1); Isaiah (5); Jeremiah (3); Zechariah (1); Malachi (2). As can be seen, the six books with multiple allusions in the Letter of James are Psalms (5), Isaiah (5), Jeremiah (3), Exodus (2), 1 Kings (2), and Malachi (2), accounting for nineteen of the twenty-seven listed total allusions. There is no obvious reason why Psalms, Isaiah, and Jeremiah are echoed more than the other books.

Of all the allusions in any of those three books, only Isa 40:6-7 (echoes in Jas 1:10-11) is particularly well-known: "All people are grass, their constancy is like the flower of the field. The grass withers, the flower fades, when the breath of the Lord blows upon it; surely the people are grass" (Isa 40:6b-7). The only other familiar allusions come from 1 Kgs 17:1 and 18:42 (alluded to in Jas 5:17-18), which speak of the beginning and end of the drought related to Elijah's ministry.

Of the passages in the Letter of James in which the allusions are found, four are in Jas 1 (in 1:10-11; 1:19; 1:26 [2]). Three allusions are in Jas 2 (in 2:11; 2:23; 2:25). Two are in Jas 3 (3:8; 3:18). James 4 contains six allusions (4:5; 4:8 [3]; 4:10; 4:13-14). James 5 easily contains the most allusions with twelve (5:3; 5:4 [5]; 5:5 [2]; 5:7; 5:11; 5:17; 5:18).

Since these allusions are but "echoes" of earlier scripture, it cannot be actually proven whether they were truly in the mind of James as his letter was being written. Thus, it ultimately accomplishes little to speculate about any of them. However, it is thought-provoking that the highest numbers of alleged allusions are found in Jas 5:4 (5) and 4:8 (3).

James 5:4 reads: "Listen! The wages of the laborers who moved your fields, which you kept back by fraud, cry out, and the cries of the harvesters have reached the ears of the Lord of hosts." If nothing else, the possibility of five allusions in Jas 5:4 marks it off as sounding an alarm that was a consistent theme in the Hebrew Bible.

James 4:8 says, "Draw near to God, and he will draw near to you. Cleanse your hands, you sinners, and purify your hearts." This is very much in keeping with James's earlier appeal for "religion that is pure and undefiled before God, the Father" (1:27).

---

37. For a substantial discussion of the allusions in roughly the order of the Hebrew Bible (i.e., "The Law," "Prophecy," "Wisdom"), see Johnson, *Letter of James*, 30-34. Johnson also surveys in detail numerous other Jewish sources that, to him, have noticeable similarities to the Letter of James (*Letter of James*, 34-48).

As with the scripture citations in the Letter of James, there is nothing related to the allusions that necessarily would lead to a later dating of the letter. Nor is there anything that would lessen the Jewish feel of James or provide a basis for a supersessionist perspective on James—unless, of course, a pre-existing supersessionist viewpoint was "dropped upon" the book and it is seen through interpretive "lenses" colored in advance by supersessionist assumptions.

Other likely allusions to the Hebrew Bible in the Letter of James

Forty years ago, Luke Timothy Johnson offered a strong argument for an extensive use of Lev 19 in the Letter of James,[38] beyond the citation of Lev 19:18b (i.e., "You shall love your neighbor as yourself") in 2:8. In the order of verses from Lev 19, Johnson lists six additional allusions and the verses in James where they are "echoed"[39]:

(1)	Lev 19:12	Jas 5:12	
(2)	Lev 19:13	Jas 5:4	
(3)	Lev 19:15	Jas 2:1, 9	
(4)	Lev 19:16	Jas 4:11	
(5)	Lev 19:17b	Jas 5:20*	(*Johnson considers this to be a less likely allusion.)
(6)	Lev 19:18a	Jas 5:9*	(* Johnson considers this to be a less likely allusion.)

Even if only the first four of Johnson's listed possible allusions to Lev 19 in the Letter of James are valid, though, a major implication flows from his work with Lev 19. Beyond the "You shall love your neighbor as yourself" command" in 19:18b, that section of Lev 19 (i.e., 19:12–18) has to do with how to relate to "your neighbor (19:13, 15, 16, 17), which category apparently includes "a laborer" (19:13), "the deaf" (19:14), "the blind" (19:14), "the poor" (19:15), "the great" (19:15), "your people" (19:16, 18), and "your kin" (19:16). It is also strengthened in its commands (i.e., "you shall not swear," you shall not defraud," "you shall not steal," etc.) by the authoritative repetition of "I am the Lord" four times

---

38. Johnson, "Use of Leviticus 19 in the Letter of James," 391–401. Since then, this material has been handled succinctly in his 1995 commentary on James (*Letter of James*, 31) as well as reprinted in his volume of essays, *Brother of Jesus, Friend of God*, 123–35.

39. Johnson, *Brother of Jesus, Friend of God*, 132.

in those seven verses (19:12, 14, 16, 18). The significant implication, in Johnson's words, is that "James regarded the 'Royal Law' . . . and the 'Law of Liberty' . . . as explicated concretely and specifically not only by the Decalogue (2:11) but by the immediate context of the Law of Love, the commands found in Lev 19:12–18."[40]

In other words, because of the apparent "echoes" of Lev 19:12, 13, 15, 16, 17, and 18a in the Letter of James, alongside the clear quotation of "You shall love your neighbor as yourself" (Lev 19:18b) in Jas 2:8, it seems that, as far as James is concerned, keeping the "love command" includes obeying the rest of the context in Lev 19:12–18,[41] a phenomenon that can be called "widening context," that has been much discussed by scholars in recent decades.[42] And, if such intended wider contextual usage beyond a citation itself is the case, any secessionist (conscious or unconscious) attempt at reducing the Torah to the "love command," and thus minimizing the Jewishness of the Letter of James, will not work.

Parallels to the words of Jesus in the Gospels in the Letter of James

The footnotes of the Greek text of the Letter of James of the *UBS Greek New Testament* (5th rev. ed.) contain the following thirty-seven passages in the Gospels the editors believed are paralleled in James:[43] Matt 5:7, 9, 19, 21, 27, 34–37; 6:13, 19; 7:7, 11, 21, 26; 8:29; 12:36–37; 15:11, 18, 19; 18:22–35; 19:18; 19:19; 22:39; 23:12; 24:33; Mark 1:24; 5:7; 6:13; 10:19; 12:31; Luke 4:25, 34; 6:24; 10:27; 12:18, 47; 18:20; John 1:13; 13:17.[44] That the *UBS Greek New Testament* editors listed all these Gospels passages

---

40. Johnson, *Brother of Jesus, Friend of God*, 133.

41. It is obvious that the content of most of the other commands (i.e., beyond the "love command" [in 19:18b]) in 19:12–18 is quite similar to the Decalogue.

42. The best succinct summary of this important hermeneutical trend and its implications that I have seen is the recent volume by Abner Chou, *Hermeneutics of the Biblical Writers*.

43. *UBS Greek New Testament*, 5th rev. ed., 750–760.

44. Longer lists of the purported words of Jesus in the Letter of James are presented by Joseph Mayor (*Epistle of St. James*, 2nd ed.), with a total of sixty-five parallels, and Peter Davids (*Epistle of James*, 66–67), who offers a listing of forty-seven. Allison (*James*, 56, fn 304) considers the treatments of the relevant issues by Dean Deppe (*Sayings of Jesus in the Epistle of James*) and Patrick Hartin (*James and the Q Sayings of Jesus*) as "the two most important surveys."

does not, of course, guarantee that James directly had all of that content in mind as he wrote his letter.

However, before considering a notably shorter list of (in this case) parallels to the Synoptic Gospels[45] in James, still it is noteworthy that twenty-three of the thirty-seven passages included (i.e., well over 60 percent) are from the Gospel of Matthew. The possible significance of this statistic will be discussed in the next section of this chapter.

At the opposite end of the spectrum, a listing compiled by Dale Allison posits seventeen Gospels passages containing "the Jesus tradition"[46] in the Letter of James, only eight of which are in Matthew. His list is set forth in the following chart[47] (which is organized using nomenclature for common Synoptic critical categories):[48]

Sayings found in Q

Matt 5:3 = Luke 6:20	Jas 2:5
Matt 5:11–12 = Luke 6:22–23	Jas 1:2; cf. 1:12
Matt 7:1–5 = Luke 6:37, 41–42	Jas 4:11–12
Matt 7:24–27 = Luke 6:47–49	Jas 1:22–23
Matt 7:7–11 = Luke 11:9–13	Jas 1:5, 17; 4:3
Matt 6:19–21 = Luke 12:33–34[50]	Jas 5:1–3

---

45. This decision is based on there being only some 10 percent of overlap in content between the Gospel of John and the Synoptic Gospels (i.e., Matthew, Mark, and Luke), minimizing the likelihood of significant intertextuality between John and the Synoptics. In addition, because "most scholars favor a date for John's Gospel at or around 90" (Bernier, *Rethinking the Dates of the New Testament*, 87), whatever perceived parallels exist between the Gospel of John and the Letter of James should be viewed as John echoing James.

46. Allison, *James*, 56.

47. Allison, *James*, 56–57.

48. E.g., "Sayings found in Q," "Sayings found in Mark and Matthew," "Sayings found only in Matthew," "Sayings found only in Luke." "Q" is the hypothetical source of at least the saying of Jesus used by the authors of Matthew, Mark and Luke. Also, Allison's placement of Mark before Matthew apparently reflects his assumption of Markan Priority (i.e., the hypothesis that Mark was written before Matthew and Luke).

49. Allison's wording "See on. . ." in this column refers the reader to where the passages are discussed in the commentary section of his volume.

50. For some unstated reason, Allison orders the listing on the left after the sequence of the Gospel of Luke instead of the Gospel of Matthew, even though he placed the passages in Matt first. Whether this represents a conviction of some sort related to the Synoptic Problem is unknown.

Saying found in Mark and Matthew

| Mark 11:23 = Matt 21:21 | Jas 1:6 |

Saying found only in Matthew

| Matt 5:33–37 | Jas 5:12 |

Sayings found only in Luke

| Luke 6:24 | Jas 5:1–3 |
| Luke 6:25 | Jas 4:9; 5:1 |

The somewhat dramatic differences among scholars in the perceived number of parallels between the Letter of James and the Synoptic Gospels certainly gives pause to attempts to determine possible dependence between James and the Synoptics. However, it seems even-handed to hazard conjecture on two things from the above brief survey: 1) Conservatively, the number of actual parallels is probably at least as close to the list compiled from the UBS footnotes (i.e., thirty-seven; see above) than the seventeen listed in Allison's chart (see above). If so, that would place the number of such parallels somewhere between twenty-five and thirty; and 2) As opposed to the eight parallels with the Letter of James that Allison offers for both Matthew and Luke, it seems somewhat more likely that there are more from the First Gospel.

If there indeed are more parallels between James and Matthew, it may strengthen the idea put forward earlier in this book. That idea was that it makes sense that James, the brother of Yeshua, and the apostle Matthew, both likely being in Jerusalem for an extended period (i.e., perhaps roughly twenty years)[51] after the Day of Pentecost and both serving as leaders in the Jerusalem congregation, interacted extensively over time on the historical and theological data which Matthew later published as the First Gospel. Certainly, interaction in depth, especially over a substantial length of time, between James, on the one hand, and Mark or Luke, on the other hand, was much more unlikely.

Regarding whether the consideration of parallels to the words of Yeshua in the Synoptic Gospels strengthens the supersessionist case related to the Letter of James, the answer must be No. The only way to attempt to

---

51. If the crucifixion and resurrection took place in 33 CE, and the apostles stayed in Jerusalem until sometime after the Jerusalem Council, the apostle Matthew's time in residence there could have been somewhat less than twenty years. If, however, the crucifixion/resurrection is dated as early as 29, the length of Matthew's stay in Jerusalem could have been well over twenty years.

frame such a contention would be to lift the words of Yeshua completely out of their Jewish context in the Synoptics. However, from a hermeneutical standpoint, one of the most well-known basic truths in biblical hermeneutics is that "a text without a context is a pretext." In such a case, the fallacious hermeneutical impact would be the ignoring of the Jewishness of Yeshua and the Synoptic Gospels in a supersessionist attempt to create a "Christian Jesus" for an exclusively gentile church.

The presence of parallels to the Letter of James in 1 Peter

The footnotes of the Greek text of the Letter of James in the *UBS Greek New Testament* (5th rev. ed.) list fifteen parallels between the Letter of James and 1 Peter.[52] Those possible parallels are presented in the following chart:

Passage in the Letter of James	Possible parallel passage in the Letter of 1 Peter
1:1	1:1
1:2	1:6
1:3	1:7
1:10–11	1:24
1:12	5:4
1:18	1:23
1:21	2:1
1:25	2:16
2:12	2:16
4:1	2:11
4:6	5:5
4:7	5:8–9
4:10	5:6
5:8	4:7
5:20	4:8

All fifteen items in the list above are not equally persuasive as being true parallels between the Letters of James and 1 Peter. However, as will be seen just below, at least nine of the fifteen probably should be considered parallels. The wording (from the NRSV) of those nine perceived parallel passages is presented in the following chart:

52. *UBS Greek New Testament*, 5th rev. ed., 750–60.

Wording in the passage in James	Wording in the passage in 1 Peter
"To the twelve tribes in the Dispersion" (1:1)	"To the exiles of the Dispersion" (1:1)
"whenever you face trials of any kind" (1:2)	"... even if now for a little while you have had to face various trials" (1:6)
"For the sun rises with its scorching heat and withers the field; its flower falls." (1:11a)	"The grass withers and the flower falls." (1:24b)
"Rid yourselves . . . ." (1:21a)	"Rid yourselves . . . ." (2:1a)
"God opposes the proud, but gives grace to the humble." (4:6b, citing Prov 3:34 LXX)	"God opposes the proud, but gives grace to the humble." (5:5b, citing Prov 3:34 LXX)
"Resist the devil, and he will flee from you." (4:7b)	"Like a roaring lion, your adversary the devil prowls around, looking for someone to devour. Resist him." (5:9)
"Humble yourselves before the Lord, and he will exalt you." (4:10)	"Humble yourselves therefore under the mighty hand of God, so that he may exalt you in due time." (5:6)
"... for the coming of the Lord is near." (5:8)	"The end of all things is near." (4:7a)
"... will cover a multitude of sins." (5:20b)	"... covers a multitude of sins." (4:8b)[53]

The striking similarity of the wording seen above in these nine passages from the Letter of James and the corresponding nine passages in 1 Peter is difficult to escape. How may these similarities best be explained?

There are four obvious possibilities. They are: 1) The Letters of James and 1 Peter are completely independent of each other and their highly similar portions are strictly coincidental; 2) James and 1 Peter are both dependent on an unknown source; 3) James is dependent on 1 Peter; or 4) 1 Peter is dependent on James.

The first two possibilities can be dispensed with quickly: With Option 1) the similarities simply are too close to be merely coincidental. Option 2) is logically possible, but there is no way to prove it—one way or the other—unless and until relevant information concerning such a common source for the Letters of James and 1 Peter would be discovered.

53. This list of similar passages in the Letters of James and 1 Peter are very close to the similar passages discussed by Johnson, *Letter of James*, 54–55.

The remaining views, Options 3) and 4), are both worthy of discussion. There is evidence in favor of both positions, as will be seen, but the external evidence for neither is compelling. On the one hand, fairly early attestation for 1 Peter related to extracanonical works is extensive.[54] On the other hand, not every New Testament scholar agrees with early attestation for the Letter of James. For example, according to Dale Allison, "The Epistle of James lacks unequivocal attestation prior to the time of Origen in the third century."[55] However, Davids makes a statistical point that tends toward neutralizing the seeming external attestation advantage of 1 Peter over James: "J. B. Mayor . . . fills fourteen pages with allusions to James by the early church fathers, the clearest being those in 1 Clement and the Shepherd of Hermas."[56]

As far as other ways of dating James vis-a-vis 1 Peter, as thoroughly argued in chapter 1 of this book, a better case can be made for an early date of the Letter of James than for 1 Peter. The position taken in this volume is that James was most likely written in 44–45 CE. By contrast, the latest work exhaustively arguing the dates of all the New Testament books, Jonathan Bernier's *Rethinking the Dates of the New Testament: The Evidence for Early Composition,* after utilizing rigorous historical methodology, ends its section on 1 Peter in this way: "we conclude that 1 Peter was written no earlier than 60 and no later than 69."[57]

Conclusion

At the end of this extensive discussion, it can be safely affirmed that there was no issue treated in this chapter for which the weight of the evidence pointed in the direction of a supersessionist perspective. Whether it be: 1) the citations of the Hebrew Bible—including the "paraphrase" from Num 11; 2) the agreed upon allusions from the Hebrew Bible; 3) the numerous apparent "echoes" of the words of Yeshua, especially from the Gospel of Matthew, in the Letter of James; or 4) the nine relatively clear parallels between the Letters of James and 1 Peter, no compelling reasons for either late-dating the Letter of James or interpreting its phenomena

---

54. Bernier, *Rethinking the Dates of the New Testament*, 214.
55. Allison, *James*, 69–70.
56. Davids, *Epistle of James*, 8, citing Mayor, *Epistle of St. James*, 2nd ed., lxix–lxxxiv.
57. Bernier, *Rethinking the Dates of the New Testament*, 223.

as applying to the church instead of messianic Jewish believers have been found.

8

James on faith, works, and justification

"You see that a person is justified by works and not by faith alone." (Jas 2:24)

"[W]e know that a person is justified not by the works of the law but through faith in Jesus Christ...." (Gal 2:16a)

THE ABOVE VERSES ARE at the heart of what is almost certainly the most widely written on and lingering exegetical/theological controversy related to the Letter of James.[1] To cite only the classic (and best known) historical example, the father of the Protestant Reformation, Martin Luther, described the Letter of James as "an epistle of straw" because of his understanding of the teaching of "works salvation," in 2:14–26. In addition, he relegated the letter to a location at the end of the New Testament in his translation of the German Bible.[2] Luther even went so far as to assert that the Letter of James "mangles the Scriptures and thereby opposes Paul and all Scripture."[3]

A first glance comparison does indeed indicate that what each of the two verses affirms appear irreconcilable with the affirmation of the other passage. That is, James affirms that a person is justified by works, not by faith alone; conversely, Paul affirms that a person is *not* justified by works, but through faith in Yeshua Messiah (alone). This certainly seems

---

1. Allison states: "the relevant books, chapters, and articles [i.e., on the meaning of Jas 2:14–26] are as the sands of the sea. Indeed, the secondary literature on Jas 2.14–26 seemingly exceeds that dedicated to the rest of James put together" (*James*, 426).

2. Moo, *Letter of James*, 2nd ed., 5.

3. Cited by Moo, *Letter of James*, 2nd ed., 5.

to be a classic "never the twain should meet" disagreement, and one with huge practical implications regarding how a person comes into a right (or righteous) relationship with God!

Certainly, it is fair to say that the question of whether a person is justified by faith or by faith and works is one of the most heated theological topics in church history. And, in many cases, the various writers have chosen to side with either James and his wording or Paul and his words (i.e., often—though not always—assuming one or the other of the two was mistaken in what he said [or that one or the other had an erroneous understanding of the other's view]).

Such an approach—that either James or Paul was right and the other wrong—has proven less than helpful, given two factors that believers in Yeshua should hold dear: 1) It does not honor God, who "breathed out" the content of "all scripture" (2 Tim 3:16), to assume that it contains mistakes or contradictions—especially an apparent major theological contradiction such as the nature of the believer in Yeshua Messiah's justification before God; and 2) It does not reflect reverence toward the scriptures themselves, and how they were written and divinely superintended (2 Pet 1:20–21) to assume they contain such contradiction.

Does it not instead glorify the Lord to assume that, *somehow*, the words of James and Paul are complementary, rather than contradictory? That is what the remainder of this chapter seeks to demonstrate.

Before laying out the progress of the contents of this chapter, though, one other angle is worth mentioning here. Though it is subtle—and probably occurs most commonly at the subconscious level—the view that sees Paul in the right and James in the wrong regarding faith, works, and justification can easily be a "soft supersessionist"[4] perspective, depreciating the value of early messianic Jewish thought, and thus very much a concern of this volume.

The remaining contents of this chapter entitled "James on Faith, Works, and Justification" are: first, discussing possible relationships between the Letter of James and Paul's Letter to the Galatians from logical and sequential angles; second, providing a plausible chronological sequencing of biblical events related to the Letter of James, Galatians, and the Book of Acts; third, before moving into exegesis of the text of Jas 2:14–26, exploring several other important considerations: the differing audiences/circumstances of the Letters of James and Galatians;

---

4. See chapter 3 above for an explanation of the meaning of "soft supersessionism" employed in this volume.

undertaking a survey of the uses of the focal terms "faith," "works," "justify," and "law" in James and Galatians; exploring the previous context of the Letter of James before 2:14–26 and in its mirroring section, 3:13–18; considering the help provided by an interpretation of the chiastic structuring of Jas 2:14–26; and, after all of these factors/areas have been considered, an interpretive paraphrase of Jas 2:14–26, followed by the chapter conclusion.

Possible logical and sequential relationships between the Letters of James and Galatians

Regarding the "apparent contradiction" between the focal wording of James and that of Paul, according to Dale Allison, "there are at least six ways of accounting for" it:[5]

i. James and Paul wrote independently of other, so neither was concerned with the other; and if one did know what the other taught, he was not consciously being oppositional.

ii. Paul responded to James or followers of James in order to correct or rebut him or them.

iii. Paul agreed with James but sought "to prevent a mischievous use" of his words, which the apostle "thought likely to be perverted by the Judaizers who were corrupting the Gospel of Christ."

iv. James responded to Paul in a polemical fashion.

v. James responded to Paul but sought to clarify his teaching, not counter it.

vi. James reacted negatively not to Paul but to some form of (distorted) Pauline antinomianism . . . .[6]

These six possible understandings can be placed in three simple categories: 1) James and Paul wrote independently of each other (view i); 2) Paul responded to James (views ii and iii); and 3) James responded to Paul (views iv, v, and vi).

To succinctly analyze these three categories:

---

5. Allison, *James*, 426.
6. Allison, *James*, 426–28.

- The amount of terminology in common employed by James and Paul is simply too much to responsibly conclude that the Letter of James and Paul's Letter to the Galatians were written "independently" (i.e., view 1).

- To conclude that James was responding to Paul (in whatever sense) runs counter to the stated position of this volume that the Letter of James was the first New Testament book written, in the mid-40s CE (i.e., views 4, 5, and 6).[7]

- Thus, it is concluded that Paul wrote the Letter to the Galatians in reaction to the Letter of James *in some sense* (i.e., either views 2 or 3, in general).

A plausible wider chronological sequence as background for James 2:14–26

The following section represents this writer's meticulously considered understanding of the timing of the relevant events and documents related to accurately placing the Letters of James and Galatians in their proper New Testament chronology and sequence:

- Paul visits Jerusalem and meets with Peter and James (Gal 1:18–19, paralleled by Acts 9:26–30)

- Paul again visits Jerusalem, this time meeting with James, Peter, and John, who acknowledged his gospel mission to the gentiles and their gospel mission to the Jews (Gal 2:1–10, paralleled by Acts 11:27–30)[8]

---

7. This is the perspective taken by the clear majority of those who have written in some detail on this topic.

8. In addition, for around a decade leading up to this time, the migratory process spoken of in Acts 11:19 had been taking place: "Now those who were scattered because of the persecution that took place over Stephen traveled as far as Phoenicia, Cyprus, and Antioch, and they spoke the word to no one except Jews." While 11:20–21 goes on to speak of evangelism done by some messianic Jews which resulted in the founding of the church in Syrian Antioch, the key point to be noticed here is that not all the messianic Jewish migrants in that part of the Diaspora began to mix and worship with gentiles. Indeed, it is almost a surety that the majority did not. This majority would have been those who founded their own messianic synagogues or who chose to participate in existing synagogues (whether in Syrian Antioch or elsewhere in the region) that were at least somewhat open to the message of Yeshua as Messiah.

- Peter miraculously is released from jail in Jerusalem[9] and then "went to another place" (Acts 12:17b), which likely ends up being Syrian Antioch, after an unknown journey route and time length.[10]
- James authors the Letter of James[11] and it is sent out to "the twelve tribes in the Dispersion" (Jas 1:1).[12]
- Paul and Barnabas are sent out by the church at Syrian Antioch on their first missionary journey (Acts 13–14).[13]
- Upon Peter's arrival in Syrian Antioch, he has table fellowship with gentile messianic believers (Gal 2:12a).[14]
- Paul and Barnabas return to Syrian Antioch at the end of the first missionary journey (Acts 14:26-28).
- Whether the following arrivals in Syrian Antioch happened simultaneously cannot be known, but the Letter of James—undoubtedly carried by official couriers from the church of Jerusalem (i.e., "certain people from James" [Gal 2:12a], the leader of the Jerusalem church)—and men representing "the circumcision faction"[15] (Gal 2:12b, paralleled by Acts 15:1) both arrive on the scene.

---

9. Peter's imprisonment and release in Acts 12 likely took place between 42 and 44 CE.

10. It would have been natural for Peter to return and visit for periods of time at the various ministry stops—and the messianic believers in each location—that are seen in Acts 8:14-25 and 9:32—10:47. However, because the attention of the narrative of the Book of Acts has shifted to exclusively following Paul's ministry, Peter's travels and ministry during this period are not recorded.

11. As argued in chapter 1 above, the Letter of James was likely written in 44 or 45 CE.

12. Without question, Syrian Antioch was a major Jewish gathering point in the Diaspora, with a significant percentage of the city being Jewish and several synagogues there. Thus, it would be expected that the Letter of James would be delivered to at least the messianic Jews in the Jewish community in Syrian Antioch within a reasonable amount of time after it was published.

13. It is likely not possible to date Paul's first missionary journey any more specifically than that it took place in 46 or 47 CE.

14. Peter's willingness to have table fellowship with gentiles in Syrian Antioch (Gal 2:12) must have primarily had to do with his vision in Acts 10 and the resulting conversion of Cornelius, the gentile centurion, and his household (Acts 10–11). Though the wording in Acts 10:48b does not mention table fellowship specifically, it is unlikely that, if Peter stayed with Cornelius in his home "for several days," after all that had taken place in coming to that point (i.e., 10:1-48a), Peter would *not* have eaten with the family.

15. It may have been mere coincidence that "certain people from James" and "the

- Peter withdraws from table fellowship with gentile believers and is sternly rebuked by Paul (Gal 2:11) for his "hypocrisy" (2:13), which Paul terms as being inconsistent with "the truth of the gospel" (2:14)[16]
- Paul (and Barnabas, somewhat ironically, after his own hypocrisy alongside Peter [Gal 2:13]) "debate" (Acts 15:2) those who taught that circumcision is required for salvation (Acts 15:1)
- a) Paul's experience with Peter's hypocrisy, b) very possibly the vagueness of wording in the Letter of James regarding faith, works, and justification, as well as its silence on issues like circumcision, and c) Paul's debates with "the circumcision faction" in Syrian Antioch are major contributing factors,[17] though the tipping point is most likely Paul receiving word about the impact of teaching like that of "the circumcision faction" within the Galatian churches he had planted mere months before, news which prompted the writing of the letter to the Galatians[18]

---

circumcision faction," likely also from Jerusalem—especially given the characterization in Acts 15:1 as teachers who "came down from Judea" that focused on the necessity of circumcision for salvation—ended up in Syrian Antioch at the same point in time (Gal 2:11–14). It is mildly speculative (but hardly impossible), though, that, given that the Letter of James mentions nothing about circumcision, leaders of "the circumcision faction" in Jerusalem—perhaps Pharisees who believed in Yeshua as Messiah, such as those who spoke up at the Jerusalem Council in favor of gentiles being circumcised and keeping the Torah of Moses (Acts 15:5)—dispatched some of their faction to follow those who delivered the Letter of James, in order for them to make sure their views on circumcision would be made clear to those who were receiving the content of the Letter of James (which has absolutely nothing to say about circumcision, so "the circumcision faction" would have been filling in a blank spot in James's Letter that he may well have intended to stay blank).

16. After the end of the incident involving Paul, Peter, "certain people from James," and "the circumcision faction" in Gal 2:11–14, Peter is not again mentioned in Galatians. It cannot be known whether he left Syrian Antioch immediately after being rebuked by Paul (2:11, 14). However, Peter does appear in the narrative of Acts some months later when he speaks at the Jerusalem Council (Acts 15:6–11) toward the same end (i.e., that gentiles did not have to effectively become Jews to be saved) that Paul did.

17. Paul's Letter to the Galatians most likely dates from sometime in 48 CE.

18. There is no biblical information by which to determine how and exactly when Paul found out about the theological defection of (at least many in) the Galatian churches. However, Paul's depiction of the teaching of those who had arrived in the Galatian cities and infiltrated the young churches soon after he left makes it clear that what he heard was more than vague rumors. In addition, Paul speaks specifically about the less than godly motivations of these teachers: "They make much of you, but for no good purpose; they want to exclude you, so that you may make much of them" (Gal 4:17). In Gal 6:12, Paul ties this wrong motivation to the teaching about the necessity

- Paul and Barnabas are appointed by the church at Syrian Antioch to go to Jerusalem for a meeting (usually called "the Jerusalem Council"),[19] the focal topic of which is whether gentiles had to be circumcised and keep the Torah to be saved (Acts 15:1–29)—the same subject Paul had focused on in his recent Letter to the Galatians.

- The findings of the Jerusalem Council—which decidedly favor Paul's perspective—are written up as a fully authoritative letter,[20] which is then delivered to "the believers of [g]entile origin in Antioch and Syria and Cilicia" (15:23) to (hopefully) finally answer the questions raised by the previous debates stirred up by "the circumcision faction" in those geographical locations.[21]

If the above chronology is reasonably accurate, the anchor point here is that the Letter of James was written some three or four years before Paul's Letter to the Galatians. Another important implication to be drawn here from the chronological reasoning above is that the "relationship" between the Letters of James and Galatians needs to be resolved between *those two documents alone*, without bringing Romans[22] (or any of Paul's other letters, for that matter) into the discussion.

---

of circumcision: "It is those who want to make a good showing in the flesh that try to compel you to be circumcised."

19. The Jerusalem Council is probably best dated in 49 CE (though some evangelical scholars today date it as early as 48 and others as late as 50).

20. It is difficult to decide whether this missive can be rightly referred to as an "apostolic letter," at least in the sense that the Letters of James and Galatians both are in that category. The reason is that the Jerusalem Council letter is stated as originating from "the brothers, both the apostles and the elders" (Acts 15:23). Even though there is hesitancy about how to classify the Jerusalem Council letter, there need not be any doubt about its authority, because it ultimately was not the human authors, but the Holy Spirit, who was the final authority (15:28).

21. Apparently, the circulation of the authoritative letter from the Jerusalem Council did not solve completely the issue having to do with the influence of Jewish teachers with views like "the circumcision faction" in other places. For example, a few portions of Paul's Letter to the Romans sounds remarkably like Galatians, quite possibly indicating that the same—or markedly similar—ideas related to "works of the law" (i.e., circumcision and keeping the Torah) were still circulating in Rome in both believing gentile and Jewish circles.

22. Bernier (*Rethinking the Dates of the New Testament*, 156) concludes "Romans was written in the winter of 56/57." If Galatians was written in 48 CE, as argued above, Romans was authored at least eight years later: well after the Jerusalem Council (49 CE), as well as Paul's second (50–52) and third missionary journeys (53–56) had taken

The reason for setting that limitation is that the concerns related to faith, works, and justification being considered in this chapter were brought up and officially debated and settled at the Jerusalem Council where both Paul and James had their says (see Acts 15:1–29)—relatively soon after both the Letter of James and the Letter to the Galatians had set forth the views of the two leaders: James, in regard to the messianic Jewish community in the "Diaspora" outside Jerusalem (Jas 1:1); and Paul, regarding the new predominantly gentile local churches in Galatia.

Unfortunately, even given the amount of detail carefully assembled in chronological/sequential reasoning above, there is no information having to do with what happened when Paul first encountered the Letter of James. Thus, it is not possible to be any more specific than to conclude, because of the striking similarity in terminology in certain parts of both letters, that Paul had access to the Letter of James before he wrote Galatians.

Even given that lack of detail, it is still possible to proceed further in seeking to better understand the relationship between the Letter of James and Galatians (though tentatively in certain areas). The four angles that follow each contribute to that process: 1) exploring the different audiences of the Letter of James and Galatians; 2) pondering carefully the various inclusions of the terms "faith," "works" and "justify"/"justification" in both James and Galatians, and "law" in Galatians; 3) carefully observing the prior literary context of Jas 2:14–26 and its "mirror" passage: 3:13–18; and 4) learning from the chiastic structuring Jas 2:14–26.

Interpretative help from the differing audiences of the Letters of James and Galatians

In certain respects, approaching James and Galatians is like comparing apples and oranges. In order to be sensitized to such—sometimes significant—differences, the following listing of helpful contrasts is offered here:

place. It is hardly likely Paul would still be attempting to counter the views of James of Jerusalem at such a late date, especially given that the two clearly were on the same side (i.e., regarding how gentiles could be saved without being circumcised or keeping the Torah) at the Jerusalem Council and also cooperated in Acts 21:18–26—after Romans was written—in Paul demonstrating his own Torah commitment to the Torah-observant messianic Jewish community in Jerusalem. Thus, whatever remarks Paul makes in Romans which *sound like* wording in Galatians are aimed at Jewish teachers (and those who followed them) whose expressed views remained—almost a decade later—like "the circumcision faction" in Syrian Antioch described by Paul in Gal 2:11–14.

Obvious Differences between the Audiences of Jas and Galatians

Letter of James		Letter to the Galatians
James, whose mission was, along with Peter and John, to the Jews (Gal 2:8–9)	**Author**	Paul, whose mission was to the gentiles (Gal 2:8, 10)
Exclusively Jewish	**Ethnicity of Audience**	Almost exclusively gentile
The Jewish Diaspora (1:1)	**Location of Audience**	Four cities in the Roman province of Galatia (Acts 13–14)[23]
ca. 44 or 45 CE	**Date of Writing**	ca. 48 CE
From "brotherly" to stern exhortation	**Tone of Letter**	Initially angry, but occasionally emotionally paternal
Designed to speak to *general* issues of a messianic Jewish audience in the Diaspora	**Letter's Message**	Designed to speak regarding a very *specific* type of teaching contrary to "the truth of the gospel" (2:6, 14)

Besides the comparative dates of the Letters of James and Galatians, and their different ethnic audiences (see just above), the differing tones and messages of the two letters point in the direction that Paul's *immediate* reasons for writing Galatians were: 1) his encountering and debating "the circumcision faction" in Syrian Antioch (Gal 2:11–14; Acts 15:1); and 2) his becoming aware (though it is not known how that happened) that the teachers of the circumcision faction—or others related to their group—had followed his ministry in Galatia and that their views had been received with surprising openness by many in the new Galatian churches.

The uses of "faith," "works," "justification" and "law" in the Letters of James and Galatians

The most significant terms in this discussion related to the meaning of Jas 2:14–26 and Gal 2:16 (and its context) are "faith," "works," "justify/

---

23. This wording is reflective of the "South Galatian" view of the location of the readers of Paul's letter. If the North Galatian is correct, little is known of their location other than that it would be somewhere in the northern part of what is central Turkey today.

justification," and "law."[24] The following mini-charts list the number and locations of the uses of these four major terms in James and Galatians.

"Faith" in the Letters of James and Galatians

As will be seen below, there are fifteen uses of the noun "faith" in the Letter of James, as well as three uses of the verb "to believe." That compares with twenty-two uses of "faith" in the Letter to the Galatians and four uses of "to believe."

Of the total uses in each letter (i.e., eighteen relevant uses in James; twenty-six in Galatians), ten of the uses of "faith" and all three uses of "to believe" in James are in the focal passage of this chapter: 2:14–26. That compares to only three uses of "faith" and one use of "to believe" in Gal 2:11–21, the passage in which the focal verse 2:16 is located.

Uses of "faith" in the Letter of James	Uses of "faith" in the Letter to the Galatians
Noun (Greek *pistis*): 1:3, 6; 2:1, 5, 14(2),[25] *17, 18(3), 20, 22, 24, 26*; 5:15	**Noun** (Greek *pistis*): 1.23; 2:*16*(2), 20: 3:2, 5, 7, 8, 9, 11, 12, 14, 22, 23(2), 24, 25, 26; 5:5, 6, 22; 6:10
Verb (Greek *pisteuo*): 2:*19*(2), *23*	**Verb** (Greek *pisteuo*): 2:7, *16*; 3:6, 22

Comparing these statistics regarding the use of "faith" in the Letters of James and Galatians makes the point (at least generally) that both "faith" and its kindred verb "to believe" are more a part of the focused issue in Jas 2:14–26 than the same wording in the immediate context of Gal 2:16. If anything, though, the density of usage of most of the "faith" terminology in the Letter of James in 2:14–26, which, by comparison, is spread throughout the middle chapters of Galatians, implies Paul's discussion there is, overall, more detailed and urgent, as well as seemingly theologically weightier.

---

24. It is necessary to bring "law" (Greek *nomos*) into this discussion, even though the term "law" is not found in Jas 2:14–26, because of Paul's multiple uses of the phrase "works of the law" in Galatians (including three times just in 2:16).

25. The verse numbers in this chart *in italics* are found in the focal passages in Jas 2:14–26 and Gal 2:11–21.

"Works" in the Letters of James and Galatians

As seen in the chart below, there are fourteen uses of the noun "work(s)" in the Letter of James, plus one use of the verb "to work." By comparison, there are eight uses of the noun "work(s)" in Galatians, and a single use of the corresponding verb.

Of the total of fifteen uses in James, eleven are in 2:14–26. Of the nine overall uses in Galatians, only three are in 2:11–21.

Uses of "works" in the Letter of James	Uses of "works" in the Letter to the Galatians
Noun (Greek *ergon*): 1:4, 25; 2:14, 17, 18(3), 20, 21, 22, 24, 25, 26; 3:13	**Noun** (Greek *ergon*): 2:16(3); 3:2, 5, 10; 5:19; 6:4
Verb (Greek *ergazomai*): 2:9	**Verb** (Greek *ergazomai*): 6:10

The cluster of eleven uses of "works" in Jas 2:14–26 versus the three inclusions of "works" in the focal passage in Gal 2:11–21 gives pause. Also, all three of those uses in Gal 2:16 employ the wording "works of the law,"[26] phraseology not used at all in the Letter of James. Thus, it appears James is, at least for the most part,[27] referring to some other angle regarding "works" than the keeping of the normally focal aspects of Torah, while the usage in Galatians apparently primarily has to do with "works" related to keeping the Torah.

"Justify" in the Letters of James and Galatians

There are three appearances of the verb "to justify" in James—all three in 2:14–26—and another three inclusions of the related noun "righteousness," one of which is in 2:14–26. In Galatians, the verb "to justify" is found eight times—four in 2:11–21—and "righteousness" four times, with one of those uses in 2:11–21.

---

26. In addition, the next three uses of "works" in Galatians after 2:16 (i.e., 3:2, 5, 10) also employ the phrase "the works of the law."

27. The lone apparent exception to that observation in the usage of "works" in the Letter of James is found in 1:25: "But those who look into the perfect law, the law of liberty, and persevere, being not hearers who forget but doers who act" (lit. "a doer of work" [Greek *poietes ergou*]). However, given that, only a few verses later, 2:8 speaks of "You shall love your neighbor as yourself" as "the royal law according to the scripture," even 1:25 may have to do with "works" not strictly part of the traditional Jewish practice of the Torah.

Uses of "justify" in the Letter of James	Uses of "justify" in the Letter to the Galatians
Verb (Greek *dikaioo*): 2:21, 24, 25	**Verb** (Greek *dikaioo*): 2:16(3), 17; 3:8, 11, 24; 5:8
Noun (Greek *dikaiosune*): 1:20; 2:23; 3:18	**Noun** (Greek *dikaiosune*) 2:21; 3:6, 21; 5:5

At first glance, due to a simple comparison of the overall number of uses in each letter, it appears that "justification" is a bigger issue in Galatians than in James. For the most part, "justification" terminology in James is limited to 2:14–26. However, in Galatians, it is used not only in 2:11–21, but also in Paul's argumentation in Gal 3 and 5.

"Law" in the Letters of James and Galatians

The noun "law" appears ten times in James—*none of which* are in 2:14–26. In Galatians, though, "law" is used twenty-two times, with *six* of those inclusions being found in 2:11–21.

Use of "law" in the Letter of James	Uses of "law" in the Letter to the Galatians
Noun (Greek *nomos*): 1:25; 2:8, 9, 10, 11, 12; 4:11(4)	**Noun** (Greek *nomos*): 2:16(3), 19(2), 21; 3:2, 5, 10(2), 11, 12, 13, 17, 18, 19, 21(3), 25; 6:2, 13

Given that Paul's Letter to the Galatians is not much longer than the Letter of James, it is unusual that Galatians contains more than double the number of uses of "law" than does James (i.e., twenty-two to ten). That sense of oddity only grows with the realization that: 1) James is a letter written to a messianic Jewish audience, with which 2) expectation of discussion of the Torah in Jas 2:14–26 is natural, but does not take place at all. On the other hand, since Galatians is written to a predominantly gentile audience, there would not be the same *natural* expectation of extensive discourse on the Torah. Yet, Galatians refers to the Torah twenty-two times, with six of those uses in 2:11–21.

What conclusions emerge from these statistics on word usage?

In light of these comparisons of usage of the key terminology in James and Galatians, several tentative observations may be offered: 1) Although there are more uses of the "faith" terminology in Galatians (twenty-six) than in James (eighteen), those uses are spread throughout Galatians while, in James, there is a clustering of ten uses in 2:14-26; 2) Amazingly, though eleven of the fourteen uses of "work(s)" in James are found in 2:14-26, none contain the wording "works *of the law*," as in Gal 2,[28] which is strange *if* Paul is indeed talking about the same thing as James; 3) Statistically speaking, the amount of emphasis on the term "justify" is roughly the same in both Jas 2:14-26 and Gal 2:11-21; and 4) To reiterate the point above regarding the phrase "works of the law," there is no mention at all of "law" in Jas 2:14-26, while there are six inclusions in Gal 2:11-21, including three uses of "works of the law" clustered in the focal verse (2:16), then three more uses of "works of the law" in the immediately following section (i.e., 3:2, 5, 10).

For the purpose of simplification (without *over*simplifying, hopefully), the statistics just discussed are visualized in the following chart:

	Number of uses in Jas 2:14-26	Number of uses in Gal 2:11-21
Faith	10	3
Works	11	3 (all 3 read "works of the law")
Justify	3	4
Law	0	6 (3 of the 6 being "works of the law")

Two more tentative observation emerge at this point: 1) The issue of "justification" appears to arise—and be treated with roughly equal emphasis—in connection with the discussion of the roles of "faith" and "works" in both Jas 2 and Gal 2; and 2) Jas 2 includes much more about both "faith" *and* "works" than Gal 2, but Jas 2 is silent on "works of the law," while all three uses of "works" in Gal 2 are in the phrase "works of the law."

Although it is a calculated risk at best to draw even tentative conclusions from statistics alone, it can be cautiously stated that the numbers set forth above appear to point in the following two directions: 1) The question of how "justification" relates to the elements of "faith" and "works" *began* with the earlier passage, Jas 2, with its far greater concentration of the use of both terms and its more practical orientation; then 2) Paul later *applied* and *adjusted* James' practical discussion of "faith," "works," and "justification" as part of the argumentation in the Letter of Galatians in his already heated theological debate with "the circumcision faction,"

28. As well as in the immediately succeeding context, in Gal 3:2, 5, 10.

in the process shrewdly expanding James's original wording "works" to "works of the law."

Interpretative help from the earlier context of James and the parallel chiastic passage to James 2:14–26

From the beginning of the body of the Letter of James, there is an emphasis on "faith," but not on "faith" *by itself*. Instead, the focus is on the continuing *growth* of faith, notably through some kind of *action or works*.

Passages closely related thematically to 2:14–26 in the earlier context of James

The first of such passages is Jas 1:2–4:

> My brothers and sisters, whenever you face trials of any kind, consider it nothing but joy, because you know that the testing of your faith (Greek *tes pisteos*) produces (Greek *katergazetai*, lit. "does, works out") endurance; and let endurance have its full effect (Greek *ergon . . . echeto*, lit. "have [its] work"[29]), so that you may be mature (Greek *teleion*)[30] and complete, lacking in nothing.

James's lead-off thought in his letter (i.e., 1:2–4) is that, in lives that are inevitably filled with trials, faith must *grow*. The ongoing "working out" of such *enduring faith* eventually accomplishes its "work" of bringing about *maturity* (Greek *teleion*, which is also used in 2:22, in the heart of the key passage focused on in this chapter) that lacks nothing.

Those last words lead to the next relevant passage in the "daisy chain" about faith and works found through the first two chapters of James in 1:5–6:

> If any of you is lacking wisdom, ask God, who gives to all generously and ungrudgingly, and it will be given you. But ask in faith

---

29. The major idea James is expressing here seems to be that enduring faith "works out" into maturity.

30. The semantic range of the Greek *teleios* is "perfect, complete, mature." Since another word clearly meaning "complete" (Greek *holokleroi*) is used just after *teleios* in Jas 1:4, the use of *teleios* here cannot also mean "complete." Nor can it mean "perfect," because such perfection is not possible for mankind in this life. Thus, the correct shade of meaning is "mature," as in NRSV, CSB, and NIV.

JAMES ON FAITH, WORKS, AND JUSTIFICATION

> (Greek en *pistei*), never doubting, for the one who doubts is like a wave of the sea, driven and tossed by the wind . . . .

Among the truly significant things in life that could be lacking in the growth to maturity (Jas 1:2–4) is wisdom. However, God is always willing to grant wisdom to his child, *if* he or she asks in *faith*, without doubting. In fact, one of the most important ways that faith grows on the road of endurance to full maturity is by *praying for wisdom* while going through the many and varied trials encountered along the way.

Next in the order is Jas 1:17:

> Every generous act of giving, and every perfect (Greek *teleion*) gift, is from above, coming down from the Father of lights, with whom there is no variation or shadow due to change.

It is clear from Jas 1:5–6 that wisdom is granted by God as a gift in response to *the action of the prayer of faith*. James 1:17 adds that it is a "perfect" (Greek *teleion*) gift, which causes it to fit seamlessly into the "maturity" that is the product of the process outlined in 1:2–4 by taking care of the lack of wisdom through the *action* of the prayer of faith. (This verse also will be clearly seen to fit with the section that is parallel to 2:14–26 in the overall chiastic structure of the Letter of James: 3:13–18).

Next comes Jas 1:22–25:

> But be doers (Greek *poietes*) of the word, and not merely hearers who deceive themselves. For if any are hearers of the word and not doers (Greek *poietes*), they are like those who look at themselves in a mirror; for they look at themselves and, on going away, immediately forget what they are like. But those who look into the perfect (Greek *teleion*) law, the law of liberty, and persevere, being not hearers who forget but doers (Greek *poietes*) who act (Greek *ergou*, "work")—they will be blessed in their doing (Greek *poiesei*).

The focus of Jas 1:22–25 is on doing/acting (i.e., works). Also in evidence is the necessity of perseverance in the process, as in 1:3. Further, the doing/acting is described as "work" (Greek *ergou*), which seems to be more than coincidence, given the extensive use of the term "work" only a few verses later: twelve times in the key passage considered in this chapter—in 2:14, 17, 18 (three uses), 20, 21, 22 (two uses), 24, 25, 26. Finally, since the "law of liberty" is described as *teleios*, it is implied that the faith growth process set forth in 1:2–4 must include—at least to some extent—the keeping of the *teleios* law of liberty (which appears to be defined—at least narrowly, for this context—in 2:8 as "You shall love your neighbor as yourself" [i.e., including acts/works of love]).

The last verses in the previous context that set up 2:14–26 are 2:1 and 2:12:

> My brothers and sisters, do you with your acts of favoritism (Greek *prosopolempsiais* simply means "partiality or favoritism," and the wording "acts of. . ." in the NRSV rendering is an unwarranted interpretive paraphrase) really believe (Greek *echete ten pistin* is more properly to be rendered as "have, hold, or possess the faith," not as "*really* believe" [NRSV]) in our glorious Lord Jesus Christ?

An additional problem with the NRSV translation of Jas 2:1 is that it is not a question, but a command. What James is getting across in 2:1 is "My brethren, with partiality, do not hold the faith in our glorious Lord Jesus Christ." This sentence leads into an embarrassing example of such partiality in both word and deed in 2:2–4, which 2:9 says in so many words is committing sin, making the person displaying such partiality a transgressor of the law. What "law" is being transgressed? In this context, it is clearly the command to "love your neighbor as yourself" (Jas 2:8; See Lev 19:18), following up on the preceding context in 2:1–13.

An important theological question here is whether it is possible to mix faith with sin (i.e., in this case, transgressing the law of love). The obvious answer is No. According to Jas 1–2, it is not a legitimate option for faith to stand pat—to do nothing. From the initial commands of his letter (i.e., in 1:2–4), James clearly states his expectation that faith "works out" toward the eventual "work" of maturity. This is not double-talk.

As seen in Jas 1:22, those who are merely hearers of the word and not doers are self-deceived. So, it is with those who claim to have faith, but do not have *matching works that flow from faith*. They are likewise self-deceived. That point leads to 2:12.

> So speak and so act (Greek *poieite*) as those who are to be judged by the law of liberty.

This verse is located near the end of the section 2:1–13, in which an act of blatant partiality has been labelled by James as a clear transgression of the law that requires love for one's neighbor. In 2:12, he goes on to say to his audience that they must "So *speak* and so *act* as those who . . ." realize fully that they too will be judged as transgressors of the law, if they do not love their neighbors as they love themselves.

One thing particularly striking about the wording in 2:12 is the way "speak" and "act" there set the stage for the unsettling example of "speaking" and "acting" in 2:15-16, on the one hand, which, in turn, is playing off the earlier example of partiality in speech and action in 2:2-3. What is the point James is making in this progression? It seems to be that the person who professes *faith* in "our glorious Lord Jesus Christ" will indeed *speak and act*, but that does not automatically mean the speech and actions that flow forth will be kindly judged by "the law of freedom" (2:12). If such speech and actions are not merciful, no amount of protest that one possesses faith will avail in the final judgment (2:13), which will be merciless for such a self-deceived person. In other words, such words will be found to be hollow.

The key verses in James 2:14-26 linking up with the preceding context

> What good is it, my brothers and sisters, if you say you have faith (Greek *pistin*) but do not have works (Greek *erga*)? Can faith (Greek *he pistis* [lit. "the faith"—or the slightly paraphrased "that faith"[31] or "such faith"[32]] save you? (Jas 2:14)

The exact wording in 2:12 has changed from "speak" (Greek *laleo*) and "act (or do)" (Greek *poieo*) to "say" (Greek *lego*) and "works" (Greek *ergon*) in 2:14, but what James is doing in 2:14 is skillfully using different terms to make a closely related point, which is approached from a different angle: just as no matter what a person says (2:12), "judgment will be without mercy to anyone who has shown (Greek *poieo* [lit. "done"] no mercy" [2:13]); likewise, there will be a "judgment" of no salvation for a person whose faith is not acted upon in works (i.e., acts or doing [2:14]).

Also crucial to be understood here is that the "works" in question in 2:14-26 are not to be confused with the "works of the law" about which Paul is deeply concerned in Gal 2:16; 3:5, 10. In the immediately preceding context and in Jas 2:14-26, the "works" in view are unquestionably practical works that flow out from love (2:8-13; 2:15-16), not religious requirements of the Torah.

---

31. So NASB; ESV.
32. So NIV; CSB.

> So faith (Greek *he pistis*) by itself, if it has no works (Greek *erga*), is dead. (Jas 2:17)

Verse 17 here also should be paired with verse 26, due to the clearly intended bracketed (i.e., bookends) use of the word "dead" at the end of both 2:17 and 2:26.

> For just as the body without the spirit is dead, so faith without works is dead. (Jas 2:26)

The comparison in 2:26 makes abundantly clear the meaning of what James set forth in 2:17: just as a human body without a spirit is dead (i.e., without life, because it lacks a source of animation: the spirit), so faith without works is without life because it lacks the activated force of works. "Works" are the only *visible* proof (i.e., "Show me" [Greek *deixo*; 2:18]) which can demonstrate effectively that faith actually exists and is more than mere words (2:18).

Finally in this section is the highly significant wording in 2:22:

> You see (Greek *blepo*) that faith (Greek *he pistis*) was active with (Greek *synergei*) his works (Greek *tois ergois autou*) and faith (Greek *he pistis*) was brought to completion (Greek *eteleiothe* [or "brought to maturity"]) by the works (Greek *ek ton ergon*). (Jas 2:22)

As was seen in chapter 1, in setting forth the overall chiastic structure of the Letter of James, it was shown that each section of the book also has an inverted internal structure. As laid out in a section below, 2:22 is part of the pairing that immediately surrounds the central focus of the section 2:14–26.

That proves to be the case, including the most helpful clarification it provides regarding the relationship of faith and works in 2:14–16. The first word of the Greek text of 2:22 (*blepo*; "to see") looks back to the latter half of 2:18: ". . . I by my works will show (Greek *deixo*) you my faith." In James's interaction with his unnamed dialogue partner in 2:18ff., James is *showing* Abraham's faith through the example of his willingness to sacrifice his son, Isaac, on the altar in Gen 22—an example that, in their first-century Jewish context, would be impossible for the interlocutor not to "see" and agree with.

The NRSV rendering of the Greek *synergeo* as "was active with" obscures James's apparently intended play on words, which is literally translated as "worked with his works." The point here, though, is *not* what easily might be inferred from the use of the Greek verb *synergeo*, from which comes the idea of *synergism*, with the false conclusion that faith and works are, so to speak, co-equal partners in salvation. Rather the correct conclusion is, as James says in the latter half of 2:22, that the faith was "brought to maturity" (Greek *teleioo*) by the works.

This wording in the latter part of Jas 2:22 looks back to 1:3-4: "the testing of your faith produces (Greek *katergazomai*, "works out") endurance, and let endurance have its full (Greek *teleios*, "mature") effect (Greek *ergon*, "work"), so that you may be mature (Greek *teleios*) and complete, lacking in nothing." The following paraphrase clarifies this portion of Jas 1:3-4: "The testing of your faith works out into endurance, with the mature work of endurance being maturity and completeness . . . ." Though this paraphrase sounds almost like double-talk, it makes the point here well: *testing stretches faith through developing endurance and, eventually, maturity.*

The example of Abraham in Jas 2:21, 23 is employed to the same end as what has just been said. When James says Abraham was "justified by works when he offered his son Isaac on the altar" (2:21), that incident took place in Gen 22:1ff., some *thirty years after* "Abraham believed God and it was reckoned to him as righteousness" (Jas 2:23), which wording is cited from Gen 15:6. In Gal 3:6-8, Paul's point in quoting Gen 15:6 there is that Abraham was justified by faith at the time of Abraham's belief in God in Gen 15. Thus, James must be employing the concept of "justification" with a different meaning than does Paul, given the thirty-year difference in when the two of them understand the point of "justification" in Abraham's life. So, if Paul sticks closely to the apparent stated meaning of Gen 15:6 regarding Abraham's justification by faith, where does the view James advances in 2:21-23 come from?

Fortunately, the passages James cites from Gen 15 and 22 provide help in understanding his perspective expressed in Jas 2:21-23. Certainly, Abraham (actually "Abram" in Gen 15)[33] was "justified" in some important sense in Gen 15:6. However, at that point in his life, Abram apparently had not yet been "tested" in the way God intended. That focal "testing" takes place in Gen 22, which begins with the wording "After these things God tested Abraham."

Interestingly, in the LXX of Gen 22:1, the verb rendered in English as "tested" (Greek *peirazo*) is cognate to the term in Jas 1:3 in the phrase

---

33. His name was not changed from "Abram" to "Abraham" until Gen 17.

"the testing (Greek *peirasmos*) of your faith." Thus, through the lens of Jas 1:3-4, Abraham, who had faith from at least Gen 15 forward, was tested in Gen 22—in the incident the Jews call "the Akedah"—toward the end of stretching his faith and endurance (Jas 1:3, 4) to its intended "completed work" (Greek *ergon teleion* [Jas 1:4]) of a "mature" (Greek *teleioi* [Jas 1:4]) Abraham.

That understanding certainly sounds like what happened in Gen 22. Verse 12 of that passage states: "now I *know* that you fear God, since you have not withheld your son, your only son, from me." Now, obviously, God already knew that Abraham trusted him from Gen 15:6, but the undeniable *observable* knowledge of that trust only came about through the Akedah in Gen 22.

The understanding stated just above also sounds very much like what is expressed in Jas 2:21–23:

- James states that Abraham was "justified by works" by offering Isaac in Gen 22 (2:21)

- However, those "works" are understood by James to be *the observable* (Greek *blepo*, "to see" [2:22]) *evidence of faith* being brought to "maturity" (Greek *teleioo* [2:22]).

- James then concludes that Abram's faith in 15:6 was "made full" (Greek *pleroo* [its only use in the Letter of James, so the best translation is the nuance in the word's semantic range[34] that best fits the context]) through his *climactically tested* choice to trust God and mature through his action (i.e., work) of offering Isaac—which is what James means by Abram being "justified by works" (2:23).

The parallel section to James 2:14–26 in the overall structure of James: 3:13–18

This idea of the progression of faith initially mapped out in Jas 1:3–4 and which is played out through the Letter of James is encountered again in 3:13–18. However, 3:13–18 also echoes four other earlier, but closely connected, passages in Jas 1 and the earlier part of Jas 2 (all of which were catalogued and discussed earlier in this chapter). The first two earlier

---

34. BAGD, S.v., "*pleroo*," 670. The first (and most basic) possible nuance of *pleroo* listed is "make full, fill (full)."

passages interact with 3:13 and the latter two with the structural parallel (see the diagram below) of 3:13 (a) and 3:17–18 (a').

The first explores the situation of one whose faith has not yet been stretched through the work of endurance to the point of maturity (1:3–4), who "is lacking in wisdom" (1:5). James's answer to that dilemma is to "ask God who gives to all generously" (1:5) "in faith" (1:6). If that is done, a major lack (i.e., "wisdom") in the faith being tested (1:3) is removed over time by endurance (1:3–4) in praying in faith (1:5–6). The second passage is Jas 1:17, which describes God's "generous" answers to the prayers of 1:5–6—along with his other *teleios* gifts to his people (i.e., which may imply that such "gifts" are part of how the prayerful person moves through testing by faith to "maturity" [also *teleios*; 1:3–4])—as "coming down from the Father of lights" (1:17). That observation leads directly into the wider wording of 3:13–18. The third passage is 1:22–25, which emphasizes being "doers (Greek *poietes*) of the word"—the "law of liberty" (i.e., the love command) in that context—doers who "act" (Greek *ergou* ["work"]). The fourth passage, 2:12, very similarly to 1:22–25, states: "So speak and so act (Greek *poieite*) as those who are to be judged by the law of liberty." In both passages, James's exhortation is to the effect that one must not just hear or speak, but act (i.e., work [1:25; 2:12])—and that action is to be in keeping with the "law of liberty" (1:25; 2:12).

The paragraph (3:13–18) just below clearly differentiates between heavenly wisdom and earthly "wisdom" (i.e., the attitudes and corresponding behavior that flow from that which is "earthly, unspiritual, demonic" [3:15b; so ESV; NIV; CSB]) as a polar opposite of heavenly wisdom. In stating "Such wisdom (i.e., false earthly wisdom) does not come down from above . . ." (3:15a)—which is the focal point (c) of the inverted parallel structure of 3:13–18—James is clearly contrasting with 1:17: "Every good gift, with every perfect gift, is from above, coming down from the Father of lights . . . ."

The observations already made in this section of the chapter are sufficient to make the point that 3:13–18 further develops several themes introduced earlier in the Letter of James. Regarding the topic of this chapter (i.e., the meaning of faith, works, and justification in 2:14–26), though, the most helpful portion of 3:13–18 is the outer layer of the structure: a (3:13) and a' (3:17–18). Those verses will be discussed just below the structural diagram of 3:13–18.

a (3:13) Who is wise and understanding among you? Show (Greek *deixo*) by your good life (Greek *anastrophe*) that your works (Greek *ergon*) are done with gentleness (*prauteti*) born of wisdom.

b (3:14) But if you have bitter <u>envy</u> and <u>selfish ambition</u> in your hearts, do not be boastful and false to the truth.

> c (3:15) Such wisdom does not come down from above, but is earthly, unspiritual, devilish.

b' (3:16) For where there is <u>envy</u> and <u>selfish ambition</u>, there will also be disorder and wickedness of every kind.

a' (3:17-18) But the wisdom from above is first pure, then peaceable, gentle (*epieikeis*), willing to yield, full of mercy and good fruits, without a trace of partiality or hypocrisy. And a harvest of righteousness is sown in peace for those who make (Greek *poieo*) peace.

In the wake of the emphasis in Jas 1-2 on observable works, not just words, the question with which 3:13 begins is understandably asking for *tangible evidence* that a person is indeed "wise and understanding." The Greek imperative *deixo* ("to show, demonstrate") in 3:13 is only used elsewhere in the Letter of James in 2:18 (twice): "Show me your faith apart from your works"—*which is impossible to do*—"and I by my works will show you my faith." Thus, the use of *deixo* in 3:13 is likely intended to recall the emphasis of 2:18 on displaying on the outside (i.e., by works) what is claimed to be present on the inside (i.e., faith in 2:18 and wisdom in 3:13).

And the "works" in view in 3:13 are of a very specific kind: those that flow out from a good lifestyle (Greek *anastrophe*) and that are carried out "with gentleness born of wisdom." From what source does such "wisdom" come? James's earlier answer was from "God" (1:5) in answer to the prayer of faith of the one who lacks wisdom (1:5-6) along the road of enduring faith toward maturity" (1:3-4).

The point here in 3:13 (a) is what has been seen over and over in the early chapters of the Letter of James—that faith *works* . . . whether by enduring trials (1:2-3), asking for wisdom in prayer (1:5-6), persevering as doers of the word (1:25), acting as those who are to be judged by the law of liberty (2:12), or by demonstrating works reflecting the gentleness of wisdom (3:13). And much the same thing is seen in 3:17-18 (a').

In 3:17, the wisdom that God gives in answer to prayer is described, filling out precisely what is meant in 3:13 by the phrase "gentleness born of wisdom." But 3:18 is even closer to the discussion at hand: in the phrase "those who make peace," the Greek word translated "make" is *poieo*, cognate forms of which are used several times in the earlier passages studied above for *action/works* (e.g., 1:22, 23, 25; 2:12). Also of interest is the way the outcome of those who make peace is expressed: as "a harvest of righteousness." Though the Greek term in 3:18 rendered "harvest" (*karpos*) can just as well be interpreted as "fruit," the significance is the same: *action* taken in making peace over time produces "fruit" or a "harvest," the nature of which is "righteousness" (Greek *dikaiosyne*).

There are only three uses of "righteousness" in the Letter of James: in 1:20; 2:23; and here in 3:18. There are also only three inclusions of the cousin idea, "to justify" (Greek *dikaioo*): all in 2:14–26 (2:21, 24, 25). And, given that James's concept of "justification" in 2:21–23 was one in which justification could be extended over some thirty years—from Gen 15:6 to the Akedah in 22:1–18—the idea of "righteousness" being the product of a *process* of peacemaking in 3:18 is not at all strange. If this observation is correct, it fits seamlessly with what has been observed through Jas 1, 2, and 3 about James's repeated teaching on the necessity of *action* in the activating of faith or "the word"/"law of liberty" or "wisdom."

Interpretative help from the chiastic structuring of Jas 2:14–26

The inverted parallel structure of Jas 2:14–26 is particularly helpful in understanding what James is seeking to get across in this passage. An interpretation of the significance of each layer of the center-facing shape of the passage is found immediately below the following structural diagram.

> a (2:14–17) *What good is it*, my brothers and sisters, if you say you have faith but do not have works? Can (that) faith save you? If a brother or sister is naked and lacks daily food, and one of you says to them, "Go in peace; keep warm and eat your fill," and yet you do not supply their bodily needs, *what is the good of that*? So faith by itself, if it has no works, is dead.
>> b (2:18) But someone will say, "You have faith and I have works." <u>Show me your faith apart from your works, and I by my works will show you my faith.</u>
>>> c (2:19–22) You believe that God is one; you do well. Even the demons believe—and shudder. Do you want to be shown, you senseless person, that faith apart from works is barren? <u>Was not our ancestor Abraham justified by works when he offered his son Isaac on the altar? You see (Greek *blepo*) that faith was active along with his works, and faith was brought to completion (Greek *teleios*) by the works.</u>

> d' (2:23) *Thus the scripture was fulfilled (Greek pleroo) which says,* "Abraham believed God, and it was reckoned to him as righteousness," *and he was called the friend of God.*
>   c' (2:24) You see (Greek *orao*) that a person is justified by works, and not by faith alone.
>   b' (2:25) Likewise, was not Rahab the prostitute also justified by works when she welcomed the messengers and sent them out by another road?
>   a' (2:26) For just as the body without the spirit is dead, so faith without works is also dead.

The a layer (2:14–17; 2:26): The a portion of this layer (2:14–17) sets up the whole passage. By reading those four verses, it become clear that the issue is not simply faith and how it relates to any or all types of works, but faith expected to *express* itself in works that confront the need in front of the believer. Unless faith is expressed in that type of works, it is dead. In parallel, a' (2:26) observes that faith without works is as dead as a body without a spirit, because it is not animated.

The b layer (2:18; 2:25): The main point of 2:18 (b) is that faith *cannot* be demonstrated without works. The b' portion of the pairing (2:25) describes Rahab as a classic example of her faith being demonstrated by her "works" of protecting the two Jewish messengers. (Note: Josh 2 makes no direct statement of faith on Rahab's part, but she certainly *acts* as if she is a believer in the one true God of Israel. Also, in Heb 11:31, it says, "By faith Rahab the prostitute did not perish with those who were disobedient, because she had received the spies in peace.")

The c layer (2:19–22; 2:24): The largest of the various pairings in 2:14–26 is c (2:19–22). The reason all this material fits together structurally is because these verses develop the classic—almost comical—contrast between the "bare" (i.e., "barren") belief of demons in the existence of God and Abraham's faith expressed in his testing by God in which he was obedient in his "work" to sacrifice Isaac in Gen 22. The explanation of this in 2:22 is crucial: Abraham's faith was active along with his works, which resulted in the maturing (Greek *teleios*) of his faith. It is in that sense that Abraham was "justified by works" (c' [2:24]): his faith was unquestionably demonstrated by his "works" in being willing to sacrifice Isaac, as God had commanded Abraham, to test him.

The central point—d (2:23): The scripture was "filled full" (see the explanation above), which here cannot mean "fulfilled *at a point in time*." The reason for that is that there had been some thirty years between

God's declaration that Abram was "justified" in Gen 15:6 until the Akedah in Gen 22:1ff. This is a completely different understanding of "justified" from Paul's point in time concept in Galatians and Romans. The latter part of the verse brings into the discussion a scripturally unique way of referring to Abraham—as "the friend of God"—found only in Isa 41:8 and 2 Chr 20:7. Perhaps the significance is to show that Abraham's relationship with God had *matured* to the point where he was unusually close to the Lord (i.e., as with a very close friend).

A resulting interpretive paraphrase of James 2:14-26

The most succinct way to summarize the results of what has been determined regarding the meaning of Jas 2:14-26 is to reflect those findings in an interpretive paraphrase. That paraphrase follows.

> 14 Is it not useless for a person to claim to have faith but have no works to prove the faith exists? Can such a "faith" completely lacking in evidence save that person? 15 That is just as useless as encountering a brother or sister without clothes or daily food 16 and blowing them off by saying, "Peace, stay warm and eat well," without doing anything at all to help. 17 That kind of "faith" cannot present evidence that it is other than dead, because it is unaccompanied by activating force. 18 If someone were to try to start an argument by saying, "You have faith and I have works," I would not take the bait. Whatever is said, faith cannot be seen except through works. 19 Faith is not just bare belief, like believing God is One. Even demons believe that much, and it makes no positive difference in their destiny. 20 Is it not foolish to fail to acknowledge that faith without works is useless? 21 Does not the example of Abraham offering Isaac on the altar show that he was justified by works? 22 That event demonstrates how his faith was matured by working together with his works? 23 It also explains the *final* "fulfillment" of what scripture said about Abram thirty years earlier: "Abram believed God, and it was reckoned to him as righteousness." Another example of God's long-term developing relationship with Abraham was that Abraham was called God's "friend." 24 Thus, you see that a person is understood by onlookers as justified by works and cannot be justified by bare faith. 25 Is that not how we understand that Rahab was saved: because her works in receiving and protecting the spies reflect her justification? 26 For a final analogy: faith without works is just as dead as a body without the spirit.

Conclusion

In summary, the relevant sectional conclusions drawn in this chapter on James's view on the relationship between faith, works, and justification were:

- The Letter of James was probably written several years before Paul's Letter to the Galatians (i.e., James, dating from 44–45 CE and Galatians from 48 CE).

- It is plausible that Paul wrote Galatians after reading the Letter of James and realizing that it had either been misunderstood or misused by those he calls "the circumcision group" (Gal 2), or both.

- The Letters of James and Galatians were written to very different audiences, which may have been the basis for the different definitions of justification James and Paul employed.

- The primary conclusion from the survey of the uses of the focal terms "faith," "works," "justify," and "law" in James and Galatians was that there is no appreciable difference in meaning of the terms other than that Paul uses the wording "works of the law" and James does not. That is likely the case because Paul was arguing against those who were teaching that, to be saved, a person had to believe in Yeshua *plus* keep the Torah, whereas James was arguing against the view that a merely *stated* claim of faith was sufficient to be saved.

- The selective survey of relevant passages in the Letter of James before 2:14–26 and in its mirroring section, 3:13–18 demonstrated that, from the beginning of the body of the letter, James portrayed faith and other key parts of the spiritual life of the believer as growth processes.

- At the center of the chiastic structuring of Jas 2:14–26 is d (2:23): "Thus the scripture was fulfilled which says, 'Abraham believed God, and it was reckoned to him as righteousness.'" What had just been discussed in 2:21 was that Abraham's justification took place when he sacrificed Isaac in the Akedah episode, at least thirty years after the wording of faith being the basis of Abram's justification in Gen 15:6. This temporal observation leaves no doubt that James is viewing justification differently than Paul.

- The paraphrase of Jas 2:14–26 attempted to keep in mind all these smaller conclusions and embody them in its slightly expanded interpretative wording.

Finally, it can be affirmed, as suggested at the beginning of this chapter, that the views of James and Paul on faith, works, and justification indeed are complementary and not conflicting. They simply approach the overall issue from different vantage points.

James refers to "justification" as having to do with the presenting of the unmistakable evidence of works in proving the presence of faith—but the "works" James has in mind are not "works of the law" (which wording James never uses). By "justification," Paul is speaking of the point of what is often called "saving faith," which he develops in strong contrast to the phrase "works of the law" (i.e., deeds in keeping Torah). However, Paul's view cannot be far distanced from James's, as seen in Eph 2:8–10:

> For by grace you have been saved through faith, and this is not of your own doing; it is the gift of God—not the result of works, so that no one may boast. For we are what he has made us, created in Christ Jesus for good works, which God prepared beforehand to be our way of life.

In other words, while "works" do not save, they are the essence of the life that the believer in Yeshua Messiah is to live.

9

Conclusion

Review of chapter findings

IN CHAPTER 1 OF this book, I stated that my initial intention was to demonstrate that the Letter of James was the earliest written New Testament document. While the dating of the letter is certainly not the only background issue of interest—or even the most difficult with which to grapple, for that matter—it is the most *foundational* issue to be resolved in seeking an accurate understanding of James and its implications for both first century CE and contemporary Messianic Judaism.

In chapter 2, it was concluded that it is highly likely that the Letter of James was indeed the first New Testament book written, very likely in the mid-40s CE. That historical "puzzle piece" then opened the door to probable conclusions that James, the half-brother of Jesus, was the author of the Letter; that it most likely was written in Jerusalem; that its literary genre is that of a "Diaspora apostolic letter"; and that it is best understood to be structured in a beautiful book-length inverted parallel (chiastic) manner, with each section of the overall outline also an internal chiasm.

Chapter 3 asked and answered the question of what is the best understanding of the wording "To the twelve tribes in the Dispersion?" (Jas 1:1 [NRSV]). It was determined that this phraseology referred to Diaspora Jews—most likely a largely messianic Jewish audience, though a wider Jewish audience in synagogue settings containing both messianic Jews and those who did not view Yeshua as Messiah cannot be ruled out—who had fled Jerusalem during the persecution of followers of Yeshua after the stoning of Stephen (see Acts 8:1–4). Given the early dating of the Letter of James, there is no good reason to conclude that "the twelve tribes in the Diaspora" refers to the church. However, it is by just such slippery "exegesis" that the supersessionist view that the church is what is meant *spiritually* by "the twelve tribes in the Diaspora" has been arrived at over many centuries of church history.

Chapter 4 explored the meaning of "the perfect law, the law of liberty" in 1:25 (and similar wording elsewhere in the Letter of James). It was concluded that, although the presence of James's citation of "love your neighbor as yourself" from Lev 19:18 has been taken as implying a compression of the Mosaic law into the "love command" within the theological context of the new covenant, such a perspective comes largely from ignoring the rest of James's explanatory comments on the law, as well as by wrongly reading the Letter of James through the lens of Paul's Letter to the Galatians. The assumption has been that Galatians was written before James and that the definitions of the common terminology about the law in the two documents are the same. Against this, I have argued here that James predates Galatians by several years and that James's "works" are not what Galatians has in mind by "the works of the law" (a phrase that James does not use at all). Thus, the Letter of James does not teach that messianic Jews should not be Torah observant. Thus, while supersessionist thinkers undoubtedly will continue to attempt to argue that the Letter of James is meant for the "spiritual Israel" (i.e., the church), the evidence in James is decidedly not in their favor.

Chapter 5 discussed James's meaning of the wording "religion that is pure and undefiled by God" (Jas 1:27). That wording does not mean at all that the rest of the Mosaic law is to be ignored in the messianic Jewish believer's obedience. Instead, this chapter set forth an understanding of messianic Jewish "religion" that is "pure and undefiled" as a "worldview" related to purity that James was imparting to his audience in the Diaspora (Jas 1:1). This "worldview" is the polar opposite of that of "the world" (*kosmos*), which originates from the demonic realm. In addition, a powerful internal source is in direct opposition to this godly worldview concerning purity: the tongue, a *kosmos* of iniquity that "stains the whole body" (3:6). Again, the material covered in chapter 5 does not offer any hopeful means for supersessionists to argue for either the abrogation of or a new covenant redefining of the Torah for a presumed "spiritual Israel."

Chapter 6 inquired into the meaning of what is most naturally literally translated from the Greek text as "synagogue" (Greek *synagoge*) in

2:2. Specifically, it was asked why this word has been typically rendered as either "assembly" or "meeting?" As was noted, supersessionist assumptions often play a part. Chapter 6 also focused on the key wording in 5:14: "Call for the elders of the church (Greek *ekklesia*)." Much of this chapter kept the generally assumed *differences* between *synagoge* and *ekklesia* in the spotlight. However, such a perspective did not provide a reasonable answer to how James could apply both terms to the same people. As it turned out, shifting to focus on the similarities between the *synagoge* and *ekklesia* proved a much more productive approach. From that angle, the terms are readily seen to be complementary, not in the least contradictory. Thus, *synagoge* is accurately translated "synagogue" in Jas 2:2 and *ekklesia* is also correctly rendered "church" in 5:14. That means the messianic Jewish believers being addressed in the Letter of James can be referred to as the *ekklesia* ("church") Yeshua said he would build (Matt 16:18), in which there was leadership by "elders," but who gathered congregationally in the Diaspora (Jas 1:1) as "synagogues" (Greek *synagoge*). That exegetical understanding provides a strong basis for calling places of messianic Jewish worship "synagogues."

Chapter 7 dealt with citations from and allusions to the Hebrew Bible in the Letter of James. There are a limited number of actual quotations from the Hebrew Bible in James, but, if anything, that makes each citation that much more significant. The allusions to the Tanak reflect that the mind of James is undoubtedly saturated with the Hebrew scriptures. However, it also seems clear that the Letter of James is equally saturated with the teaching of Messiah Jesus, especially the Sermon on the Mount. Relatedly, it can be safely affirmed that there was no issue covered in this chapter favoring a supersessionist perspective: neither the citations of the Hebrew Bible (including the "paraphrase" from Num 11); nor the agreed upon allusions from the Hebrew Bible; nor the "echoes" of the words of Yeshua in the Letter of James; nor the reasonably clear parallels between James and 1 Peter. There is no evidence that rises to the level of a compelling reason for either a late dating of the Letter of James or otherwise spiritually interpreting its phenomena as applying to the church instead of messianic Jewish believers.

Chapter 8 explored what has been perennially the most controversial passage in the Letter of James: 2:14–26. It was admitted that the relationship between faith and works regarding "justification" as set forth by James initially *appears* to be in direct conflict with Paul's approach to justification in his letters to the Romans, Galatians, and Ephesians.

However, it was seen from a number of different angles throughout chapter 8 that the views of James and Paul on faith, works, and justification actually are *complementary* and not at all conflicting. Because of their different audiences and their different reasons for writing, James and Paul approach the overall issue, and the various smaller issues involved, from different vantage points. For example, James refers to "justification" as having to do with the need to present unmistakable evidence through works to prove the presence of faith. However, the "works" James has in mind are not "works of the law" (which wording James never uses). On the other hand, by "justification," Paul is speaking of what is often called "saving faith," which he develops in strong contrast to the phrase "works of the law" (i.e., deeds in keeping Torah). Both perspectives are vitally important to be understood as complementary and balancing, and both make good sense when considered according to their particular audience and circumstances. And, once again, there is nothing in the findings of this chapter that opens the door to supersessionist thinking.

Implications of the chapter conclusions for current Messianic Jewish faith and practice

If it is correct that the Letter of James is the earliest New Testament book—and it seems quite likely that it is—James is a unique textual base for contemporary Messianic Jews to study and apply in seeking to understand how their New Testament era messianic Jewish counterparts believed and lived. In addition, they will also find considerable insight regarding the dynamics of growth toward spiritual maturity in Yeshua Messiah. Finally, they will find perspective on facing the various spiritual and practical dangers in both their outer and inner (e.g., the tongue) worlds.

All of those aspects are apparent from a careful reading and study of the Letter of James. There is, however, a very important angle related to the letter that can so easily be overlooked: leadership. James wrote from the vantage point of what today would be the "lead pastor" of a megachurch. In his case, it was the original biblical "megachurch." But, his pastoral heart extended much further than his large and challenging congregation in Jerusalem.

James realized that many others who had been members of that original congregation prior to the persecution that broke out after the stoning of Stephen in Acts 7 had fled for their lives and left behind the caring fellowship and responsible teaching and accountability of their leaders, like James. The Letter of James is a direct result—the action he took—because of the compassion of his beating pastor's heart. And, that kind of demonstrated concern/action is the way godly Messianic Jewish and gentile leaders can make a huge difference in the time ahead as they guide their own groups and also reach out to each other in the power of the Holy Spirit, to the glory of God.

Bibliography

Adam, A. K. M. *James: A Handbook on the Greek Text*. Baylor Handbook on the Greek New Testament. Waco, TX: Baylor University Press, 2013.
Adamson, James B. *The Epistle of James*. New International Commentary on the New Testament. Grand Rapids: Eerdmans, 1976.
———. *James: The Man and His Message*. Grand Rapids: Eerdmans, 1989.
Aland, Barbara, Kurt Aland, Johannes Karavidopoulos, Carlo Martini, and Bruce Metzger, eds. *The Greek New Testament*. 5th rev, edited by Stuttgart: Deutsche Bibelgesellschaft, 2014.
Alexander, Desmond, and David W. Baker. *Dictionary of the Old Testament: Pentateuch*. Downers Grove, IL: IVP, 2003.
Alexander, Loveday. "Chronology of Paul." In *The Dictionary of Paul and His Letters*, edited by G. F. Hawthorne, R. P. Martin, and D. G. Reid, 115–23. Downers Grove, IL: IVP, 1993.
Allen, David. *Hebrews*. New American Commentary. Nashville: B & H, 2010.
Allison, Dale C., Jr. "Blessing God and Cursing People: Jas. 3:9–10." *Journal of Biblical Literature* 190 (2011) 197–205.
———. *A Critical and Exegetical Commentary on the Epistle of James*. International Critical Commentary. London: Bloomsbury T&T Clark, 2013.
———. "Eldad and Modad." *Journal for the Study of the Pseudepigrapha* 21.2 (2011) 99–131.
———. "The Fiction of James and Its *Sitz im Leben*." In *The Catholic Epistles: Critical Readings*. T&T Clark Critical Readings in Biblical Studies, edited by Darian Lockett, 39–66. London: T&T Clark, 2021.
Anderson, Kelly, and Daniel Keating. *James, 1, 2, 3 John*. Catholic Commentary on Sacred Scripture. Grand Rapids: Baker, 2017.
Aune, David E. *The New Testament in Its Literary Environment*. Library of Early Christianity. Philadelphia: Westminster, 1987.
Baker, William R. "'Above All Else': Contexts of the Call for Verbal Integrity in James 5.12." *Journal for the Study of the New Testament* 54 (1994) 57–71.
———. "Christology in the Epistle of James." *Evangelical Quarterly* 74 (2002) 47–57.
———. *Personal Speech-Ethics in the Epistle of James*. Tübingen: Mohr-Siebeck, 1995.
———. "Searching for the Holy Spirit in the Epistle of James." *Tyndale Bulletin* 59 (2008) 293–315.
Barton, John, and John Muddiman, eds. *Oxford Bible Commentary*. Oxford: Oxford University Press, 2001.

Bateman, Herbert W. IV. *Interpreting the General Letters: An Exegetical Handbook*. Handbooks for New Testament Exegesis. Grand Rapids: Kregel, 2013.

Batten, A. "God in the Letter of James: Patron or Benefactor?" *New Testament Studies* 50 (2004) 257–272.

Bauckham, Richard. "James and the Gentiles (Acts 15.13–21)." In *History, Literature, and Society in the Book of Acts*, edited by Ben Witherington III. Cambridge: Cambridge University Press, 1996: 154–184.

———. "James and the Jerusalem Church." In *The Book of Acts in Its Palestinian Setting*. The Book of Acts in Its First Century Setting, edited by Richard Bauckham, 415–80. Grand Rapids: Eerdmans, 1995.

———. "James and the Jerusalem Council Decision." In *Introduction to Messianic Judaism: Its Ecclesial Context and Biblical Foundations*, edited by David Rudolph and Joel Willitts, 178–86. Grand Rapids: Zondervan, 2013.

———. "James and Jesus." In *The Brother of Jesus: James the Just and His Mission*, edited by Bruce Chilton and Jacob Neusner, 100–137. Louisville, KY: Westminster John Knox, 2001.

———. "James, 1 and 2 Peter, Jude." In *It is Written: Scripture Citing Scripture: Essays in Honor of Barnabas Lindars*, edited by D. A. Carson and H. G. M. Williamson, 303–17. Cambridge: Cambridge University Press, 1988.

———. *James: Wisdom of James, Disciple of Jesus the Sage*. New Testament Readings. London: Routledge, 1999.

———. "James." In *Eerdmans Commentary on the Bible*, edited by J. D. G. Dunn and John W. Rogerson, 1483–92. Grand Rapids: Eerdmans, 2003.

———. *Jude and the Relatives of Jesus in the Early Church*. Edinburgh: T&T Clark, 2004.

———. "Messianic Jewish Identity in James." In *The Catholic Epistles: Critical Readings*, edited by Darian Lockett, 85–98. T&T Clark Critical Readings in Biblical Studies. London: T&T Clark, 2021.

———. "Peter, James, and the Gentiles." In *The Missions of James, Peter, and Paul: Tensions in Early Christianity*, edited by Bruce Chilton and Craig Evans, 91–142. Novum Testamentum Supplements Series 115. Leiden: Brill, 2005.

———. "The Spirit of God in Us Loathes Envy: James 4:5." In *The Holy Spirit and Christian Origins*, edited by G. N. Stanton, B. W. Longenecker, and S. C. Barton, 270–81. Grand Rapids: Eerdmans, 2004.

———. "The Tongue Set on Fire by Hell (James 3:6)." In *The Fate of the Dead: Studies on the Jewish and Christian Apocalypses*, edited by R. Bauckham, 119–31. Novum Testamentum Supplements 93. Leiden: Brill, 1998.

Bauer, Walter, W .F. Arndt, F. W. Gingrich, and Frederick W. Danker, eds. *A Greek-English Lexicon of the New Testament and Other Early Christian Literature*. Chicago: University of Chicago Press, 1979.

Beale, Gregory K., and D. A. Carson, eds. *Commentary on the New Testament Use of the Old Testament*. Grand Rapids: Baker Academic, 2007.

Becker, Jürgen, ed. *Christian Beginnings: Word and Community from Jesus to Post-Apostolic Times*. Translated by A. S. Kidder and R. Krauss. Louisville, KY: Westminster John Knox, 1993.

Bernheim, Pierre-Antoine. *James, Brother of Jesus*. Translated by J. Bowden. London: SCM, 1997.

Bernier, Jonathan. *Rethinking the Dates of the New Testament: The Evidence for Early Composition*. Grand Rapids: Baker Academic, 2022.

Biblia Hebraica Stuttgartensia. Stuttgart: Deutsche Bibelgesellschaft, 1997.
Bird, Michael F. *Evangelical Theology: A Biblical and Systematic Introduction*. 2nd ed. Grand Rapids: Zondervan, 2020.
Black, David Alan. *Why Four Gospels? The Historical Origins of the Gospels*. Grand Rapids: Kregel, 2001.
Black, David, and David Dockery, eds. *Interpreting the New Testament: Essays on Methods and Issues*. Nashville: B&H, 2001.
Blomberg, Craig L. *Matthew*. New American Commentary. Nashville: B & H, 1992.
———. *Neither Poverty nor Riches: A Biblical Theology of Material Possessions*. New Studies in Biblical Theology. Grand Rapids: Eerdmans, 1999.
Blomberg, Craig L., and Mariam J. Kamell. *James*. Zondervan Exegetical Commentary on the New Testament. Grand Rapids: Zondervan, 2008.
Bockmuehl, Marcus. *Jewish Law in Gentile Churches: Halakhah and the Beginning of Jewish Public Ethics*. Edinburgh: T&T Clark, 2000.
Bowden, A. M. "An Overview of Interpretive Approaches to James 5.13–18." *Currents in Biblical Research* 13 (2014) 67–81.
Boyarin, Daniel. *Border Lines: The Partition of Judaeo-Christianity*. Philadelphia: University of Pennsylvania Press, 2004.
Brand, Chad, Charles Draper, and Archie England, eds. *Holman Illustrated Bible Dictionary*. Nashville: Holman Bible Publishers, 2003.
Brosend, William F. II. *James and Jude*. New Cambridge Bible Commentary. Cambridge: Cambridge University Press, 2004.
Brown, Raymond. *An Introduction to the New Testament*. Anchor Bible Reference Library. New York: Doubleday, 1997.
Bruce, F. F. *I & II Corinthians*. New Century Bible Commentary. Grand Rapids: Eerdmans, 1971.
———. *The Epistle to the Hebrews*. Rev. ed. New International Commentary on the New Testament. Grand Rapids: Eerdmans, 1990.
Burchard, Christoph. *Der Jacobusbrief*. Handbuch zum Neuen Testament. Tübingen: Mohr Siebeck, 2000.
Burdick, Donald. "James." In the *Expositor's Bible Commentary*, edited by F. E. Gaebelein, 12:161–205. Grand Rapids: Zondervan, 1981.
Cadoux, A. T. *The Thought of Saint James*. London: James Clarke, 1944.
Campbell, Keith D. "Lament in James and Its Significance for the Church." *Journal of the Evangelical Theological Society* 60 (2017) 125–38.
Campbell, R. A. *The Elders: Seniority within Earliest Christianity*. Edinburgh: T&T Clark, 1994.
Campbell, William S. "Church as Israel, People of God." *Dictionary of the Later New Testament and Its Developments*, edited by R. P. Martin and Peter Davids, 204–19. Downers Grove, IL: IVP, 1997.
Cantinat, J. *Les Epitres de Saint Jacques et de Saint Jude*. Paris: Gabalda, 1973.
Cargal, T. B. *Restoring the Diaspora: Discursive Structure and Purpose in the Epistle of James*. SBL Dissertation Series. Atlanta: Scholars, 1993.
Carpenter, Craig B. "James 4.5 Reconsidered." *New Testament Studies* 47.2 (2001) 189–205.
Carson, D. A. "1 Peter." In *Commentary on the New Testament Use of the Old Testament*, edited by G. K. Beale and D. A. Carson, 1015–45. Grand Rapids: Baker Academic, 2007.

———. "James." In *Commentary on the New Testament Use of the Old Testament*, edited by G. K. Beale and D. A. Carson, 997–1013. Grand Rapids: Baker Academic, 2007.
Casey, Maurice. *From Jewish Prophet to Gentile God*. Louisville, KY: Westminster/John Knox, 1991.
Chaine, J. *L'Epitre de Saint Jacques*. Paris: Gabalda, 1927.
Charlesworth, James H., ed. *The Old Testament Pseudepigrapha*. 2 vols. Garden City, NY: Doubleday, 1983–85.
Chester, A., and R. P. Martin. *A Theology of the Letters of James, Peter, and Jude*. New Testament Theology. Cambridge: Cambridge University Press, 1994.
Cheung, L. L. *The Genre, Composition and Hermeneutics of James*. Paternoster Biblical Monographs. Carlisle, UK: Paternoster, 2006.
Chilton, Bruce, and Craig Evans, eds. *James the Just and Christian Origins*. Novum Testamentum Supplements 98. Leiden: Brill, 1999.
———. *The Missions of James, Peter, and Paul: Tensions in Early Christianity*. Novum Testamentum Supplements 115. Leiden: Brill, 2005.
Chilton, Bruce, and Jacob Neusner, eds. *The Brother of Jesus: James the Just and His Mission*. Louisville, KY: Westminster John Knox, 2001.
———. *Judaism in the New Testament: Practices and Beliefs*. London: Routledge, 1995.
Chou, Abner. *The Hermeneutics of the Biblical Writers: Learning to Interpret Scripture from the Prophets and Apostles*. Grand Rapids: Kregel, 2018.
Christensen, Duane L. *Deuteronomy 1—21:9*. 2nd ed. Word Biblical Commentary. Grand Rapids: Zondervan, 2001.
Cohen, Shaye J. D. *The Beginnings of Jewishness: Boundaries, Varieties, Uncertainties*. Berkeley: University of California Press, 1999.
Cranfield, C. E. B. "The Message of James." *Scottish Journal of Theology* 18 (1965) 182–93, 338–45.
Daniel-Rops, Henri. *Daily Life in the Time of Jesus*. Translated by P. O'Brian. Ann Arbor, MI: Servant, 1962.
Davids, Peter. *The Epistle of James*. New International Greek Testament Commentary. Grand Rapids: Eerdmans, 1982.
———. "The Epistle of James in Modern Discussion." *Aufsteig und Niedergang der romischen Welt* 2.25.5 (1988) 3621–45.
———. *A Theology of James, Peter and Jude: Living in the Light of the Coming King*. Biblical Theology of the New Testament. Grand Rapids: Zondervan, 2014.
Deppe, Dean B. *The Sayings of Jesus in the Epistle of James*. Chelsea, MI: Bookcrafters, 1989.
———. "The Sayings of Jesus in the Paraenesis of James." Ph.D. dissertation, Free University of Amsterdam, 1990.
Dibelius, Martin. *A Commentary on the Epistle of James*. Hermeneia. Translated by Michael Williams. 11th ed. Philadelphia: Fortress, 1976.
Doriani, Daniel M. *James*. Reformed Expository Commentary. Phillipsburg: P&R, 2007.
Douglas, J. D., ed. *New International Dictionary of the Christian Church*. Grand Rapids: Zondervan, 1974.
Dunn, James D. G., ed. *Jews and Christians: The Parting of the Ways A.D. 70 to 135*. Grand Rapids: Eerdmans, 1999.
———. *The Parting of the Ways between Christianity and Judaism and Their Significance for the Character of Christianity*. London: SCM, 1991.

Dunn, James D. G., and John Rogerson, eds. *Eerdmans Commentary on the Bible.* Grand Rapids: Eerdmans, 2003.

Duvall, Scott, and Daniel Hays. *Grasping God's Word: A Hands-on Approach to Reading, Interpreting, and Applying the Bible.* 4th ed. Grand Rapids: Zondervan, 2020.

Dyrness, William. "Mercy Triumphs over Justice: James 2:13 and the Theology of Faith and Works." *Themelios* 6 (1981) 11–16.

Edgar, D. H. *Has God Not Chosen the Poor? The Social Setting of the Epistle of James.* Journal for the Study of the New Testament Supplement Series 206. Sheffield, UK: Sheffield Academic, 2001.

Elkins, Kathleen Gallagher, and Thomas Bolin. "Boundaries, Intersections, and the Parting of the Ways in the Letter of James." *Interpretation* 74.4 (2020) 335–43.

Elliott, J. H. "The Epistle of James in Rhetorical and Social Science Perspective: Holiness-Wholeness and Patterns of Replication." *Biblical Theology Bulletin* 23 (1993) 71–81.

Erickson, Millard J. *Introducing Christian Doctrine.* 2nd ed. Edited by Arnold Hustad. Grand Rapids: Baker Academic, 2001.

Evans, Craig. "Christianity and Judaism: Parting of the Ways." *Dictionary of the Later New Testament and Its Developments,* edited by R. P. Martin and Peter Davids, 159–70. Downers Grove, IL: IVP, 1997.

———. "Comparing Judaisms: Qumranic, Rabbinic, and Jacobean Judaisms Compared." In *The Brother of Jesus: James the Just and His Mission,* edited by Bruce Chilton and Jacob Neusner, 161–83. Louisville, KY: Westminster John Knox, 2001.

———. "Jesus and James: Martyrs of the Temple." In *James the Just,* edited by Bruce Chilton and Craig Evans, 233–49. Louisville, KY: Westminster John Knox, 2001.

Fiorello, Michael D. "The Ethical Implications of Holiness in James 2." *Journal of the Evangelical Theological Society* 55.3 (2012) 557–72.

Forrest, Benjamin, and Chet Roden, eds. *Biblical Leadership: Theology for the Everyday Leader.* Grand Rapids: Kregel Academic, 2017.

Foster, Robert J. *The Significance of Examplars for the Interpretation of the Letter of James.* Wissenschaftliche Untersuchungen zum Neuen Testament series. Tübingen: Mohr-Siebeck, 2014.

France, R. T. *The Gospel According to Matthew.* Tyndale New Testament Commentaries. Grand Rapids: Eerdmans, 1985.

Francis, Fred O. "The Form and Function of the Opening and Closing Paragraphs of James and 1 John." *Zeitschrift fur Neutestamentliche Wissenschaft* 61 (1970) 110–26.

Frankenmolle, H. *Der Brief des Jacobus.* Gütershoh: Güterloher, 1994.

Fredriksen, Paula. "*Secundem Carnem*: History and Israel in the Theology of St. Augustine." In *Augustine and World Religions,* edited by Brian Brown, John Doody, and Kim Pappenroth, 31–52. Lanham, MD: Lexington, 2008.

Freedman, David Noel, ed. *Anchor Bible Dictionary.* 6 vols. New York: Doubleday, 1992.

Gaebelein, Frank E., ed. *Expositor's Bible Commentary.* 12 vols. Grand Rapids: Zondervan, 1976–92.

Glaser, Mitch. "The Dangers of Supersessionism." In *Israel, the Church, and the Middle East,* edited by D. Bock and M. Glaser, 101–18. Grand Rapids: Kregel, 2018.

Gordon, R. P. "*kai to telos kuriou eidete* (Jas. 5.11)." *Journal of Theological Studies* 26 (1975) 91–95.

Grudem, Wayne. *1 Peter*. Tyndale New Testament Commentaries. Grand Rapids: Eerdmans, 1988.
Gunter, J. J. "The Family of Jesus." *Evangelical Quarterly* 46 (1974) 25–41.
Guthrie, George H. "James." In *The Expositor's Bible Commentary*, edited by Tremper Longman III and David E. Garland, 13:197–273. Rev. ed. Grand Rapids: Zondervan, 2006.
Hanson, K. C., and Douglas E. Oakman. *Palestine in the Time of Jesus: Social Structures and Social Conflicts*. Minneapolis: Fortress, 1998.
Harland, Philip A. *Associations, Synagogues, Congregations: Claiming a Place in Ancient Mediterranean Society*. Minneapolis: Fortress, 2003.
Harris, Murray J. *Slave of Christ: A New Testament Metaphor for Total Devotion to Christ*. New Studies in Biblical Theology. Downers Grove, IL: IVP, 1999.
Hart, Larry D. *Truth Aflame: Theology for the Church in Renewal*. Rev. ed. Grand Rapids: Zondervan, 2005.
Hartin, Patrick J. *James*. Sacra Pagina 14. Collegeville, MN: Liturgical, 2003.
———. *James and the Q Sayings of Jesus*. Sheffield, UK: JSOT Press, 1991.
———. *James of Jerusalem: Heir to Jesus of Nazareth*. Interfaces. Collegeville, MN: Liturgical, 2004.
Hartley, John. "Holy and Holiness, Clean and Unclean." *Dictionary of the Old Testament: Pentateuch*, edited by Desmond Alexander and David Baker, 420–31. Downers Grove, IL: IVP, 2003.
Hawthorne, Gerald F., Ralph P. Martin, and Daniel Reid, eds. *Dictionary of Paul and His Letters*. Downers Grove, IL: IVP, 1993.
Hayden, D. R. "Calling the Elders to Pray." *Bibliotheca Sacra* 138 (1981) 258–86.
Heide, G. Z. "The Soteriology of James 2:14." *Grace Theological Journal* 12 (1982) 69–97.
Hengel, Martin. "Der Jacobusbrief als antipaulinsche Polemik." In *Tradition and Interpretation in the New Testament*, edited by Gerald F. Hawthorne and Otto Betz, 248–78. Grand Rapids: Eerdmans, 1987.
———. *Judaism and Hellenism*. 2 vols. Philadelphia: Fortress, 1974.
Hennecke, Edgar, ed. *New Testament Apocrypha*. Vol. 1. Translated by R. McLaren Wilson. Philadelphia: Westminster, 1963.
Hiebert, D. Edmond. *The Epistle of James: Tests of a Living Faith*. Chicago: Moody, 1979.
Hodges, Zane C. *Dead Faith: What Is It?* Dallas: Redencion Viva, 1987.
Holmes, Michael W., ed. and transl. *The Apostolic Fathers: Greek Texts and English Translations*. 3rd ed. Grand Rapids: Baker, 2007.
Hort, F. J. A. *The Epistle of St. James: The Greek Text with Introduction, Commentary as Far as Chapter IV, Verse Seven, and Additional Notes*. London: Macmillan, 1909.
Instone-Brewer, David. "James as a Sermon on the Trials of Abraham." In *The New Testament in Its First Century Setting: Essays on Context and Background in Honor of B. W. Winter on His 65th Birthday*, edited by P. J. Williams, A. D. Clarke, P. M. Head, and D. Instone-Brewer, 250–68. Grand Rapids: Eerdmans, 2004.
Isaacs, Marie E. *Reading Hebrews and James: A Literary and Theological Commentary*. Macon, GA: Smyth and Helwys, 2002.
Jackson-McCabe, M. A. *Logos and Law in the Letter of James: The Law of Nature, the Law of Moses, and the Law of Freedom*. Leiden: Brill, 2001.
Jobes, Karen H. *Letters to the Church: A Survey of Hebrews and the General Epistles*. Grand Rapids: Zondervan, 2011.

Johnson, Luke Timothy. *Brother of Jesus, Friend of God: Studies in the Letter of James.* Grand Rapids: Eerdmans, 2004.

———. "James 3:13—4:10 and the Topos PERI PHTHNOS." *Novum Testamentum* 25 (1983) 327–47.

———. *The Letter of James: A New Translation with Introduction and Commentary.* Anchor Bible. New York: Doubleday, 1995.

———. "The Mirror of Remembrance (James 1:22–25)." *Catholic Biblical Quarterly* 50 (1988) 632–45.

———. "The Use of Leviticus 19 in the Letter of James." *Journal of Biblical Literature* 101 (1982) 391–401.

Johnston, J. W. "James 4:5 and the Jealous Spirit." *Bibliotheca Sacra* 170 (2013) 344–60.

Juel, Donald. *Messianic Exegesis: Christological Interpretation of the Old Testament in Early Christianity.* Library of Early Christology. Waco, TX: Baylor University Press, 2017.

Kaiser, Walter, and Moises Silva. *An Introduction to Biblical Hermeneutics: The Search for Meaning.* Grand Rapids: Zondervan, 1994.

Kamell, Mariam. "The Nature of Eternal Security in James: Divine Grace Pairs with the Imitatio Dei." *Testamentum Imperium* 2 (2009) 1–28.

Keener, Craig S. *The IVP Bible Background Commentary: New Testament.* 2nd ed. Downers Grove, IL: IVP Academic, 2014.

———. *Matthew.* IVP New Testament Commentary. Downers Grove, IL: IVP, 1997.

———. *Miracles: The Credibility of the New Testament Accounts.* Grand Rapids: Baker, 2011.

———. *Revelation.* NIV Application Commentary. Grand Rapids: Zondervan, 2000.

Klein, William, Craig Blomberg, and Robert Hubbard. *Introduction to Biblical Interpretation.* Rev. ed. Nashville: Thomas Nelson, 2004.

Konradt, Matthias. *Christliche Existenz nach dem Jakobusbrief. Eine Studie zu seiner Soteriologischen und ethischen Konzeption.* Göttingen: Vanderhoeck and Ruprect, 1998.

———. *Israel, Church, and the Gentiles in the Gospel of Matthew.* Translated by Kathleen Ess. Studies in Early Christianity. Waco, TX: Baylor University Press, 2014.

Korner, Ralph. *The Origin and Meaning of* Ekklesia *in the Early Jesus Movement.* Ancient Judaism and Early Christianity. Leiden: Brill, 2017.

Kummel, W. G. *Introduction to the New Testament.* Rev. ed. Nashville: Abingdon, 1975.

Kirk, J. A. "The Meaning of Wisdom in James: Examination of a Hypothesis." *New Testament Studies* 16 (1969–70) 24–38.

Kistemaker, Simon J. *Exposition of the Epistle of James and the Epistles of John.* New Testament Commentary. Grand Rapids: Baker, 1986.

Kovalishyn, Mariam Kammel. "The Prayer of Elijah in James 5: An Example of Intertextuality." *Journal of Biblical Literature* 137 (2018) 1027–45.

Kuhatschek, Jack. *Applying the Bible.* Grand Rapids: Zondervan, 1990.

Kümmel, W. G. *Introduction to the New Testament.* Rev, ed. Nashville: Abingdon, 1975.

Laato, T. "Justification according to James: A Comparison with Paul." *Trinity Journal* 18 (1997) 43–84.

Lappenga, B. "James 3:13—4:10 and the Language of Envy in Proverbs 3." *Journal of Biblical Literature* 136 (2017) 989–1006.

Laws, Sophie. *A Commentary on the Epistle of James.* Harper's New Testament Commentaries. Peabody, MA: Hendrickson, 1980.

———. "Does Scripture Speak in Vain? A Reconsideration of James IV.5." *New Testament Studies* 30 (1974) 10–15.

Lockett, Darian, ed. *The Catholic Epistles: Critical Readings*. T&T Clark Critical Readings in Biblical Studies. London: T&T Clark, 2021.

———. *An Introduction to the Catholic Epistles*. Approaches to Biblical Studies. London: T&T Clark, 2012.

———. *Letters from the Pillar Apostles: The Formation of the Catholic Epistles in a Canonical Collection*. Eugene, OR: Pickwick, 2016.

———. *Purity and Worldview in the Epistle of James*. Library of New Testament Studies. Edinburgh: T&T Clark, 2008.

———. "Salvation in James: Gift and Responsibility." Unpublished paper, 2011.

———. "Wholeness in Intertextual Perspective: James's Use of Scripture in Developing a Theme." *Midwestern Journal of Theology* 15 (2016) 92–106.

Lodge, J. C. "James and Paul at Cross-Purposes." *Biblica* 62 (1981) 195–213.

Longenecker, Richard. "Acts." In *The Expositor's Bible Commentary*, Vol. 9. Grand Rapids: Zondervan, 1981.

———. *The Christology of Early Jewish Christianity*. London: SCM Press, 1970.

———. "The 'Faith of Abraham' Theme in Paul, James, and Hebrews: A Study in the Circumstantial Nature of New Testament Teaching." *Journal of the Evangelical Theological Society* 20 (1977) 203–12.

Luter, A. Boyd. "The Fulfillment of Israel's Land Promise and Hebrews: 'Transformed' or 'On Hold'?" *Kesher* 34 (2019) 37–48.

———. *God's Land Promise to Israel: Its Continuation from Genesis to Revelation*. Southlake, TX: TKU Press, 2021.

———. "'The Holy Catholic Church': A Test Case for the Theological Interpretation of Scripture." *Criswell Theological Review* NS (2017) 79–88.

———. *Song of Songs*. Evangelical Exegetical Commentary. Bellingham, WA: Logos Software, 2013. (This commentary, which was initially published digitally, will be releaed in hardcover later this year as A. Boyd Luter, *Song of Songs*. Evangelical Exegetical Commentary. Bellingham, WA: Lexham Press.)

———. "Revelation Introduction and Notes." In the *Christian Standard Bible Study Bible*, edited by Edwin Blum and Trevin Wax, 2016–47. Nashville: Holman Bible Publishers, 2017.

Luter, A. Boyd, and Barry C. Davis. *Ruth and Esther: God behind the Seen*. 2nd ed. Focus on the Bible series. Fearn, UK: Christian Focus, 2003.

Luter, A. Boyd, and Michelle V. Lee. "Philippians as Chiasmus: Key to the Unity, Structure and Theme." *New Testament Studies* 41 (1995) 89–101.

MacArthur, John F., Jr. "Faith According to the Apostle James." *Journal of the Evangelical Theological Society* 33 (1990) 13–34.

Maier, Paul L. "Chronology." In *The Dictionary of the Later New Testament and Its Developments*, edited by R. P. Martin and P. H. Davids, 184–94. Downers Grove, IL: IVP, 1997.

———. *Eusebius: The Church History*. Grand Rapids: Kregel, 1999.

Marcus, Joel. "The Evil Inclination in the Epistle of James." *Catholic Biblical Quarterly* 44 (1982) 607–21.

———. "'The Twelve Tribes in the Diaspora' (James 1.1)" *New Testament Studies* 60 (2014) 433–47.

Martin, Ralph P. *James*. Word Biblical Commentary 48. Waco, TX: Word, 1988.

Maynard-Reid, Pedrito. *Poverty and Wealth in James*. Maryknoll, NY: Orbis, 1987.
Mayor, Joseph B. *The Epistle of St. James*. 2nd ed. London: Macmillan, 1913.
McCartney, Dan G. *James*. Baker Exegetical Commentary on the New Testament. Grand Rapids: Baker Academic, 2009.
McConville, J. G. *Deuteronomy*. Apollos OT Commentaries. Leicester, UK: Apollos, 2002.
McDermott, Gerald. *Israel Matters: Why Christians Must Think Differently about the People and the Land*. Grand Rapids: Brazos, 2017.
———. "Getting the Big Picture Wrong." In *The New Christian Zionism: Fresh Perspective on Israel and the Land*, edited by G. McDermott, 33–44. Downers Grove, IL: IVP Academic, 2016.
McKnight, Scot. *Galatians*. NIV Application Commentary. Grand Rapids: Zondervan, 1995.
———. "James 2:18a: The Unidentifiable Interlocutor." *Westminster Theological Journal* 52 (1990) 355–464.
———. *The Jesus Creed: Loving God, Loving Others*. Brewster, MA: Paraclete, 2004.
———. *The Letter of James*. New International Commentary on the New Testament. Grand Rapids: Eerdmans, 2011.
———. "A Parting within the Way: Jesus and James on Israel and Purity." In *James the Just*, edited by Bruce Chilton and Craig Evans, 83–129. Louisville, KY: Westminster John Knox, 2001.
Metzger, Bruce, ed. *New Revised Standard Version*. 1989. Reprint, Grand Rapids: Zondervan, 2007.
Michaels, J. Ramsey. *Revelation*. IVP New Testament Commentary. Downers Grove, IL: IVP, 1997.
Mitton, C. Leslie. *The Epistle of James*. Grand Rapids: Eerdmans, 1966.
Montefiore, Hugh. "Thou Shalt Love Thy Neighbor as Thyself." *Novum Testamentum* 5 (1962) 157–70.
Moo, Douglas J. "Genesis 15:6 in the New Testament." In *From Creation to New Creation: Biblical Theology and Exegesis; Essays in Honor of G. K. Beale*, edited by D. M. Gurtner and B. L. Gladd, 147–62. Peabody, MA: Hendrickson, 2013.
———. "Jesus and the Authority of the Mosaic Law." *Journal for the Study of the New Testament* 20 (1984) 3–49.
———. "The Law of Christ as the Fulfilment of the Law of Moses: A Modified Lutheran View." In *Five Views on Law and Gospel*, edited by Wayne G. Strickland, 319–76. Grand Rapids: Zondervan, 1996.
———. *The Letter of James*. 2nd ed. Pillar New Testament Commentaries. Grand Rapids: Eerdmans, 2021.
———. *The Letter of James*. Tyndale New Testament Commentaries. Grand Rapids: Eerdmans, 1985.
———. *The Letter of James*. Rev. ed. Tyndale New Testament Commentaries. Grand Rapids: Eerdmans, 2015.
———. *The Letter of James*. Pillar New Testament Commentaries. Grand Rapids: Eerdmans, 2000.
Moore, Carey. "Judith, Book of." In *Anchor Bible Dictionary*, edited by David Noel Freedman, 3:1117–25. New York: Doubleday, 1992.

Morales, N. R. *Poor and Rich in James: A Relevance Theory Approach to James's Use of the Old Testament*. Bulletin for Biblical Research Supplements 20. Winona Lake, IN: Eisenbrauns, 2018.

Morgan, Christopher W. *A Theology of James: Wisdom for God's People*. Phillipsburg, PA: P&R, 2010.

Mussner, Franz. *Der Jacobusbrief*. 5th ed. Freiberg: Heider, 1987.

Ng, E. Y. L. "Father-God Language and Old Testament Allusions in James." *Tyndale Bulletin* 54 (2003) 41–54.

Niebuhr, Karl-Wilhelm. "The Epistle of James in Light of Early Jewish Diaspora Letters." In *The Catholic Epistles: Critical Readings*, edited by Darian Lockett, 67–84. London: T&T Clark, 2021.

Nystrom, David. *James*. NIV Application Commentary. Grand Rapids: Zondervan, 1997.

O'Brien, Peter. "Church." In *Dictionary of Paul and His Letters*, edited by Gerald Hawthorne, Ralph Martin and Daniel Reed, 123–31. Downers Grove, IL: IVP, 1993.

Olson, Roger E. *The Mosaic of Christian Belief: Twenty Centuries of Unity and Diversity*. 2nd ed. Downers Grove, IL: IVP, 2016.

Painter, John. "James as the First of the Catholic Epistles." *Interpretation* 60 (2006) 245–59.

———. "James and Peter: Models of Leadership and Mission." In *The Missions of James, Peter, and Paul*, edited by Bruce Chilton and Craig Evans, 143–209. Leiden: Brill, 2005.

———. "Who Was James? Footprints as a Means of Identification." In *The Brother of Jesus: James the Just and His Mission*, edited by Bruce Chilton and Jacob Neusner, 10–65. Louisville, KY: Westminster John Knox, 2001.

Painter, John, and David DeSilva. *James and Jude*. Paideia Commentaries on the New Testament. Grand Rapids: Baker Academic, 2012.

Pao, David. *Colossians & Philemon*. Zondervan Exegetical Commentary on the New Testament. Grand Rapids: Zondervan, 2012.

Penner, T. C. *The Epistle of James and Eschatology: Re-reading an Ancient Christian Letter*. Sheffield, UK: Sheffield Academic, 1996.

Penner, T. C., and Robert W. Wall. "James as Apocalyptic Paraenesis." *Restoration Quarterly* 32 (1990) 11–22.

Perdue, Leo G. "Paraenesis and the Epistle of James." *Zeitschrift für die neutestamentliche Wissenschaft* 72 (1981) 241–56.

Perkins, Pheme. *First and Second Peter, James and Jude*. Interpretation. Louisville, KY: John Knox, 1995.

Pickar, C. "Is Anyone Sick among You?" *Catholic Biblical Quarterly* 7 (1945) 165–74.

Poirier, J. C. "Symbols of Wisdom in James 1:17." *Journal of Theological Studies* 57 (2006) 57–75.

Polhill, John. *Acts*. New American Commentary. Nashville: Broadman, 1992.

Plummer, Alfred. *The General Epistles of St. James and Sr. Jude*. The Expositor's Bible. London: Hodder and Stoughton, 1889.

Porter, Stanley E. "Is *dipsuchos* (James 1, 8; 4, 8) a 'Christian' Word?" *Biblica* 71 (1990) 469–98.

Rahlfs, Alfred. *Septuaginta*. Edited by R. Hanhart. Stuttgart: Deutsche Bibelgesellschaft, 2006.

Rakestraw, Robert T. "James 2:14–26: Does James Contradict the Pauline Soteriology?" *Criswell Theological Review* 1 (1986) 31–50.
Reicke. Bo. *The Epistles of James, Peter, and Jude.* Anchor Bible 37. Garden City, NY: Doubleday, 1964.
Reisner, Rainer. "James." In the *Oxford Bible Commentary*, edited by John Barton and John Muddiman, 1255–62. Oxford: Oxford University Press, 2001.
———. *Paul's Early Period: Chronology, Mission Strategy, Theology.* Grand Rapids: Eerdmans, 1998.
Rendall, George H. *The Epistle of St. James and Judaistic Christianity.* Cambridge: Cambridge University Press, 1927.
Richardson, Peter. *Israel in the Apostolic Church.* Society of New Testament Studies Monograph Series. Cambridge: Cambridge University Press, 1969.
Robbins, Vernon K. "Making Christian Culture in the Epistle of James." *Scriptura* 59 (1996) 341–51.
Robinson, John A. T. *Redating the New Testament.* London: SCM, 1976.
Robinson, Richard, ed. *God, Torah, Messiah: The Messianic Jewish Theology of Dr. Louis Goldberg.* San Francisco: Purple Pomegranate, 2009.
Rogers, Cleon Jr., and Cleon Rogers III. *The New Linguistic and Exegetical Key to the Greek New Testament.* Grand Rapids: Zondervan, 1998.
Robertson, A. T. *Studies in the Epistle of James.* New York: Doran, 1915.
Ropes, James H. *A Critical and Exegetical Commentary on the Epistle of St. James.* International Critical Commentary. Edinburgh: T&T Clark, 1916.
Ross, Allen. *Holiness to the Lord: A Guide to the Exposition of the Book of Leviticus.* Grand Rapids: Baker Academic, 2002.
Ross, Alexander. *The Epistles of James and John.* New International Commentary on the New Testament. Grand Rapids: Eerdmans, 1954.
Rudolph, David, and Joel Willitts, eds. *Introduction to Messianic Judaism: Its Ecclesial Context and Biblical Foundations.* Grand Rapids: Zondervan, 2013.
Sanders, E. P. *Paul and Palestinian Judaism: A Comparison of Patterns of Religion.* Philadelphia: Fortress, 1977.
Sandt, H. van de. "James 4,1–4 in the Light of the Jewish Two Ways Tradition 3,1–6." *Biblica* 88 (2007) 38–63.
Schlatter, Adolf. *Der Brief des Jacobus.* Stuttgart: Calwer, 1956.
Schmitt, John J. "You Adulteresses: The Image in James 4:4." *Novum Testamentum* 28 (1986) 327–37.
Schnabel, Eckhard. *Early Christian Mission.* Vol. 2. *Paul and the Early Church.* Downers Grove, IL: IVP, 2004.
Shogren, Gary. "Will God Heal Us? A Re-examination of James 5:14–16a." *Evangelical Quarterly* 61 (1989) 99–108.
Sidebottom, E. M. *James, Jude, 2 Peter.* New Century Bible Commentary. Grand Rapids: Eerdmans, 1967.
Skarsaune, Oskar. *In the Shadow of the Temple: Jewish Influences on Early Christianity.* Downers Grove, IL: IVP, 2002.
Skarsaune, Oskar, and Reidar Jvalvik, eds. *Jewish Believers in Jesus: The Early Centuries.* Peabody, MA: Hendrickson, 2007.
Sleeper, C. Freeman. *James.* Abingdon New Testament Commentary. Nashville: Abingdon, 1998.

Spencer, Aida Besancon. *A Commentary on James*. Kregel Exegetical Library. Grand Rapids: Kregel, 2020.

Stewart, Alexander. "James, Soteriology, and Synergism." *Tyndale Bulletin* 61 (2010) 293–310.

Stibbs, Alan M. *The First Epistle General of Peter*. Tyndale New Testament Commentaries. Grand Rapids: Eerdmans, 1959.

Tamez, Elsa. *The Scandalous Message of James: Faith without Works is Dead*. Rev. ed. New York: Crossroad, 2002.

Tasker, R. V. G. *The General Epistle of James*. Tyndale New Testament Commentaries. Grand Rapids: Eerdmans, 1957.

Taylor, Mark E. "Recent Scholarship on the Structure of James." *Currents in Biblical Research* 3 (2004) 86–115.

———. *A Text-Linguistic Investigation into the Discourse Structure of James*. Library of New Testament Studies. London: T&T Clark, 2006.

Taylor, Mark E., and George H. Guthrie. "The Structure of James." *Catholic Biblical Quarterly* 68 (2006) 681–705.

Thuren, Lauri. "Risky Rhetoric in James?" *Novum Testamentum* 37 (1995) 262–84.

Townsend, Michael J. *The Epistle of James*. Epworth Commentaries. London: Epworth, 1994.

———. "James 4:1–4: A Warning against Zealotry?" *Expository Times* 87 (1976) 211–13.

Trafton, Joseph. "Solomon, Psalms of." In *Anchor Bible Dictionary*, edited by David Noel Freedman, 6:115–17. New York: Doubleday, 1992.

Tucker, J. Brian. *Reading Romans after Supersessionism: The Continuation of Jewish Covenantal Identity*. New Testament after Supersessionism series. Eugene, OR: Cascade, 2018.

Tucker, J. Brian, and Coleman A. Baker, eds. *T&T Clark Handbook to Social Identity in the New Testament*. London: Bloomsbury, 2014.

Verseput, Donald J. "Genre and Story: The Community Setting of the Epistle of James." *Catholic Biblical Quarterly* 62 (2000) 96–110.

———. "Reworking the Puzzle of Faith and Deeds in James 2.14–26." *New Testament Studies* 43 (1997) 97–115.

———. "Wisdom, 4Q185, and the Epistle of James." *Journal of Biblical Literature* 117 (1998) 691–707.

Vik, Peter J. "Letting the Objector Have His Say (James 2:18–19)." Unpublished paper presented to the Evangelical Theological Society: Southwest Region, 2009.

Virkler, Henry. *Hermeneutics: Principles and Processes of Biblical Interpretation*. Grand Rapids: Baker, 1981.

Vlachos, Chris A. *James*. B&H Exegetical Guides to the Greek New Testament. Nashville: B & H Academic, 2013.

Vouga, Francois. *L'Epitre de S. Jacques*. Commentaire du Nouveau Testament. Geneva: Labor et Fides, 1984.

Wachob, Wesley H. *The Voice of Jesus in the Social Rhetoric of James*. Society of New Testament Studies Monograph Series 106. Cambridge: Cambridge University Press, 2000.

Wall, Robert W. *Community of the Wise: The Letter of James*. The New Testament in Context. London: Bloomsbury Academic, 1997.

———. "James, Letter of." In *Dictionary of the Later New Testament and Its Developments*, edited by Ralph P. Martin and Peter H. Davids, 545–61. Downers Grove, IL: IVP, 1997.

Wallace, Daniel. *Greek Grammar Beyond the Basics: An Exegetical Syntax of the New Testament*. Grand Rapids: Zondervan, 1996.

Ward, Roy B. "Partiality in the Assembly: James 2:2–4." *Harvard Theological Review* 62 (1969) 87–97.

———. "The Works of Abraham: James 2:14–26." *Harvard Theological Review* 61 (1968) 283–90.

Warrington, K. "James 5:14–18: Healing Then and Now." *International Review of Missions* 93 (2004) 346–67.

Watson, Duane F. "The Rhetoric of James 3:1–12 and a Classical Pattern of Argumentation." *Novum Testamentum* 35 (1993) 48–64.

Wells, C. Richard, and A. Boyd Luter. *Inspired Preaching: A Survey of Preaching Found in the New Testament*. Nashville: B&H, 2002.

Wenham, John. *Redating Matthew, Mark & Luke: A Fresh Assault on the Synoptic Problem*. Downers Grov, ILe: IVP, 1992.

———. "The Relatives of Jesus." *Evangelical Quarterly* 47 (1975) 6–15.

Whiston, William, transl. *The Works of Josephus*. Peabody, MA: Hendrickson, 1987.

Whitlark, J. A. "*Emphutos logos*: A New Covenant Motif in the Letter of James." *Horizons in Biblical Theology* 32 (2010) 144–65.

Wilder, Terry. "Pseudonymity and the New Testament." In *Interpreting the New Testament: Essays on Methods and Issues*, edited by D. A. Black and D. S. Dockery, 296–335. Nashville: B&H, 2001.

Witherington, Ben III. *Letters and Homilies for Jewish Christians: A Socio-Rhetorical Commentary on Hebrews, James, and Jude*. Downers Grove, IL: IVP Academic, 2007.

Wood, A. Skevington. "Ephesians." In the *Expositor's Bible Commentary*, edited by Frank E. Gaebelein, 11:3–92. Grand Rapids: Zondervan, 1978.

Yamauchi, Edwin. "Synagogue." In *Dictionary of Jesus and the Gospels* edited by Joel Green, Scot McKnight and I. H. Marshall, 781–84. Downers Grove, IL: IVP, 1992.

Author Index

Alexander, Loveday, 115n32, 118n45
Allen, David, 112n24
Allison, Dale C., Jr., 1nn1–2, 8, 8nn2–3, 18n48, 19n49, 64, 64n13, 66, 66n22, 67n24, 74–75, 75n44, 76, 76nn50–51, 77n52, 82–84, 82n1, 83n2, 89, 89n23, 90n25, 91, 91n30, 94, 94n37, 94n39, 95, 95n42, 100n56, 131, 131n24, 131n28, 132n33, 135n36, 138n44, 139nn46–50, 140, 143, 143n55, 145n1, 147, 147nn5–6

Bauckham, Richard, 8, 8nn3–5, 19, 19n50, 40n3, 99, 131, 131nn29–30
Bernier, Jonathan, 43n11, 115n33, 118, 118nn40–144, 119n47, 125n4, 139n45, 143, 143n54, 143n57, 151n22
Black, David Alan, 119n47
Blomberg, Craig L., 9, 9n9, 46n26, 47nn27–29, 57, 57n59, 58, 58n63, 84, 84nn4–6, 84n8, 88n14, 97n47, 99, 99n53, 131n26
Bolin, Thomas, 121, 121nn51–52, 122n53
Braund, David, 12n26
Brown, Raymond, 1–2, 1n3, 2nn4–8
Bruce, F. F., 78nn55–56, 112n24
Burdick, Donald, 20n54, 89, 90n24

Campbell, William S., 116n35
Carson, D. A., 42–43, 42nn8–9, 44, 44nn17–18, 125–26, 125n6, 126n7, 127n11, 128nn15–16
Casey, Maurice, 92nn31–32, 93
Chou, Abner, 138n42
Church, Christopher, 96n43

Davids, Peter, 56, 56n58, 88, 88n16, 130n20, 138n44, 143, 143n56
Davis, Barry C., 21n61
Deppe, Dean B., 138n44
Dibelius, Martin, 20n53
Dunn, James D. G., 116–17, 116n36
Duvall, Scott, 84n3

Elkins, Kathleen Gallagher, 121, 121nn51–52, 122n53
Evans, Craig, 116, 117n37

Forrest, Benjamin, 14n36
France, R. T., 49, 49n39
Francis, Fred O., 88, 88n17
Fredriksen, Paula, 46n23

Grudem, Wayne, 41–42, 42n7
Guthrie, George H., 21, 21n59, 22

Hartin, Patrick J., 138n44
Hartley, John, 92n33
Hays, Daniel, 84n3
Hubbard, Robert, 46n26, 47nn27–29, 84, 84nn4–6, 84n8

Johnson, Luke Timothy, 2n5, 8–9, 8n7,
    9n8, 10n18, 13n33, 19n49, 63,
    63n5, 64, 64nn14–15, 72–73,
    72n36, 73nn38–39, 89, 89n22,
    130n18, 131, 131nn26–27,
    136n37, 137–38, 137nn38–39,
    138n40, 142n53

Kaiser, Walter, 47, 47n31, 48n32, 50,
    50n40
Kamell, Mariam J., 9, 9n9, 57, 57n59,
    58, 58n63, 88n14, 97n47, 99,
    99n53, 131n26
Keener, Craig S., 45, 45n19, 53n54,
    108n16
Klein, William, 46n26, 47nn27–29, 84,
    84nn4–6, 84n8
Konradt, Matthias, 119n49
Korner, Ralph, 103, 103nn6–7
Kuhatschek, Jack, 86n11
Kümmel, W. G., 18n48

Lampe, G. W. H., 49
Lee, M., 21n61
Lockett, Darian, 93–94, 93nn35–36, 95,
    100, 101, 101n61
Luter, A. Boyd, 21n61, 45, 45n20, 47n30,
    48, 48nn33–34, 50n42, 50n44
Luther, Martin, 145

Maier, Paul L., 118n45
Marshall, I. Howard, 2n9
Mayor, Joseph B., 138n44, 143
McCartney, Dan G., 9, 9n10
McDermott, Gerald, 4n14, 46n22
McKnight, Scot, 9, 9n11, 15, 15n41, 20,
    20nn56–57, 21n60, 63, 63n7,
    64, 64nn8–9, 64nn11–12, 65–
    66, 65n18, 67–68, 67n26, 75,
    75n45, 88n14, 90, 90n26, 95,
    95nn40–41, 117, 117nn38–39,
    130n19, 131nn25–26
Michaels, J. Ramsey, 108, 108n17
Moo, Douglas J., 9, 9n13, 17, 17n45,
    17n47, 64–65, 65nn16–17, 66,
    66n19, 68n29, 80nn59–60,
    88nn13–14, 88n19, 97n46,
    101n59, 130n21, 131n26,
    145nn2–3
Moore, Carey, 135n35

Niebuhr, Karl-Wilhelm, 19, 20, 20n51
Nystrom, David, 52–54, 52nn49–50

O'Brien, Peter, 104, 104n9, 109n19,
    111, 111n21

Pao, David, 89n21
Polhill, John, 114, 114n31

Reisner, Rainer, 8n6, 12n25, 14–15,
    15nn37–38, 17n46
Richardson, Peter, 50, 50n41
Robinson, John A. T., 118
Roden, Chet, 14n36
Rogers, Cleon III., 111n23
Rogers, Cleon Jr., 111n23
Ross, Allen, 92, 93n34, 94n38

Schmitt, John J., 101n60
Silva, M., 47n31, 50, 50n40
Spencer, Aida Besancon, 9, 9n12, 12,
    12nn27–28, 13n29, 13n33, 57,
    57n61, 58, 58n62, 58n64, 88,
    88n15, 107, 107n13, 131n26
Stabnow, David, 96n43
Stibbs, Alan M., 41, 41n6

Tasker, R. V. G., 51–52, 51nn45–46
Taylor, Mark E., 20n55, 21, 21n59, 22
Tucker, J. Brian, 43n11

Virkler, Henry, 84n7

Wall, Robert W., 54–56, 54n55,
    55nn56–57, 63, 63n4
Wells, C. Richard, 21n61
Wenham, John, 119n47
Wilder, Terry, 2n9

Yamauchi, Edwin, 103, 104n8, 116n34

Scripture Index

OLD TESTAMENT

Genesis

	136
15	127n12, 163, 164
15:6	34, 66, 77, 125, 127, 127n12, 128, 163, 164, 167, 169, 170
16	127n12
16:16	127n12
17	163n33
20:5	127n14
22	34, 127, 128, 128n17, 162, 164, 168
22:1 LXX	163
22:1–18	167
22:1–19	127n13
22:1ff	34, 163, 169
22:11	127n14
22:12	127n14
22:22	127n14
26:5	128n17
49	57

Exodus

	136
12:3	103
19:5	43
19:6	43
20	123, 126, 127
20:1–17	96
20:13	125, 126, 126n9
20:13–14	66
20:14	125, 126, 126n9
21:1	96
22:22	96
22:23–24	96

Leviticus

	136
7:20–21	94
11	92
11–15	92
12	92
13	92
14	92
15	92
19	73n39, 137
19:12	137, 138
19:12–18	137, 138, 138n41
19:13	137, 138
19:14	137, 138
19:15	126, 137, 138
19:16	72, 72n37, 137, 138
19:16a	72
19:17	137, 138
19:17b	137
19:18	66, 69, 70n32, 71, 73, 125, 126, 127, 137, 138, 160, 173
19:18a	137, 138
19:18b	137, 138, 138n41

SCRIPTURE INDEX

Numbers

2	134
11	131, 133, 134, 174
11:2	143
11:16	14, 134
11:16–17	134
11:16–30	113n29
11:24	133, 134
11:24–30	125, 131, 133, 134, 135
11:25	131n25, 133, 134
11:25–30	131n25
11:26	130, 131n25, 133, 134
11:27	130
11:27–28	133
11:28	134
11:28–29	134
11:29	131n25, 133, 134
11:30	133, 134
19	92

Deuteronomy

	136
5	123, 126, 127
5:17–18	66, 125, 126
5:18	126, 126n10
5:19	126n9
5:20	126n9
10:18	96
14:28–29	96
24:19–21	96
26:12–13	96
27:26	79
32:18	75

Joshua

	136
2	33, 168
13	57
15–19	57

Judges

17–18	57n60

Ruth

	21n61

1 Samuel

17:47	104

1 Kings

	136
17:1	136
18:42	136

2 Chronicles

20:7	34, 169
28:14	104
29	39
30:1	39
30:10	39
30:11	39
30:18	40
30:25	40

Job

	136

Psalms

	136
19:7	65
22:22	111
26 [LXX 25]:5	104
68:5	95, 96
119	75

Proverbs

	7, 136
3:34	125, 129
3:34 LXX	66, 125, 129, 142

Ecclesiastes

	135n36, 136

Isaiah

	136
11:11–12	42

40:6–7	136
40:6b–7	136
41:8	34, 169

Jeremiah

	136
2:3	75
3:18	56
31:8–14	42
31:33	76, 77

Ezekiel

37:19	39
37:19–23	39
37:19–24	56
37:21–22	42

Joel

2:32	77

Zechariah

	136
10:6–12	42

Malachi

	136

DEUTEROCANONICAL BOOKS

Judith	135, 135n35
Wisdom	135n36

PSEUDEPIGRAPHA (OLD TESTAMENT)

Psalms of Solomon

	135, 135n35
17:26–28	42
17:28	56

APOCRYPHA (OLD TESTAMENT)

Book of Eldad and Modab

130, 130n23, 131

ANCIENT JEWISH WRITERS

Josephus	11n18

RABBINIC WORKS

Mishnah m. Avot.

6:2	65

Tanakh

6, 66

Testament of Benjamin

9:2	42

NEW TESTAMENT

Matthew

66, 67n23, 118, 119n47, 120, 123, 139, 139n45, 139n48, 139n50, 140, 143

4:23	105
5	68
5:3	67, 121, 139
5:7	138
5:9	138
5:10	121
5:11–12	67, 139
5:17–20	65, 68
5:19	138
5:21	138
5:21–26	127
5:22	127
5:27	138
5:27–30	127
5:28	127
5:33–37	67, 140

Matthew (continued)

5:34–37	138
5:48	65, 68
6:2	105
6:5	105
6:13	138
6:19	138
6:19–21	67, 139
7:1–5	139
7:7	138
7:7–11	67, 139
7:11	138
7:21	138
7:24–27	67, 139
7:26	138
8:1–5	67
8:29	138
9:9	119
9:35	105
10:3	17, 119
10:5–6	119
10:7	121
10:17	105
10:23	120
12:9	104, 105
12:36–37	138
13	77
13:1–9	77
13:23	77
13:40–42	120
13:49–50	120
13:54	104, 105
13:55	16, 18
15:10	100
15:11	138
15:16–20	100
15:18	138
15:19	138
15:24	124
16	118, 121
16:15	120
16:15–16	120
16:16	120n50
16:16 CSB	120
16:18	14, 103, 109, 110, 117, 120, 174
16:19a	120, 121
16:19b	121
17:1–7	17n44
18:17	103, 109
18:18	121
18:22–35	138
19:19	138
19:28	38, 39, 53n52, 54
21:21	67, 140
21:23	14
22:36–40	67, 67n27, 126, 126n8
22:39	138
23:6	105
23:12	138
23:25b	83
23:34	105, 105n10
24:33	138
25:46	120
26:14–15	16
26:26–37	17n44
26:47–50	16
28:19–20	120

Mark

	66, 67n23, 123, 139n45, 139n48, 140
1:21	104, 105
1:23	105
1:24	138
1:29	104, 105
1:39	105
3:1	104, 105
3:18	17
5:7	138
6:2	104, 105
6:3	16
6:13	138
10:19	138
10:28–31	126n8
11:23	67, 140
12:28–32	65
12:31	138
12:39	105
13:9	105
15:40	17

Luke

14n36, 66, 67n23, 123, 139n45, 139n48, 139n50, 140

4:15	105
4:16	104, 105
4:20	104, 105
4:25	138
4:28	104, 105
4:33	104, 105
4:34	138
4:38	104, 105
4:44	105
6:6	104, 105
6:15	17
6:16	17
6:20	67, 139
6:22–23	67, 139
6:24	67, 138, 140
6:25	67, 140
6:37	67, 139
6:41–42	67, 139
6:47–49	67, 139
7:3	14
7:5	13, 104, 105
8:4	105
8:41	104
9:41	116n34
9:49	116n34
10:27	138
10:46	105
11:9–13	67, 139
11:43	105
12:11	105
12:18	138
12:33–34	67, 139
12:47	138
13:10	105
15:25	113
18:20	138
20:46	105
21:12	105
22:30	38, 39, 53n52, 54

John

123, 139n45

1:13	138
6:59	104, 105
7:5	17
7:10	40
7:32	40
7:33–34	40
7:35	40, 41
7:37	40
13:17	138
18:20	105

Acts

4, 10, 11, 13, 14, 14n36, 104, 105, 106, 107, 109, 113, 114, 115, 116n34, 124n3, 146, 149n10

1:12–14	16
1:13	11n20, 17, 18
1:13–14	119
1:14	11n20, 17, 18
1:18–19	17
2	134
2:17	113
2:21	77
4:5	113
4:8	113
4:23	113
5:11	14, 109, 110
6:9	13, 105, 106, 106n12, 110
6:12	14, 113
7	106n12, 175
7:38	109, 110
8:1	13n31, 14, 107, 109, 110, 134
8:1–4	57, 173
8:3	14, 109, 110
8:4	13n31, 107
8:14–25	149n10
8–15	12, 58
9	18
9:2	13, 105, 106
9:20	13, 105, 106
9:26–30	148
9:31	109, 110
9:32–25	149n10
10	12, 120, 149n14

Acts (continued)

10:1-48a	149n14
10-11	149n14
10:48b	149n14
11:1-18	120
11:19	13n31, 44, 58, 107, 116, 134, 148n8
11:19-26	120
11:20-21	148n8
11:22	109, 110, 120
11:26	109, 110
11:27	114
11:27-30	15n37, 148
11:29	14
11:29-30	14
11:30	14, 114, 114n30, 116
12	149n9
12:1	109, 110
12:1-2	11n23, 17
12:3	12n25, 17n46
12:5	109, 110
12:17	11, 12, 18
12:17b	149
12:17ff	12
12:20-23	12
13:1	109
13:5	105, 106, 107
13:14	105, 106, 110
13-14	149, 153
13:19	106
13:43	105
14:1	105, 106
14:23	109, 110, 114
14:26-28	149
14:27	109, 110
15	11, 12, 15, 67n27, 80, 81
15:1	149, 150, 150n15, 153
15:1-29	151, 152
15:2	15, 15n39, 113, 150
15:3	109, 110
15:4	15, 15n39, 109, 110, 113
15:5	150n15
15:6	15, 15n39, 113
15:6-11	150n16
15:13	11
15:13-21	15, 67n27
15:19-21	67n27
15:20	11
15:21	13, 105, 106
15:22	15, 15n39, 81, 109, 110, 113
15:23	11, 15, 15n39, 113, 151, 151n20
15:23-29	11
15:28	151n20
15:28-29	80
15:30	11
15:41	109, 110
16:4	113
16:5	89, 109, 110
17:1	105, 106
17:10	105, 106
17:17	105, 106
18:4	105, 106
18:7	105, 106
18:11	112n26
18:19	105, 106
18:22	109, 110
18:26	105, 106
19	110, 112
19:8	105, 106, 112n27
19:10	112n27
19:32	110
19:39	110
19;39	110
19:39	110n20
19:41	110
19;41	110
20	115
20:17	14, 110, 114, 115
20:17a	14
20:28	110
20:31	112n27
21	11, 11n22, 67n27, 114n30
21:17-26	60, 80
21:18	11, 15n40, 114
21:18-26	152n22
21:20	11
21:25	11
22	18
22:19	105, 106
23:14	113

24:1	113	2:1–10	15, 148
24:12	105, 106	2:2	15
25:15	14, 113	2:6	153
26	18	2:7–8	44
26:11	105, 106	2:7–9	15
		2:8	153
		2:8–9	153
		2:8–13	161

Romans

61, 110, 151, 151n21, 151n22, 152n22, 169, 174

		2:9	15
		2:10	153
1:16	44	2:11	150, 150n16
4	56	2:11–14	150n15, 150n16, 152n22, 153
		2:11–21	154, 154n25, 155, 156, 157

1 Corinthians

17, 61, 110

		2:12	149n14
1:12	44	2:12a	149
5:1–5	78, 78n56	2:12b	149
5:5a	78n55, 78n56	2:13	150
5:5b	78n55	2:14	150, 150n16, 153
10:1–5	49	2:14–26	155
10:6	49	2:15–16	161
10:18	56	2:16	80n61, 153, 154, 154n24, 155, 155n26, 156, 157, 161
15:7	17, 18		
15:8	17		
		2:16a	145

2 Corinthians

110

		2:17	156
		2:19	156
2:6–11	78, 78n56	2:20	154
		2:21	156
		3	156

Galatians

61, 80, 80nn59–61, 111, 118n46, 146, 147, 148, 150n16, 150n17, 151, 151n20, 151n21, 151n22, 152, 152n22, 153, 154, 155, 156, 157, 169, 170, 173, 174

		3:2	80n61, 154, 155, 155n26, 156, 157, 157n28
		3:5	80n61, 154, 155, 155n26, 156, 157, 157n28, 161
		3:6	156
		3:6–8	163
		3:7	154
1:2	80	3:8	154, 156
1:11–21	155	3:9	154
1:18	10n16	3:10	60, 79, 80n61, 155, 155n26, 156, 157, 157n28, 161
1:18–19	148		
1:19	20n52		
1:23	154	3:10a	80
2	157, 170	3:11	154, 156
		3:12	154, 156

Galatians (continued)

3:13	156
3:14	154
3:17	156
3:18	156
3:19	156
3:21	156
3:22	154
3:23	154
3:24	154, 156
3:25	154, 156
3:26	154
4:17	150n18
4:21–31	56
5	156
5:5	154, 156
5:6	154
5:8	156
5:19	155
5:22	154
6:1	78
6:2	156
6:4	155
6:10	154
6:12	150n18
6:13	156

Ephesians

	61, 111, 174
2:8–10	171
4:15	91n29

Philippians

	21n61, 61, 111
3:3	56

Colossians

	111
2:18	89

1 Thessalonians

	111

2 Thessalonians

	111

1 Timothy

	61, 111
5:2	115
5:17	115
5:18	115

2 Timothy

	85nn9–10, 111
3:16	81, 85, 146

Titus

	111
1:5	115
2:2	115

Philemon

	111

Hebrews

	2n9, 21n61, 109n18, 111, 115, 124n2
1:5–18	89
2:12	111
11	112
11:2	115
11:8	128
11:8–19	128
11:9	128
11:13	56
11:17	128
11:31	34, 168
11:39	129
12:1	111
12:2	112
12:23	111
13:14	56
13:20–21	19
13:24	19

James

1	67n27, 77, 136, 164, 167
1:1	2n9, 11, 16, 19, 23, 25, 37, 38, 38n1, 39, 40, 41, 45, 50, 51, 51n45, 52, 53n53, 54, 56, 57, 58, 64n12, 75, 80, 83, 94, 97, 102, 107, 134, 141, 142, 149, 152, 153, 173, 174
1:1 NRSV	5, 172
1:1a	26
1:1b	26
1:2	26, 57, 67, 139, 141, 142
1–2	160, 166
1:2–3	166
1:2–4	23, 24, 25, 26, 27, 158, 159, 160
1:3	26, 141, 154, 159, 163, 164, 165
1:3–4	163, 164, 165, 166
1:4	155, 158n30, 164
1:4a	26
1:4b	26
1:5	67, 139, 165, 166
1:5–6	158, 159, 165, 166
1:5–8	23, 24, 26, 27
1:5a	26, 27
1:5b	26, 27
1:6	67, 140, 154, 165
1:6a	26, 27
1:6b	27
1:7	27
1:8	27
1:9–11	28
1:9–21	23, 24, 28, 29
1:10–11	136, 141
1:11a	142
1:12	28, 139, 141
1:13	135n35
1:13–15	28
1:14	127
1:14–15	90
1:14–17	167
1:15	127
1:15b	74
1:16	90
1:16–17	28
1:17	63, 67, 79, 101n62, 136, 139, 159, 165
1:18	74, 74n41, 74nn42–43, 75, 76, 79, 141
1:18a	28
1:18b	28
1:19	90, 135n35, 136
1:19–20	90, 127
1:19–21	28
1:19–27	88
1:20	156, 167
1:21	74, 74n41, 75, 76, 77, 78, 79, 141
1:21a	142
1:22	29, 30, 62, 74, 74n41, 75, 77, 79, 86, 87, 95, 160, 167
1:22–23	67, 139
1:22–24	68
1:22–25	95, 159, 165
1:22–27	23, 24, 29, 62, 63, 73, 74, 86, 87
1:23	74, 74n41, 75, 79, 167
1:23–24	29, 30, 62, 86, 87
1:25	5, 60, 61, 61n1, 62, 63, 68, 71, 74, 75, 76, 77, 79, 80, 95, 141, 155, 155n27, 156, 165, 166, 167, 173
1:25a	30, 62, 63, 65, 68, 71, 74, 86
1:25b	30, 63, 68, 71, 86, 87
1:26	24, 87, 89, 90, 91, 95, 98, 100, 136
1:26–27	30, 63, 68, 82, 83, 85, 86, 87, 88, 88n13, 91, 94, 95, 97, 98
1:26a	90
1:27	5, 83, 86, 87, 89, 95, 96, 97, 98, 99, 100, 173
2	16, 67n27, 71, 99, 127, 136, 157, 164
2:1	13, 13n32, 57, 137, 154, 160

James (continued)

2:1–4	31, 69, 99n52		148, 152, 153, 154,
2:1—5:6	21, 22		154n24, 154n25, 155,
2:1–7	70, 71, 97, 126		156, 157, 158, 159,
2:1–11	21		160, 161, 162, 164,
2:1–13	23, 24, 31, 62, 68, 69,		165, 167, 168, 169,
	70, 73, 74, 87, 160	2:15	170, 171, 174
2:2	5, 13, 14, 25, 53, 58,	2:15	97n47, 169
	75, 102, 102n3, 104,	2:15–16	161
	105, 107, 109, 116,	2:16	169
	121, 174	2:17	154, 155, 159, 162,
2:2–3	161		169
2:2–4	160	2:18	33, 154, 155, 159,
2:5	67, 99, 139, 154		162, 166, 167, 168,
2–5	98		169
2:5–7	31, 69, 70	2:18ff	162
2:8	24, 31, 61, 64n11,	2:19	154, 169
	65, 66, 69, 70, 71, 73,	2:19–22	33, 34, 167, 168
	79, 80, 125, 126, 127,	2:20	154, 155, 159, 169
	129, 135, 137, 138,	2:21	155, 156, 159, 163,
	155n27, 156, 160		164, 167, 169, 170
2:8–11	65	2:21–23	163, 164, 167
2:8–12	62, 65, 68, 97	2:22	34, 154, 155, 158,
2:9	61, 70, 71, 137, 155,		159, 162, 163, 164,
	156, 160		168, 169
2:9–10	31, 32, 69	2:23	33, 34, 66, 77, 125,
2:9–11	70		127, 128, 129, 136,
2:10	61, 64n11, 66, 70,		154, 156, 163, 164,
	70n33, 71, 156		167, 168, 169, 170
2:11	61, 66, 70, 71, 125,	2:24	33, 34, 145, 154, 155,
	126, 127, 135, 136,		156, 159, 167, 168,
	138, 156		169
2:11a	31, 69, 129	2:25	33, 136, 155, 156,
2:11b	31, 69, 129		159, 167, 168, 169
2:12	24, 61, 68, 71, 80,	2:26	33, 154, 155, 159,
	141, 156, 160, 161,		162, 168
	165, 166, 167	3	136
2:12–13	21, 31, 69	3:1	35, 36, 90
2:12b–13a	71	3:1–12	22, 23, 24, 35, 35n65,
2:13	79, 97, 120, 161		36, 37, 87, 90, 100
2:13a	68, 71, 73	3:1–18	22
2:14	77, 154, 155, 159,	3:2	35, 36, 87, 90
	161, 169	3:2b	74n41
2:14—3:12	21	3:3–4	35, 36
2:14–17	33, 97, 168	3:5	35, 36
2:14–26	6, 23, 33, 34, 127,	3:6	35n65, 88, 98, 99,
	145, 145n1, 146, 147,		100, 173
		3:6a	35, 36, 37, 37n66
		3:6b	35, 36

3:7	35, 36	4:11–17	24, 30, 62, 71, 72, 73, 74
3:8	136		
3:8–10a	35, 36	4:11a	72n37, 73
3:10b–12	36	4:12	73, 77, 78, 79, 120
3:13	34, 35, 155, 165, 166	4:12a	73
3:13–18	21, 23, 147, 152, 159, 164, 165, 170	4:13	30, 72
		4:13—5:6	21
3:13–19	34	4:13–14	136
3:14	2n10, 34, 35, 100, 166	4:14a	30, 31, 72
3:14–16	100n57, 127	4:14b	30, 31, 72
3:15	34, 35, 100, 100n57, 166	4:14c	30, 31, 72
		4:15	30, 31, 72
3:15a	165	4:16–17	30, 71, 72
3:15b	165	5	136
3:16	2n10, 34, 35, 100, 101, 166	5:1	67, 140
		5:1–3	29, 67, 120, 139, 140
3:17	87, 101n62, 166	5:1–11	24, 28, 29
3:17–18	34, 35, 165, 166	5:3	120, 135n35, 136
3:18	136, 156, 166, 167	5:4	87, 97, 136, 137
3:26	133	5:4–6	29
4	130, 136	5:5	120, 136
4:1	132, 134, 141	5:6	97
4:1–2	127	5:7	29, 120, 136
4:1–3	32, 100, 132	5:7a	29
4:1–4	129	5:7b	29
4:1–10	21, 23, 24, 32	5:8	29, 120, 141, 142
4:2	2n10, 127, 132, 134	5:9	29, 137
4:3	67, 134, 139	5:10–11	29
4:4	32, 88, 98, 99, 100, 132, 133, 134	5:11	136
		5:12	27, 67, 137, 140
4:5	32, 125, 129, 130, 131, 131n26, 132, 132n31, 133, 134, 135, 136	5:12–18	24, 27
		5:13	27
		5:14	6, 13, 14, 102, 103, 104, 111, 113, 114, 115, 116, 121, 174
4:6	66, 125, 129, 130, 135, 141		
		5:14–15	27
4:6a	32	5:15	77, 78, 78n54
4:6b	32, 142	5:16a	27
4:7	24, 129, 141	5:16b	27
4:7–8a	32	5:17	136
4:7b	100n57, 142	5:17–18	27, 136
4:8	87, 136	5:18	136
4:8b–10	32	5:19–20	24, 25, 26, 27, 78
4:9	67, 140	5:19a	26
4:10	24, 129, 136, 141, 142	5:19b	26
4:11	24, 62, 71, 72, 73, 137, 156	5:20	77, 78, 78n57, 137, 141
		5:20a	26
4:11–12	21, 30, 67, 71, 72, 73, 139	5:20b	26, 142

1 Peter

	41, 41n5, 43, 44, 109n18, 115, 123, 124, 124n2, 125, 141, 142, 142n53, 143, 174
1:1	40, 41, 42, 43, 44, 56, 141, 142
1:6	141, 142
1:7	141
1:17	56
1:23	141
1:24	141
1:24b	142
2:1	141
2:1a	142
2:9	43
2:11	56, 141
2:12	44
2:16	141
4:7	141
4:7a	142
4:8	141
4:8b	142
5:1	115
5:4	141
5:5	115, 141
5:5b	142
5:6	141, 142
5:8–9	141
5:9	142
5:13	44

2 Peter

	109n18, 124n2
1:20–21	146
3:14	98

1 John

	124n2
1	115n33

2 John

	115, 124n2
1	115

3 John

	111, 115, 124n2
1	115, 115n33
6	111
9	111
10	111

Jude

	109n18, 124n2

Revelation

	14, 21n61, 22n62, 104, 109, 111, 112, 113, 115, 124n2
1:3	22n62
1:4	112
1:11	112
1:20	112
2:1	112
2:7	112
2:8	112
2:8–11	108
2:9	107, 108, 108n15, 109
2:10	108, 108n15
2:11	112
2:12	112
2:17	112
2:18	112
2:23	112
2:29	112
3:1	112
3:2	112
3:6	112
3:7	112
3:7–13	108
3:9	107, 108, 108n15, 109
3:10	108n15
3:13	112
3:14	112
3:22	112
4:4	115
4:10	115
5:5	115
5:6	115
5:8	115
5:11	115

5:14	115	**EARLY CHRISTIAN WRITINGS**
7:5–8	57, 57n60	
7:11	115	
7:13	115	Augustine 4n14, 46, 47–48, 47n30
11:16	115	
14:3	115	Chrysostom, John 46
19:4	115	
21:2	38	Clement of Alexandria 11n18, 46
21:12	38, 39, 53, 53n52, 54, 112n25	Cyril 47
21:14	112n25	Eusebius 11n18
21–22	38, 76, 112n25	Hegesippus 11n18
22:14	22n62	Hilary 47n30
22:16	112	Irenaeus 46
		Jerome 47n30
		Justin Martyr 46, 46n21
APOCRYPHA (NEW TESTAMENT)		Origen 47, 143
		Theodore of Mopseustia 46
1 Clement	143	
Epistle of Barnabas	3n12	
The Shepherd of Hermas	3n12, 130, 130n23, 143	

www.ingramcontent.com/pod-product-compliance
Lightning Source LLC
Chambersburg PA
CBHW060607230426
43670CB00011B/2011